MW01620556

*This book is dedicated in loving memory of*
*my mother, Ilse Nitschmann Paap,*
*and my brother, Hans Horst Paap.*

– Nancy Paap

# Hans Paap

## Portraits & Landscapes

*Every continent has its own great spirit of place. Every people is polarized in some particular locality, which is home, the homeland. Different places on the face of the earth have different vital effluence, different vibration, different chemical exhalation, different polarity with different stars: call it what you like. But the spirit of place is a great reality.* – D. H. Lawrence

***Mable Dodge Lujan, Taos, New Mexico***
**oil on board**
**23 x 22¼ inches**
**Courtesy of Curt, Christina and Jonah Nonomaque**
**Tesuque, NM**

D.H. Lawrence, "The Spirit of Place," in *Studies in Classic American Literature* (1923; reprint ed., New York: Viking, 1964), 5-6.

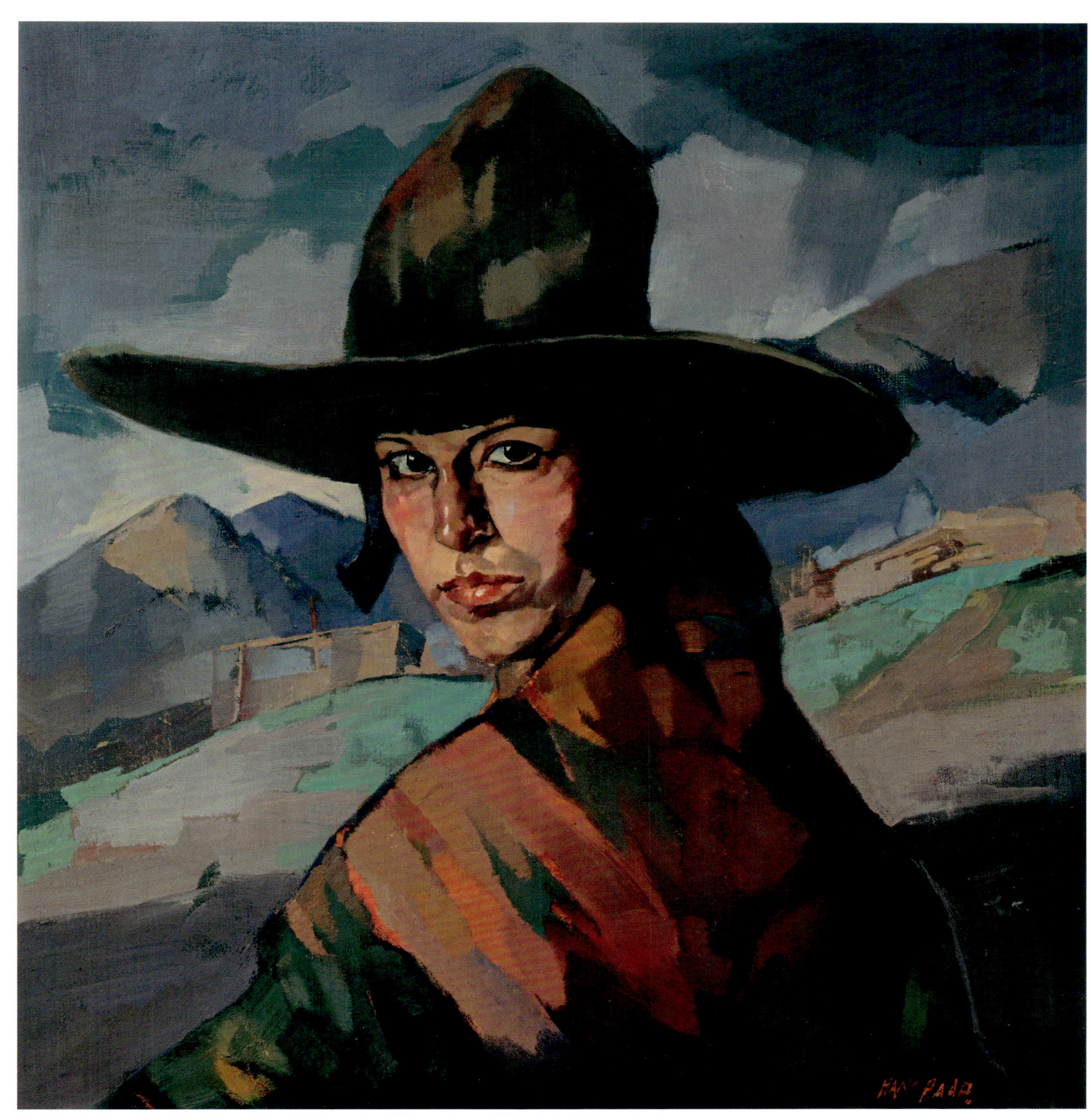

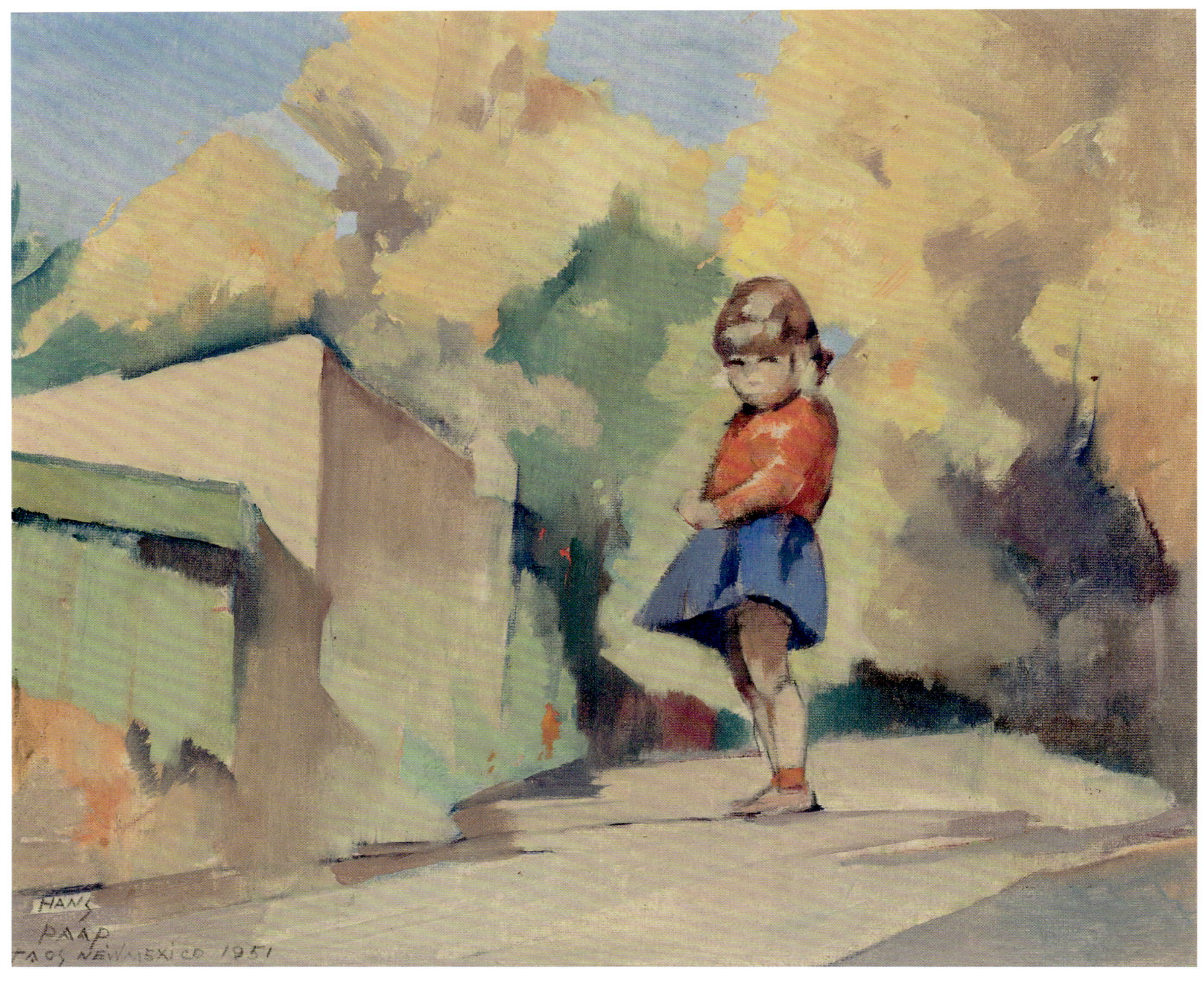


*Nancy on Taos Street*
oil on board
12 x 14 inches
1951
Courtesy of Nancy Paap
Tesuque, NM

# Meeting My Father Again through His Paintings

**by Nancy Paap**

This book arose from my quest to learn more about the life and work of my late father, the painter Hans Paap. I saw him for the last time when I was four-and-a-half years old, and it was not until I was 20 that I heard his name spoken again.

Once I began collecting his paintings and researching his life, I realized he was as gifted a portrait and landscape painter as the members of the Taos Society of Artists, who were contemporaries and friends of his. I also began to lament that his work was so little known and underappreciated. The lack of acclaim seems attributable to the fact that he never settled in one place long enough to become established and recognized. This book seeks to rectify that inequity.

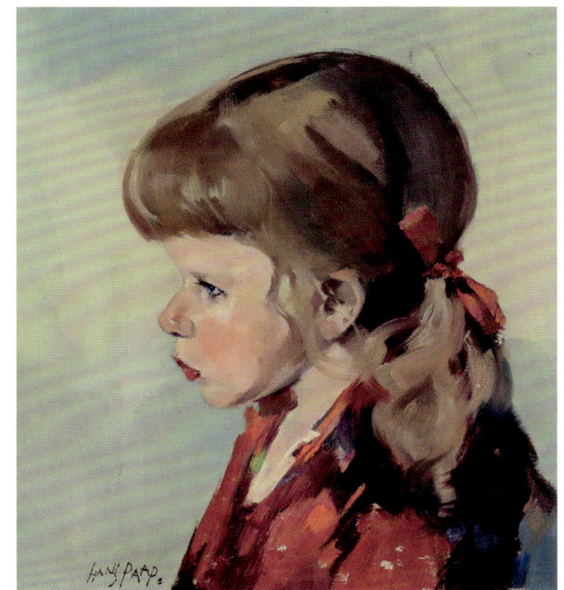


My father, who was born in Germany, lived in countless places during his life, including Europe, South America, Mexico, the United States and on various islands around the world. To certain places, such as Germany, Hawaii and Taos, New Mexico, he returned several times. He met and married my mother, Ilse (née Nitschmann), in Germany during World War II. My brother Roy, whose given name was Pancho, was born there in 1944. After leaving war-torn Germany and life in displacement camps, my parents struggled to be accepted into the United States. For nearly two years, they were held on Ellis Island, trying unsuccessfully to obtain the paperwork needed for admission to the country. Eventually they were accepted by the Dominican Republic, where I was born in 1948. In 1949, with an affidavit from my father's friend, Taos painter Martin Hennings, my parents finally gained entry to the United States. They settled in Taos, where Hans, my younger brother, was born in 1952.

My childhood memories of Taos, although limited, are happy ones. I remember the old adobe house where we lived, with the spring in the backyard and watercress growing nearby. I have a memory of digging tunnels in three-foot-deep snow. That my father loved his family is evident from his many touching portraits of us. My mother described him as loving, generous and good-hearted — except when he drank.

His alcoholism finally took its toll on their marriage, and in 1953 my mother made the difficult decision to leave him. She took her three young children and drove to Los Angeles, California, where she subsequently divorced my father and met and married an Englishman, Ivan Waight. The five of us moved to England, where we lived for nine years. My stepfather adopted us, and we took his last name. He discouraged us from talking about our father or even mentioning his name. By age 16, Roy, who did not get along with our stepfather, had left home. In 1963, the rest of the family immigrated to Cape Town, South Africa, where my mother and stepfather ran a pensione and my mother

***Portrait of Nancy Paap***
**oil on board**
**14 x 13 inches**
**1951**
**Courtesy of Nancy Paap**
**Tesuque, NM**

taught accounting at a business school for black South Africans. In 1968, when I was 20, the four of us returned to Santa Fe, New Mexico.

Unfortunately, by the time we arrived in Santa Fe, my father was no longer here, and no one knew his whereabouts. When the research for this book revealed that he had died in Hamburg, Germany, on July 5, 1967, it was a heavy blow: I was living in Munich at that particular time. I had arrived in April to work while I learned the language, and I remained there until well into the fall. It is a sad irony that I was but 100 miles from where my father was. He was staying with his sister, and had I known that before July, I might have looked for his paintings and even reconnected with him. What an amazing reunion that would have been! But it was not to be. I had always missed my father, and I know from letters he wrote to friends how acutely he felt the loss of his family.

I became a weaver, and then in 1976 three friends and I opened Santa Fe Weaving and Knitting Center on Canyon Road. With some knowledge of my artist father percolating in my head, I decided to go by the surname Paap professionally. I reasoned that he was an artist and so was I.

To supplement my income while my weaving business was getting underway, I repaired Navaho rugs. My earliest clients were Harold and Hilda Street, the owners of Streets of Taos Gallery on Canyon Road, and my first Hans Paap paintings came from them. Previously, the Streets had owned the Taos Inn in Taos and had traded with my father for many of his paintings. They sometimes compensated me in trade, giving me one of my father's paintings.

*With some knowledge of my artist father percolating in my head, I decided to go by the surname Paap professionally. I reasoned that he was an artist and so was I.*

The name Paap was recognized by the city's fine art dealers. Luckily for me, Hans Paap paintings were not expensive, and I could afford them. Soon my friends began alerting me when they saw his paintings at estate sales, in galleries or advertised in newspapers. Like my father's travels, my acquisitions were spontaneous and unplanned. I acquired several more paintings, either by purchasing them or trading my weavings for them. l was not searching for them; they showed up serendipitously, as did the paintings my brothers collected. I continued to collect my father's paintings for quite a few years. Then, at the same time I decided I could not afford to buy any more, my sources seemed to dry up.

My parents' divorce, my mother's subsequent remarriage, my growing up in England and South Africa, and certain Shakespearean twists of fate prevented me from knowing my father in person beyond my first few years. Yet as an adult, I was given the rare gift of being able to piece together significant information about him and his life from three complementary sources: my mother's memoir, *My First 70 Years*, which she wrote for her children; the research for this book; and, most importantly, his paintings. Over the years, I have become so familiar with my father's brushstrokes, palette, subject matter and backgrounds that I can recognize a Paap painting immediately.

***Honeymoon Portrait of Ilse Paap, Prerow, Germany***
**oil on board**
**15 x 13 inches**
**1943**
**Courtesy of Nancy Paap**
**Tesuque, NM**

As my collection of my father's portraits and landscapes grew, I became increasingly aware of their superior quality. Even today, when I look at his paintings, I am awed

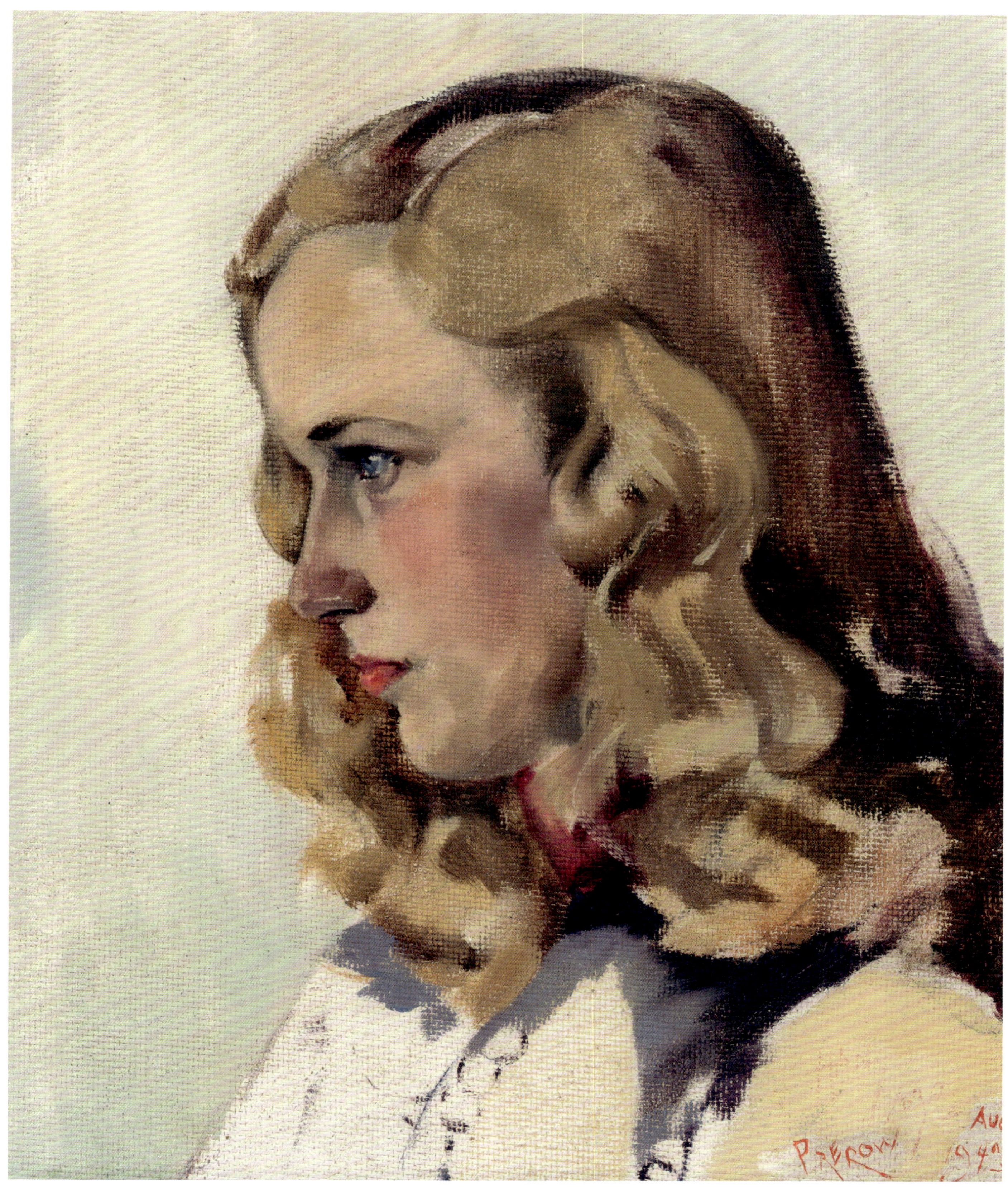

by his subtle and masterful brushstrokes, sense of perspective and deft use of color. To say his work is comparable to that of members of the Taos Society of Artists is not an overstatement, for many of them visited his studio in Taos to seek his painterly advice. I discovered dozens of articles written about him worldwide, and he was included in articles and a book by writer and historian Eberhard Axel Wilhelm of Lisbon, Portugal. However, no definitive book had been written about my father and the exceptional art he created. My family owns 53 of his paintings, and through research I was able to locate 29 more in galleries, museums and private collections. The research also shed light on my father's life during the 54 years before he met my mother in 1943 (he was 30 years older than she), as well as on his later life and travels, and on his many professional accolades.

Along the way I also realized that my father and I have certain characteristics in common. The most obvious is that we are both artists: he, a successful painter, and I, a well-known weaver. More curious is that we share a strong and unique sense of color. My weavings sell well, and I attribute this in part to my innate sense of color and the unusual combinations I create. It is as if his "color genes" were somehow passed on to me. It feels illuminating and satisfying to know that this peculiar talent of mine may have come from him. (Coincidentally, his mother was a weaver named Nancy Paap. Perhaps the "weaving gene" was also passed down from the Paap side of the family.) Moreover, my brothers, both of whom reverted to the surname Paap, also seemed to have inherited our father's creativity and artistry. Roy worked on Hollywood filmsets for many years before becoming an accomplished homebuilder in Santa Fe; Hans, who passed away in 2014, was a well-known master woodworker and woodcarver. All three of us were self-taught rather than formally trained in our vocations.

*My father's portraits and landscapes capture the souls of the individuals and the essence of the locations he painted.*

From the time I was a child, I have loved my father, and that love is in part what propelled the writing of this book. It is difficult, if not impossible, to condense a person's life to words and images, particularly if the person was complicated and gifted. For this reason, piecing together my father's life has been an intensely challenging, personal and at times painful undertaking, yet ultimately a healing and rewarding one that has brought me closer to him. I hope as a result of my longing to know him better, I have succeeded in some small way in bringing him and his art to light.

My father's portraits and landscapes capture the souls of the individuals and the essence of the locations he painted. Although circumstances prevented me from ever accompanying him to the places he lived and worked, his paintings serve as a record, a tour guide, giving me a chance to see those people and places through his eyes. His evocative portraits and landscapes enable me, even decades later, to look over his shoulder and see the same faces and vistas that compelled him to pick up his paintbrush.

Nancy Paap
August 2018
Santa Fe, New Mexico

***Ilse Paap with Hans, Jr.***
**oil on canvas**
**18 x 16 inches**
**1952**
**Collection of JoAnna Paap**
**Santa Fe, NM**

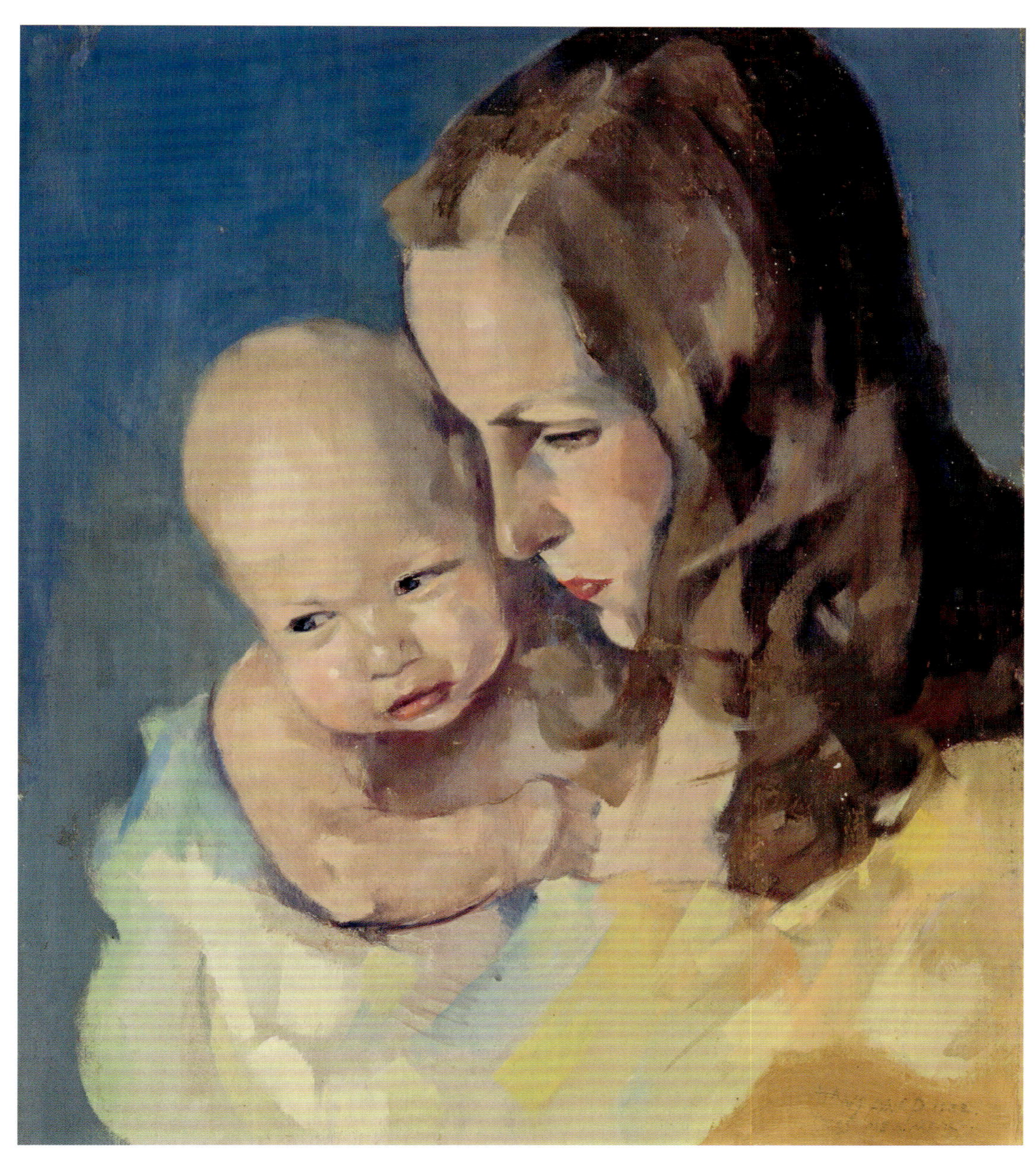

*The Mickey Mouse and Minnie Mouse hand puppets were a gift to Nancy Paap from her mother's relatives in South Africa. Nancy recalls, "My father was a fast, energetic painter, but as a three-year-old, sitting for my portrait, even an hour, felt like an eternity."*

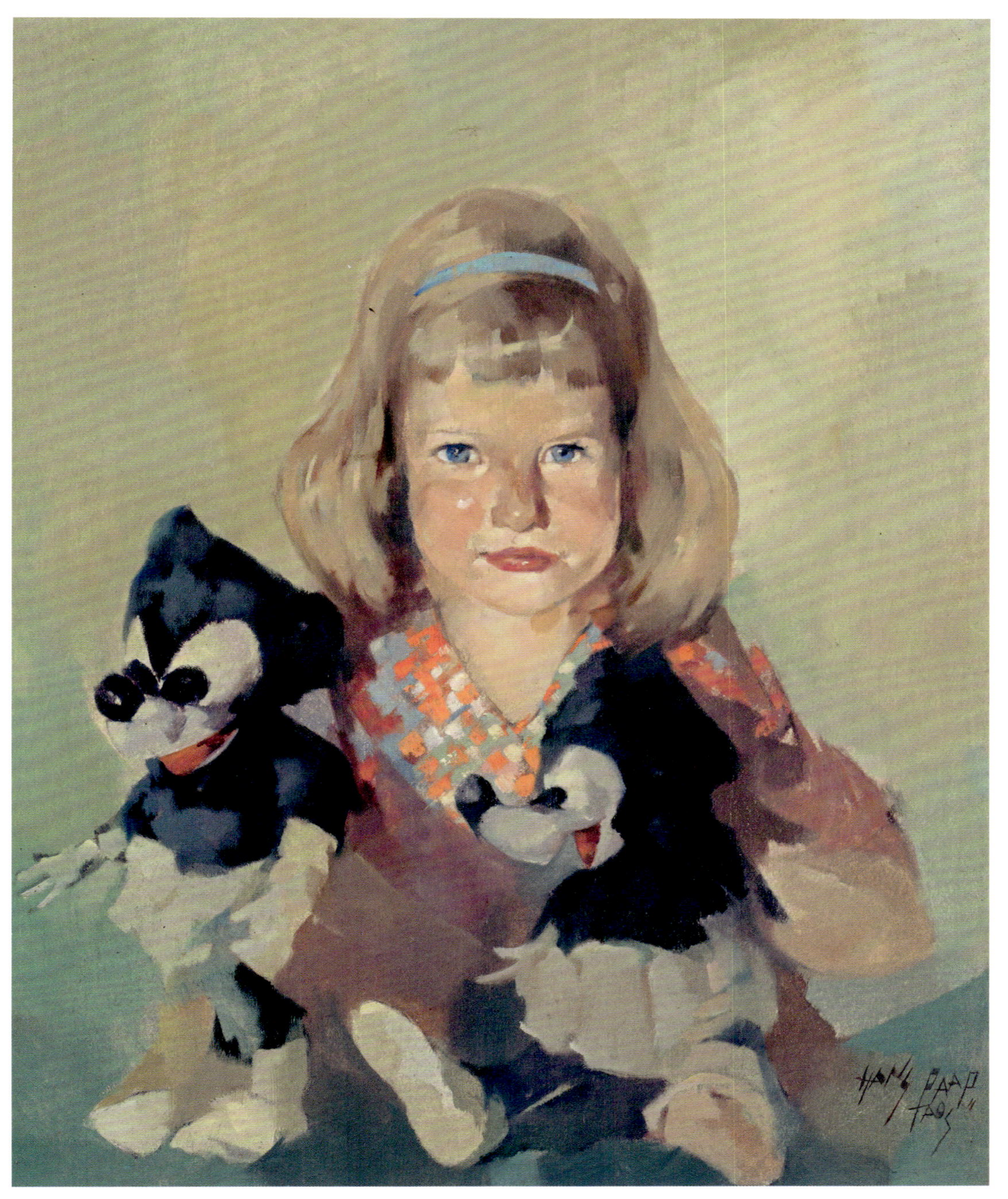

*Portrait of Nancy Paap*
*with Mickey and Minnie*
oil on canvas
22 x 18 inches
1951
Courtesy of Nancy Paap
Tesuque, NM

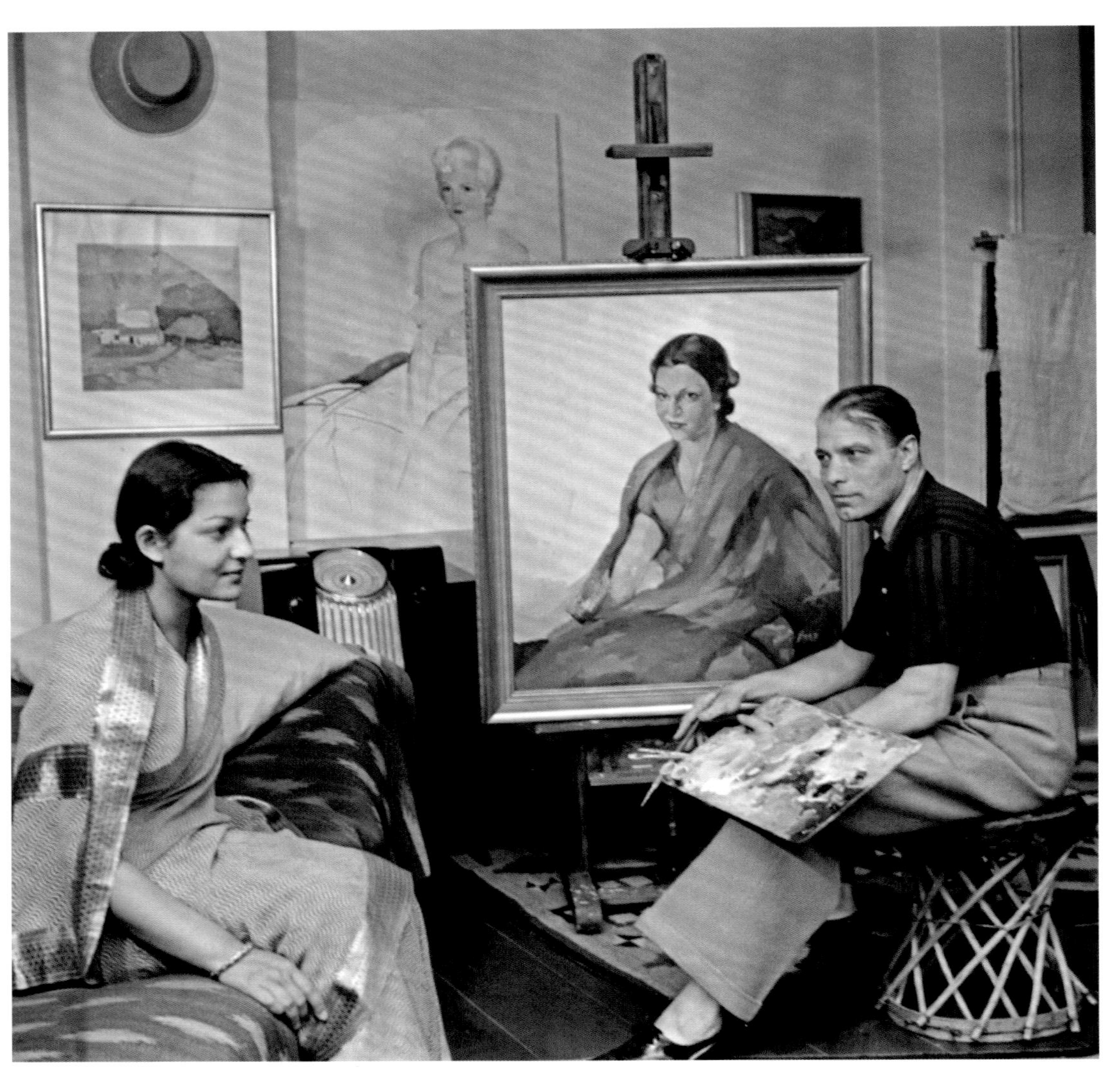

# The World through the Eyes of Hans Paap

**by Bess Murphy**

Hans Paap's life as an artist is a familiar one: one of exile, exoticism, seeking and loss. It is also a life punctuated with mystery and ambiguities. This can make the telling of his story a challenge: to tell it without falling back on clichés and unsupported assumptions. What is known is that Paap spent his entire adult life as a working artist and that his surviving legacy rests on his paintings and his daughter's drive to rebuild a connection with a father from whom she was separated at the age of four. This may seem a tenuous framework upon which to build a story. However, Paap's paintings not only provide a deeply personal narrative of his experiences, struggles and successes, they also reveal his larger position both within and on the periphery of American art. While his work was in line with general stylistic trends of the time — heading toward abstractionism, but with a healthy dose of regionalism — he was not in his lifetime accepted into the larger canon of twentieth-century American art.

Paap was born in Hamburg, Germany, in 1890, on the brink of the twentieth century, and he died in the same city in 1967. He studied painting at the Royal Academy of Fine Arts in Munich, and by the time he was in his early twenties he had moved to Veracruz, Mexico, to study and work in lithography, textiles, fabric printing and leatherwork. After that initial foray abroad, Paap spent the rest of his life on a peripatetic journey to familiar and foreign places. He seems to have been driven by the desire to find something. Clues about his life reside in his paintings, a handful of letters, the words of his third wife and many news articles from all over the world. His story is revealed first and foremost, though, through his paintings, a tangible record of the world and the people and places he encountered along the way.

Paap's biography reads as a romantic but poignant drama. In his earliest years Paap seemed to be seeking a career that allowed for both financial stability and creative expression. Choosing to study lithography in Mexico rather than in a closer, more familiar European city suggests that not only was he following his father's demand that he learn a trade, but that he was also seeking adventure. Had he been satisfied with becoming a master printer pulling images of other artists' visions, he would probably have remained there and his story would have been radically different. Instead, Paap returned to Germany, where he switched from printmaking to filmmaking. His sortie into filmmaking was relatively short lived. However, it is likely that Paap spent the war years working as an art director and production designer in the nascent German film industry. He remained in his homeland for the duration of World War I. Perhaps it was dissatisfaction with these somewhat more practical pursuits that caused him to leave Germany again, but it may simply have been to escape the lingering trauma of war-time life. By 1919 he was working full-time as a painter in Argentina.

It is at this point that both Paap's career path and personal life began to change dramatically. He married an unknown Argentine, who tragically died in childbirth. Paap did not remain in Argentina, nor did he raise his son, who was brought up by the mother's family. It is

**Paap working in his studio, Germany c. 1937–1939**

unclear whether there was a relationship between father and son, although Paap's third wife, Ilse, did remark upon communication between them much later in their lives. After the ordeal of losing his wife, Paap left Argentina and entered his first phase of traveling as a near-nomadic painter.

It is not inconsequential that Paap's creative style seemed to emerge at this time. With the end of one possible path as a husband, father and painter in Argentina came the cementing of another: the decision to focus on two primary genres, portraits and landscapes. They continued to define his artistic identity for four decades. It appears that Paap periodically returned to Germany, Argentina and Brazil throughout the 1920s. Along the way, he began exhibiting his paintings and garnering accolades. An oil painting executed sometime between 1920 and 1924, *Ocean Cottage, Santos, Brazil* (p. 39), shows the ongoing influence of late Impressionism and early Cubism and Fauvism present in Paap's landscapes in general. The swaths of brilliant blue, yellow and peach, the mottled paintwork of the beachy foreground, and the nearly abstract cottage, distinguished only by its rectangular form, recall the works of artists ranging from Monet and Turner to Gauguin and Cézanne. And yet, the structure of the scene and the more naturalistic portrayal of the large palm trees, clouds and sky are a nod to academic painting. Paap's evolving style is evident here. Stylistically his work would come in line with the post-Impressionist early European and American modern painters, even as his subject matter remained almost exclusively traditional portraits and landscapes that depicted in detail his experience of each new locale.

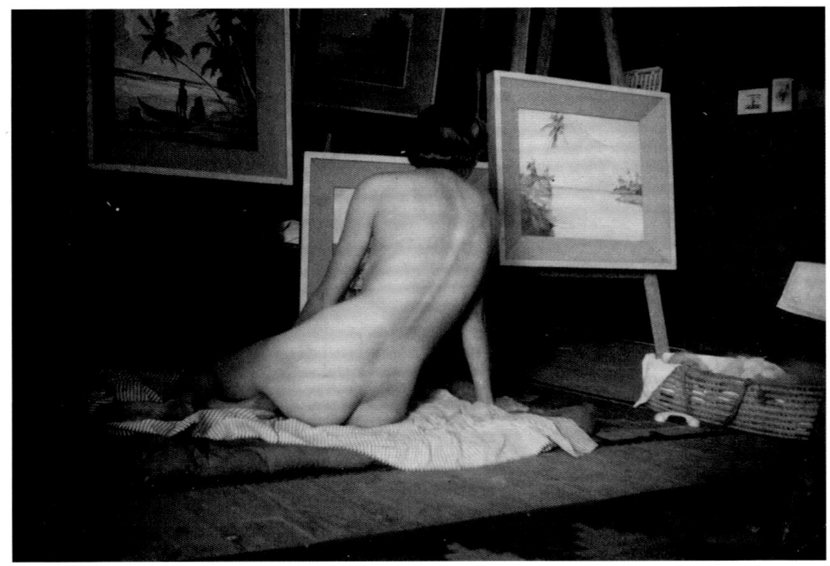

**Ilse Paap modeling for her husband, The Dominican Republic c. 1947**

For some time, Paap was dedicated primarily to life in Brazil. He would mount small exhibitions and join larger group shows, earning praise in the local newspapers for both his color and technique, and even winning a gold medal in 1927 from the Academy of Fine Arts. Moreover, as a German painter, he stood out as exotic in his own right. By 1928, though, Paap had left Brazil and landed in Los Angeles. There, he promptly presented his South American paintings in two noted exhibitions. In a review of his exhibition at the Biltmore, *The Los Angeles Times* remarked on the pure nature of both his landscapes and portraits. It also quoted the artist as planning on settling in Hollywood and painting "a series of portraits that will embody [his] conception of American life and energy."[1] Again, Paap committed to a new home in order to dig deeply into fresh artistic possibilities.

Paap remained committed to painting the land and its people, but his images of this new world, of American life and energy, show the profound influence of the West on him. Paap began to paint its indigenous people, as he had done earlier while living in other countries. In these works, he merged his sense of naturalism in the individuals portrayed, while experimenting increasingly with abstract color fields and patterns in the backgrounds and often on the individual's attire. Paap retained this sensibility in his work after he left California for the mythologized artist colony of Taos, New Mexico.

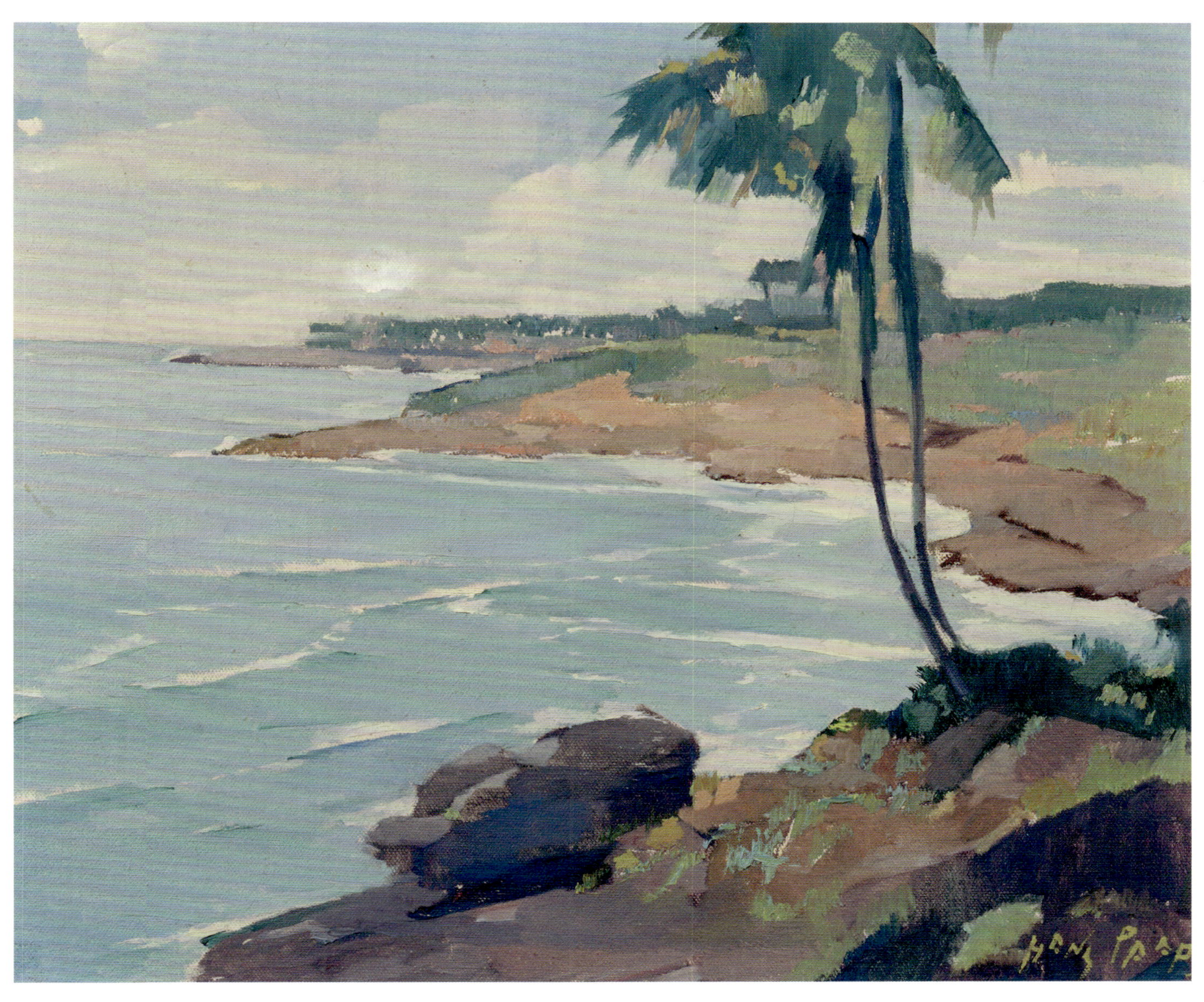

***Bay Seascape with Palm Tree***
**oil on canvas**
**14 x 16 inches**
**Courtesy of Roy Paap**
**Albuquerque, NM**

His 1929 *Portrait of an Indian Chief* (p. 75) presents a stereotypical image of a Native elder wearing a headdress and blanket, similar in subject matter, if not in style, to the paintings of prominent Taos artists. It is not known whether Paap painted this portrait while he was still in Los Angeles or when he first arrived in Taos. In any case, the image conveys his interest in people's features and individuality, and his manipulation of paint and color, particularly in the repetitive use of red, white and blue in the figure's blanket and headdress.

A June 1929 *Los Angeles Times* article situates Paap firmly within the Taos art world alongside luminaries such as Joseph Henry Sharp, E. Irving Couse, Oscar E. Berninghaus, and Walter Ufer. He was quickly befriended by the founding members of the Taos Society of Artists, studying under Kenneth Adams and Ufer, and apparently living for a time with E. Martin Hennings. Described incorrectly in the article as "a very interesting Hungarian," Paap was noted as being part of this illustrious group of painters of the Pueblo Indians.[2] The rest of Paap's personal life and career was defined by his experience in Taos.

The Taos Society of Artists, whose members had transformed the small mountain village into an international art center, was driven by a deeply romantic, exotic view of Northern New Mexico and its inhabitants. Bert Phillips, W. Herbert Dunton and Ernest Blumenschein, along with Sharp, Couse and Berninghaus, the "Taos Six," comprised the original members of the society, which organized formally as a group in 1915 and disbanded in 1927. Their paintings monumentalized Native and Hispano members of the Taos community. Typically, the artists sought to emphasize their subjects' foreignness, even going so far as to present their Taos Pueblo models in Plains Indian attire to legitimize them as "Indian" to their Anglo audience. In hindsight we can see the troubling paternalism in such actions; however, in Paap's day, members of the Taos Society of Artists were recognized as leaders in regional art.

*Regardless of the person's station in life, Paap worked to capture the sitter's individuality and humanity.*

***El Gran Espiritu Taos Indian***
**oil on canvas**
**42 x 32 inches**
**1929**
**Courtesy of Nancy Paap**
**Tesuque, NM**

**Originally in the art collection of Arthur Seligman, governor of New Mexico from 1931 to 1933, Seligman gave this painting to Walcott Lord Russell as payment for curating his collection. In 2006, Nancy Paap purchased it from Russell's great-granddaughter, Laura Pendergraft.**

The influence of the Taos painters on Paap's work is most evident in his 1929 painting, *El Gran Espiritu Taos Indian* (p. 19), which stands out in many ways from his overall body of work. This relatively somber painting features two men against a blank color field. The duo fills most of the canvas. Both are draped in ambiguous pieces of cloth that ultimately merge, joining the two figures in a mass of dark brushwork. The younger figure is identifiable as Native American from his facial features, skin tone and long braids, but unlike the figures in so many Taos Society paintings, he is not additionally defined through his clothing, action or accessories. The older figure, with his head encircled with either a well-worn cloth strip or a long single braid, could be from any number of cultures.

The unclear relationship between these two men and the uncertainty of their respective identities are heightened by the painting's title, *El Gran Espiritu Taos Indian*. For the vast majority of his works, Paap uses purely descriptive titles of the individuals or locales. Here, however, Paap's title evokes the spiritual or mystical. The positioning of the younger man slightly behind the older man suggests the younger man is a link to another

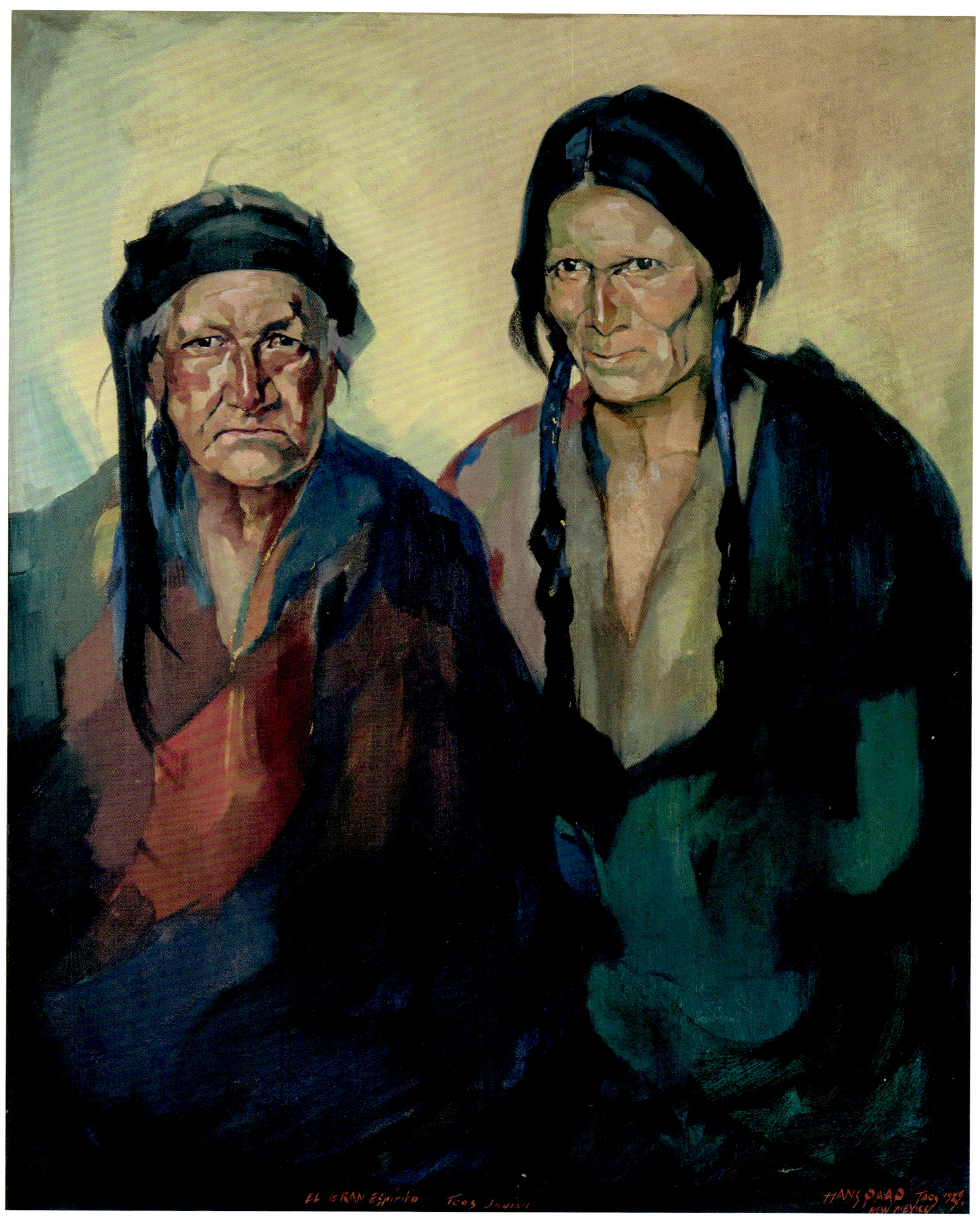
EL GRAN Espiritu Taos Indian
HANS PAAP Taos
NEW MEXICO

time or place, or perhaps that he is a spiritual presence. That this figure is more culturally identifiable may relate to the view of Pueblo culture as being more spiritual and more closely aligned with the past rather than the present, a concept that so many Taos painters espoused. Yet, this work seems more of an aberration in Paap's oeuvre, reflecting instead the direct impact of his burgeoning relationship with Taos. As Paap processed this place and its people further, his individual style emerged more clearly.

Paap's initial stay in Taos was brief, and it included an equally brief marriage to an American artist, Mildred Rackley. Together they traveled to Europe, with Paap remaining there and Rackley returning to Taos after their divorce. By 1934 Paap was working on the island of Madeira, an autonomous region of Portugal. During this period Paap's paintings once again incorporated his vibrant pastoral palette. Scenes such as *Calle San Vicente* (p. 26), painted in 1938, show his semi-abstract approach to landscapes, with bold amorphous swaths of color contrasting with strong geometric forms. In this painting, brilliantly hued blue water laps against rugged, pinkish terrain that is dotted with a few primitive structures. The image is richly evocative, and the degree of abstraction makes the scene easily accessible to all viewers. They can relate to the sense of place in such images, even though the hues are unexpected and forms are not quite natural. Although the date of Paap's *Sailboats, Portugal* (p. 29) is not known, as is the case with many of his paintings, it exemplifies his full abandonment of any vestiges of academic painting. He uses utterly vibrant colors — splotches of pastel lilacs, cerulean and chartreuse — to capture the seaside light. Moreover, his architectural forms are vaguely anonymous cubes, and the sailboats in the foreground could just as easily reside in South America or California as in Portugal. In this image there is an enthusiasm for the paint itself, for the power of color and for the emotive charge in an unexpected splash of purple on a base of tan.

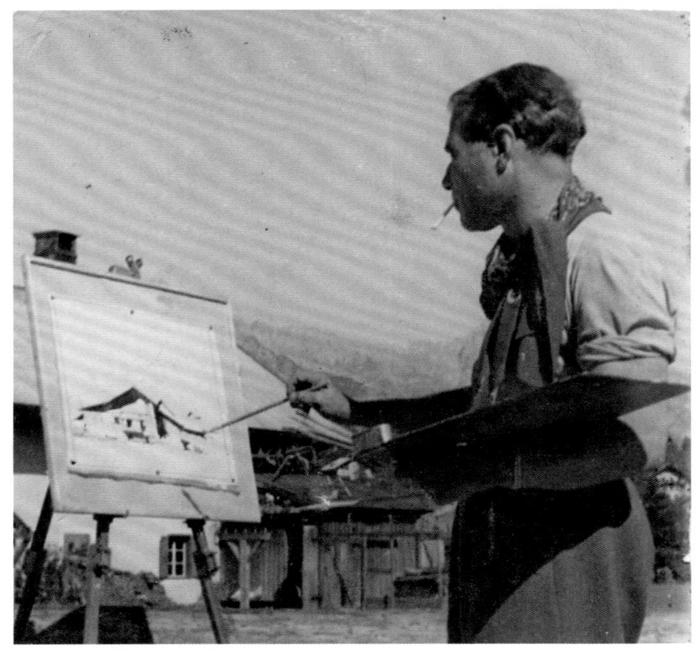

As World War II began, Paap circled back to Germany to visit his ailing mother and his sister. At this juncture, his life again took a dramatic shift. Because the German borders were subsequently closed, he was unable to leave the country and return to the United States. By some means he was able to avoid military service, and he survived primarily by painting portraits of wealthy German elites. He met his future wife, Ilse Nitschmann, at a casino in Baden Baden. Nitschmann, who was from a well-off Dutch family, was almost 30 years younger than Paap. They wed in 1943 and spent the duration of the war eking out sustenance and hoping to escape war-torn Europe. Their first son, Pancho (who later changed his name to Roy), was born in 1944, and with this increasing domesticity, Paap began to use family members as subjects in his most intimate portraits.

**Above:**
**Paap in Germany**
**c. 1945**

**Far Right:**
***Descanso de las Barcas***
**16 x 13 inches**
**oil on canvas**
**Courtesy of Nancy Paap**
**Tesuque, NM**

After Paap wed Ilse, she became the subject of many portraits, which he also apparently used as representative images when seeking portraiture commissions. In Paap's portrait of his bride on their honeymoon in Prerow in 1943, titled *Honeymoon Portrait of Ilse Paap, Prerow, Germany* (p. 9), his young wife's face is shown in profile, with her head tilted slightly down but with her gaze firmly ahead, looking into the future. She is bathed

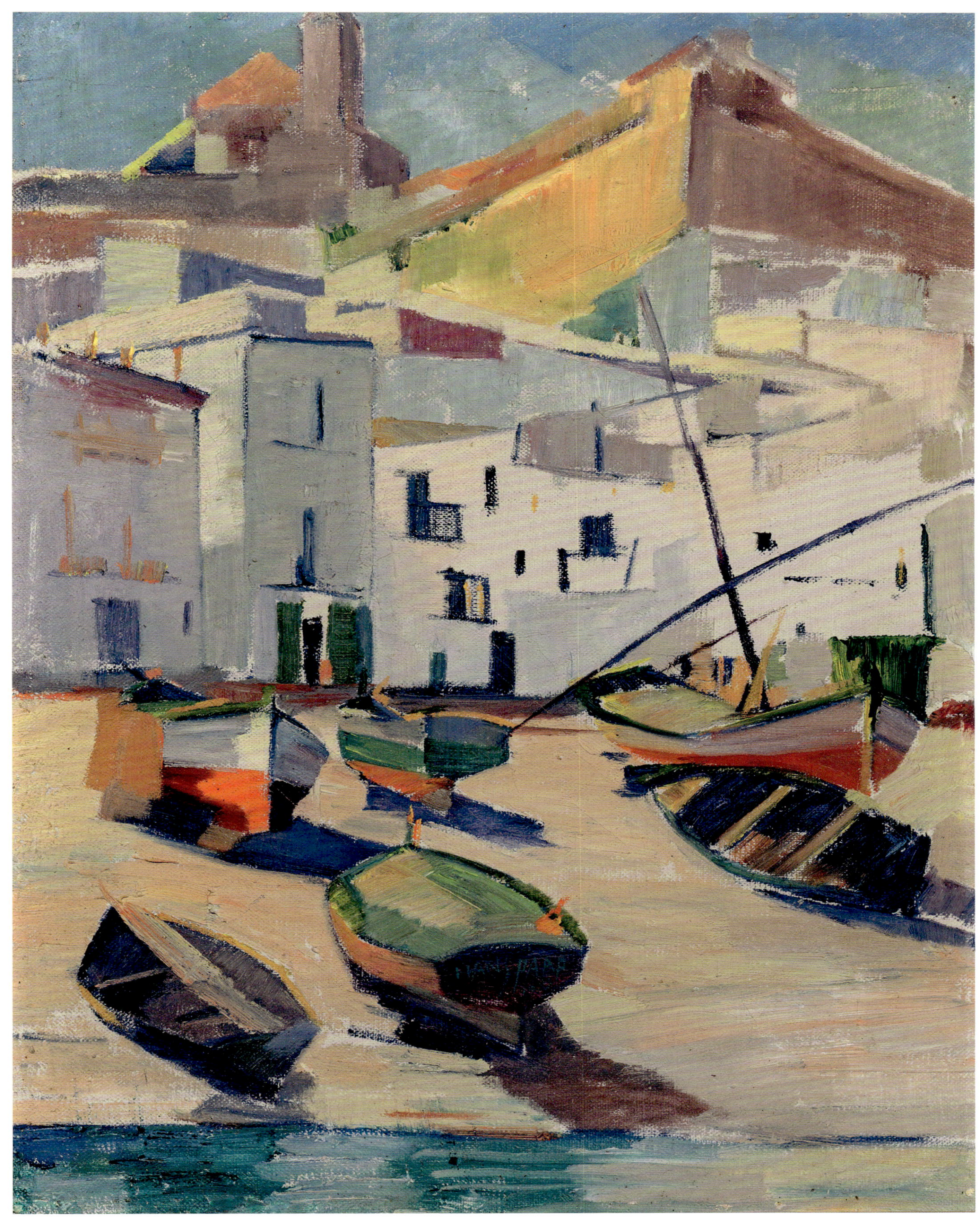

in a golden light that radiates off her blond hair and cream-colored blouse. Ilse was a striking model. A later portrait of her, posed in western attire that included a jaunty cowboy hat and a requisite red bandana (p. 104), shows what an excellent choice she was. Using family members as subjects transcended practical convenience, though: all of Paap's paintings of his family reflect love and intimacy.

Just as Paap's landscapes chronicled the places he visited, his portraiture chronicled the individuals there. Throughout his career, whenever Paap arrived in a new town, he sought out striking locals whom he could paint. His subjects reflect the extremes of society, from wealthy patrons to individuals he met on the street. Regardless of the person's station in life, Paap worked to capture the sitter's individuality and humanity. It was his habit to start each portrait by painting the subject's eyes.

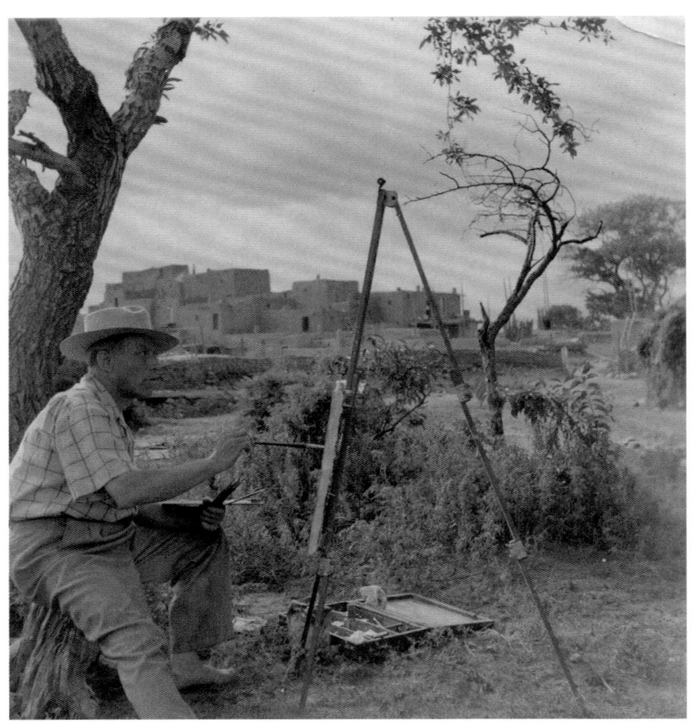

**Paap at Taos Pueblo**
**c. 1950**

After the war, Hans, Ilse and Pancho lived in Germany in displaced persons camps and then in confinement on Ellis Island for two years. This was followed by three years in the Dominican Republic, where Nancy was born in 1948. After receiving an affidavit from Martin Hennings assuring authorities that Paap had work in the United States, the family immigrated to New Mexico, finally settling in Taos in 1949. Having come full circle, Paap may have expected to finally be home. In Taos, he again threw himself into painting the people and the land, and now also his growing family. In 1952, Ilse gave birth to their third child, Hans.

At this point a subtle shift toward greater intimacy appears in Paap's portraits. It is manifested in the image of his innocent young daughter in *Nancy on Taos Street* (p. 6), painted in 1951. The image, painted looking up at the child, shows the small girl standing shyly in the middle of a dusty street, with massive bursts of autumnal gold behind her. Though her three-year-old face is not detailed, the viewer feels the painter's deep and loving connection with the subject. The angle of the view suggests a father kneeling in front of his young child, calling her to his embrace. It also makes Nancy appear almost monumental, even as she bashfully tilts her head down, juts her hips forward and clasps her tiny hands in a universal pose of childish coyness. It seems to capture the moment just before she laughs and runs to her father.

There is also depth in Paap's portraits of Taos citizens. In an undated work, titled simply *Girl with Katsina Pin* (p. 96), Paap renders a delicate depiction of a young girl whose identity and story remain unknown. Paap portrays her with vague trappings of Pueblo culture: she is wearing what is likely a Pueblo manta, or rough-textured shawl, and a woven belt. Even more compelling is the small silver-and-turquoise pin in the center of her chest. The katsina (or kachina) pin, which belonged to Paap and is owned today by his daughter, Nancy, is outsized for the girl and her dress. Her body curves over the pin ever so slightly as she stares forward, confrontationally. Viewers are left with more questions than answers. What did Paap want to convey about this child? Who was she, and what was she telling us through her eyes? How did she feel about posing for this foreigner?

The painting reflects the overall ambiguity that characterizes Paap's life and work. Was he painting his story or the sitter's? Do his landscapes accurately depict specific locales, or were they his version of what a place could or should look like?

After a decade of marriage, Ilse left Hans in 1953, and with her three children, Pancho, Nancy and Hans, moved to California. After that, Paap also left Taos, but headed to Hawaii. Later that year, an article in the *Honolulu Advertiser*, titled "'Vagabond' Will Settle Down," told of Paap's arrival. The author notes that after a lifetime of traveling the world, the artist had chosen to settle in Hawaii.[3] By 1955, though, Paap was traveling from Hamburg to New York, and by the end of the decade, he was living in Portugal. Once again, he had fully returned to his life as a wanderer, spending time in locations across Europe and Mexico, painting and exhibiting along the way.

If one were to map Hans Paap's life, it would be a series of spirals touching down repeatedly in his various "homes": Hamburg, Mexico, Argentina, Portugal and Taos, among others. Even Taos, to which he returned in his later years when he purported one last time to have settled down, would not be his final resting place. In 1967 Hans Paap died in Hamburg, his birthplace. Perhaps, in the end, he did find home, right where he had begun.

Bess Murphy, PhD
Assistant Curator, Ralph T. Coe Center
August 2018
Santa Fe, New Mexico

[1] "Hans Paap and Jack Smith at the Biltmore," *The Los Angeles Times*, April 22, 1928, Part III, 8.

[2] "Discovered on Mission," *The Los Angeles Times*, June 9, 1929, Part III, 27.

[3] Marcy Rosario, "'Vagabond' Will Settle Down: Famed Artist Decides to Make Home in Hawaii," *The Honolulu Advertiser*, May 24, 1953.

## Germany
## Spain
## Portugal

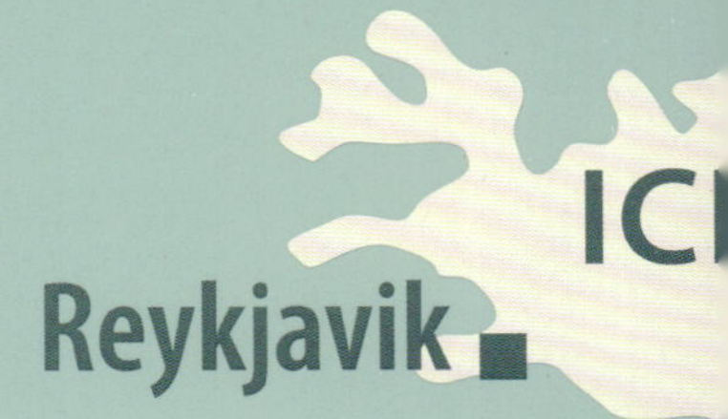


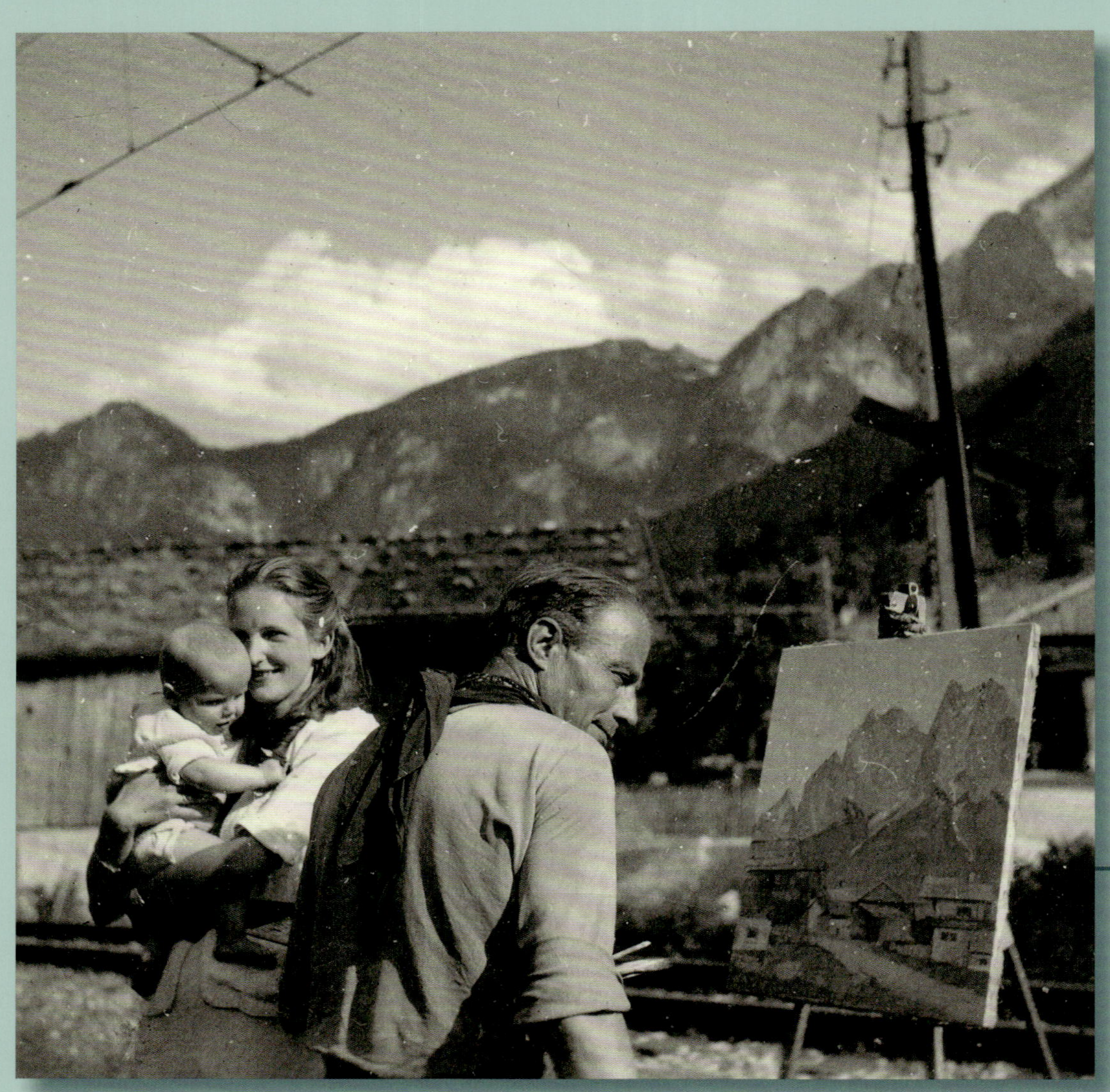

Hans, Ilse and Pancho (Roy) Paap, Germany c. 1945

*Azores (Portugal)*

*Madeira Islar (Portug*

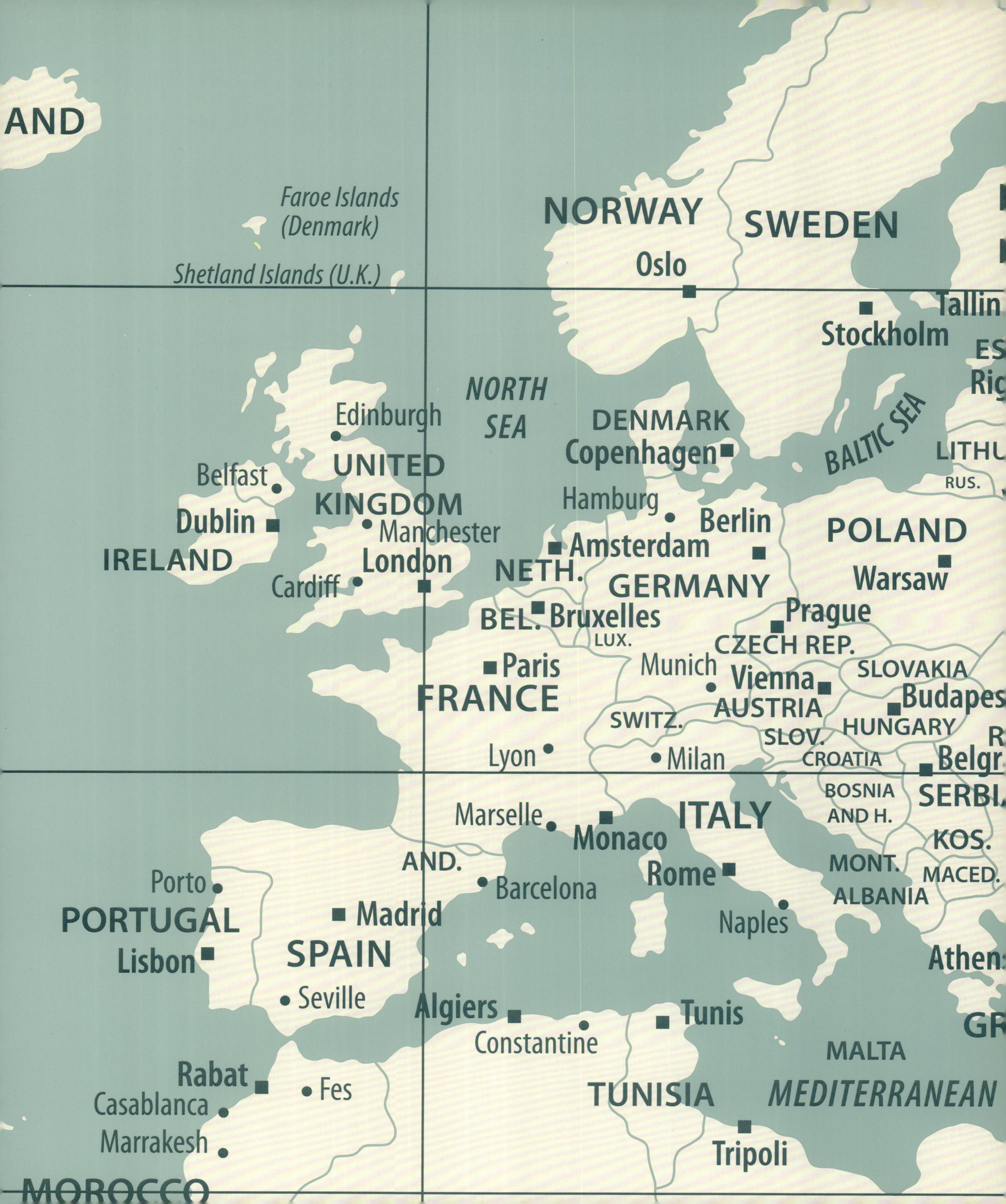

AND
Faroe Islands
(Denmark)
Shetland Islands (U.K.)
NORWAY
SWEDEN
Oslo
Tallin
Stockholm
ES
Rig
NORTH
SEA
DENMARK
Copenhagen
BALTIC SEA
LITHU
RUS.
Edinburgh
UNITED
KINGDOM
Belfast
Dublin
IRELAND
Manchester
London
Cardiff
Hamburg
Berlin
POLAND
Amsterdam
NETH.
GERMANY
Warsaw
BEL.
Bruxelles
LUX.
Prague
CZECH REP.
Paris
Munich
Vienna
SLOVAKIA
FRANCE
AUSTRIA
Budapes
SWITZ.
HUNGARY
SLOV.
R
Lyon
Milan
CROATIA
Belgr
BOSNIA
AND H.
SERBI
Marselle
Monaco
ITALY
KOS.
AND.
Rome
MONT.
MACED.
Porto
Barcelona
ALBANIA
PORTUGAL
Madrid
Naples
Lisbon
SPAIN
Athen
Seville
Algiers
Tunis
GR
Constantine
MALTA
Rabat
Fes
TUNISIA
MEDITERRANEAN
Casablanca
Tripoli
Marrakesh
MOROCCO

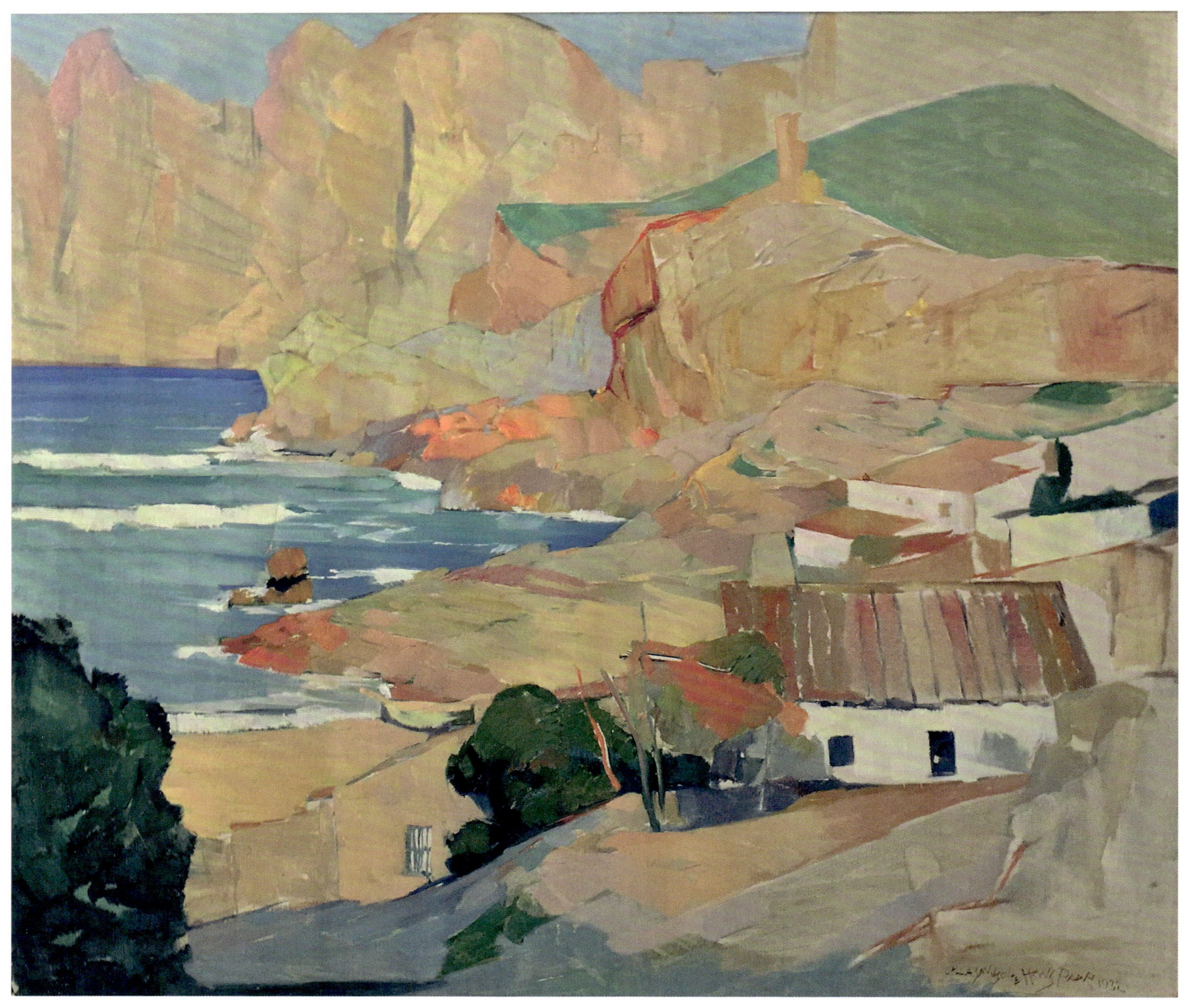

*Calle San Vicente*
oil on canvas
21¼ x 25 inches
1938
Courtesy of William Ponseti
Lincoln, CA

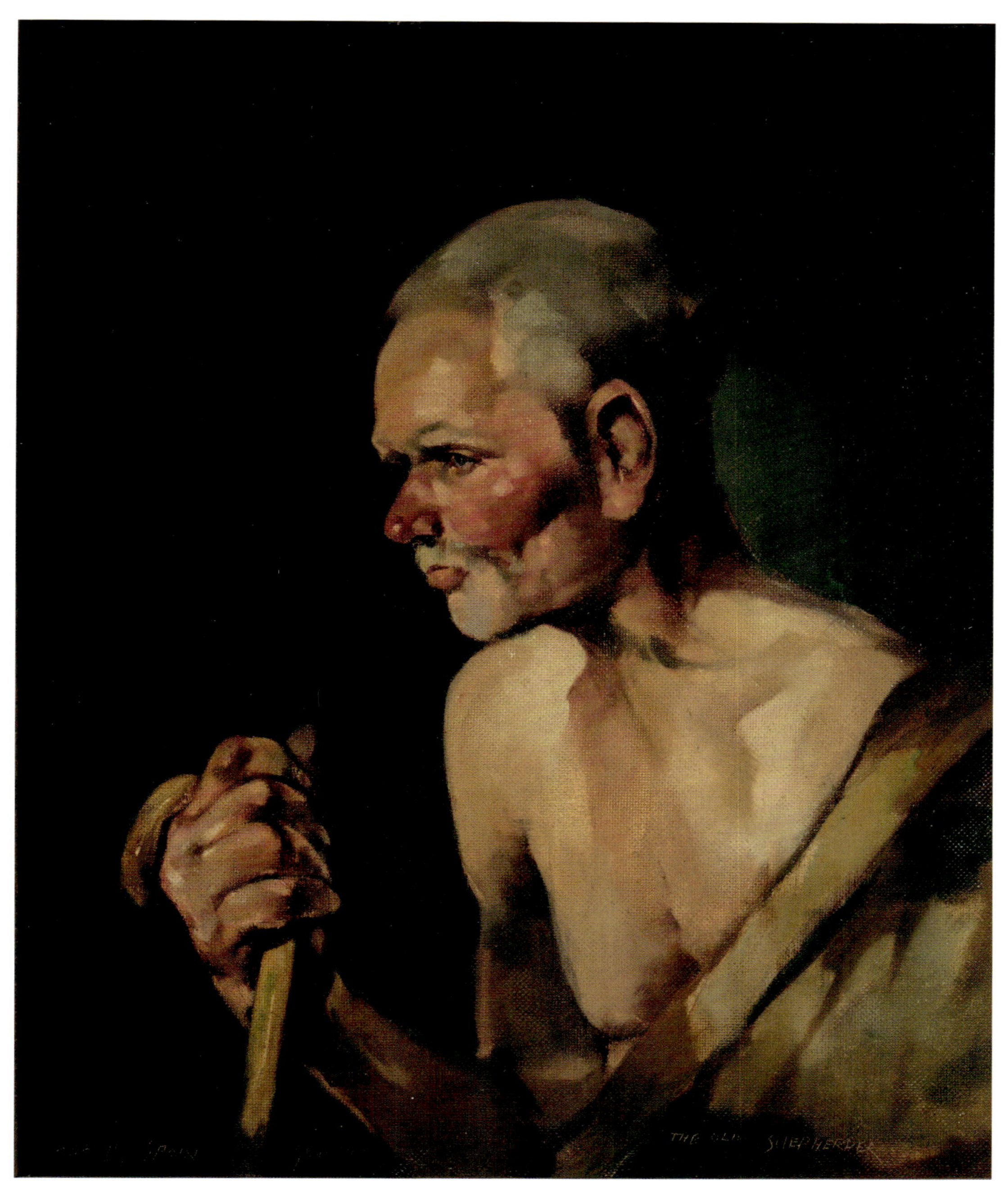

*The Old Sheep Herder, Spain*
oil on board
24 x 23 inches
Courtesy of Nancy Paap
Tesuque, NM

*Sailboats, Portugal*
oil on board
22 x 18 inches
Courtesy of Nancy Paap
Tesuque, NM

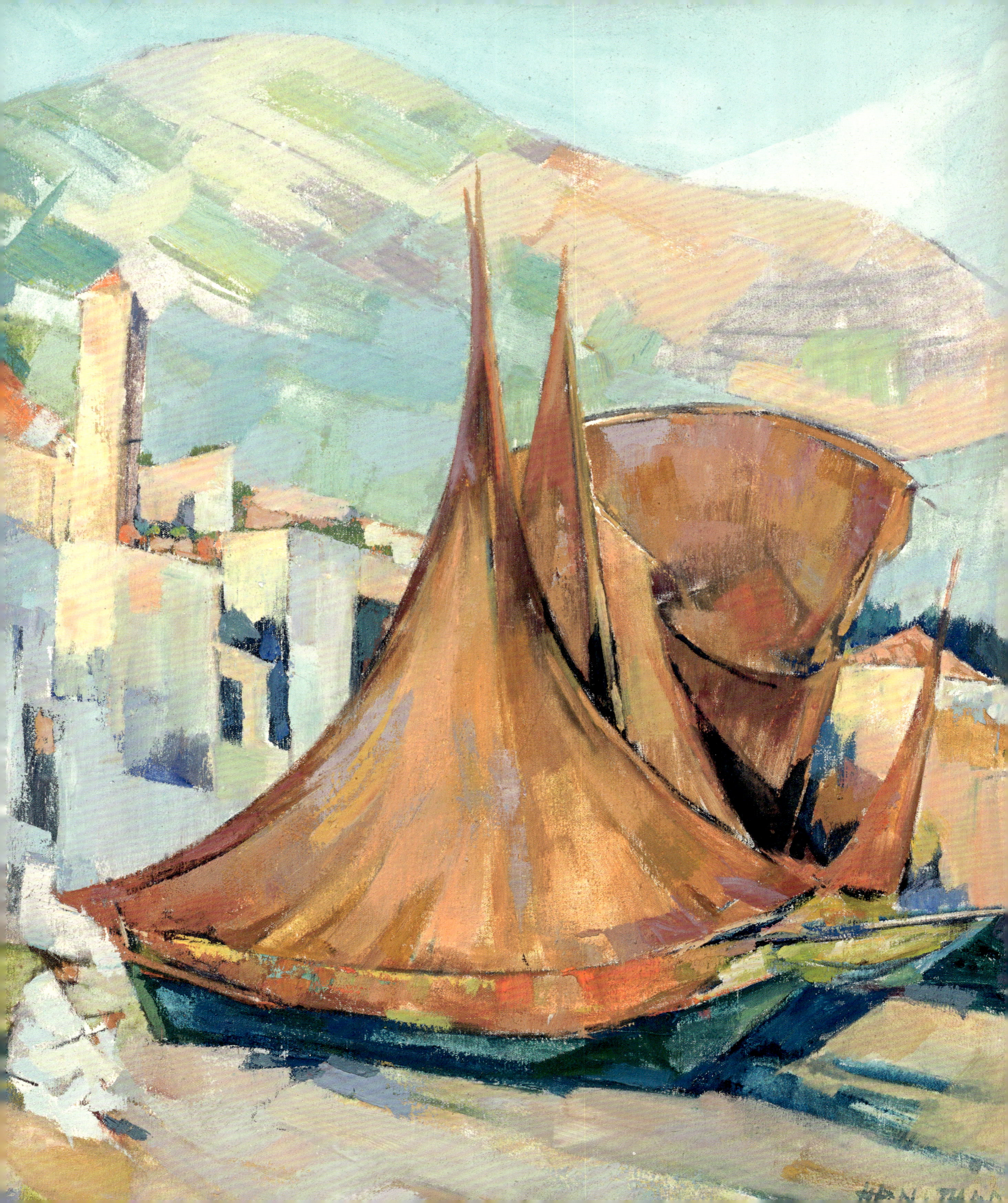

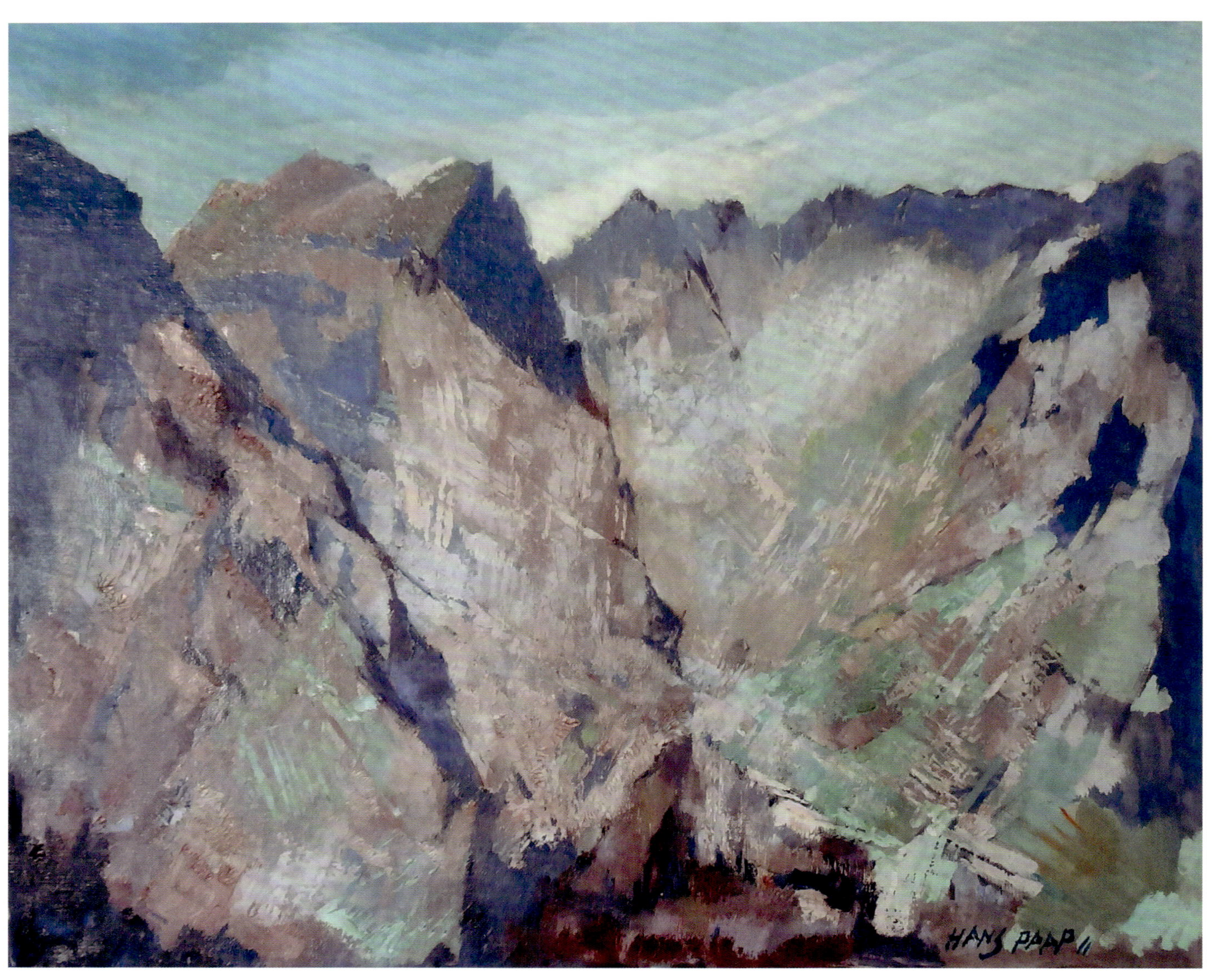
HANS PAAP 11

*Sierras da Madeira*
*(Sierras of Madeira)*
oil on canvas
20 x 24 inches
c. 1934
Courtesy of Quinta das Cruzes Museum
Madeira, Portugal

Monterrey
Culiacán
MEXICO
Guadalajara
Mexico
Acapulco

## Brazil
## Argentina
## The Dominican Republic

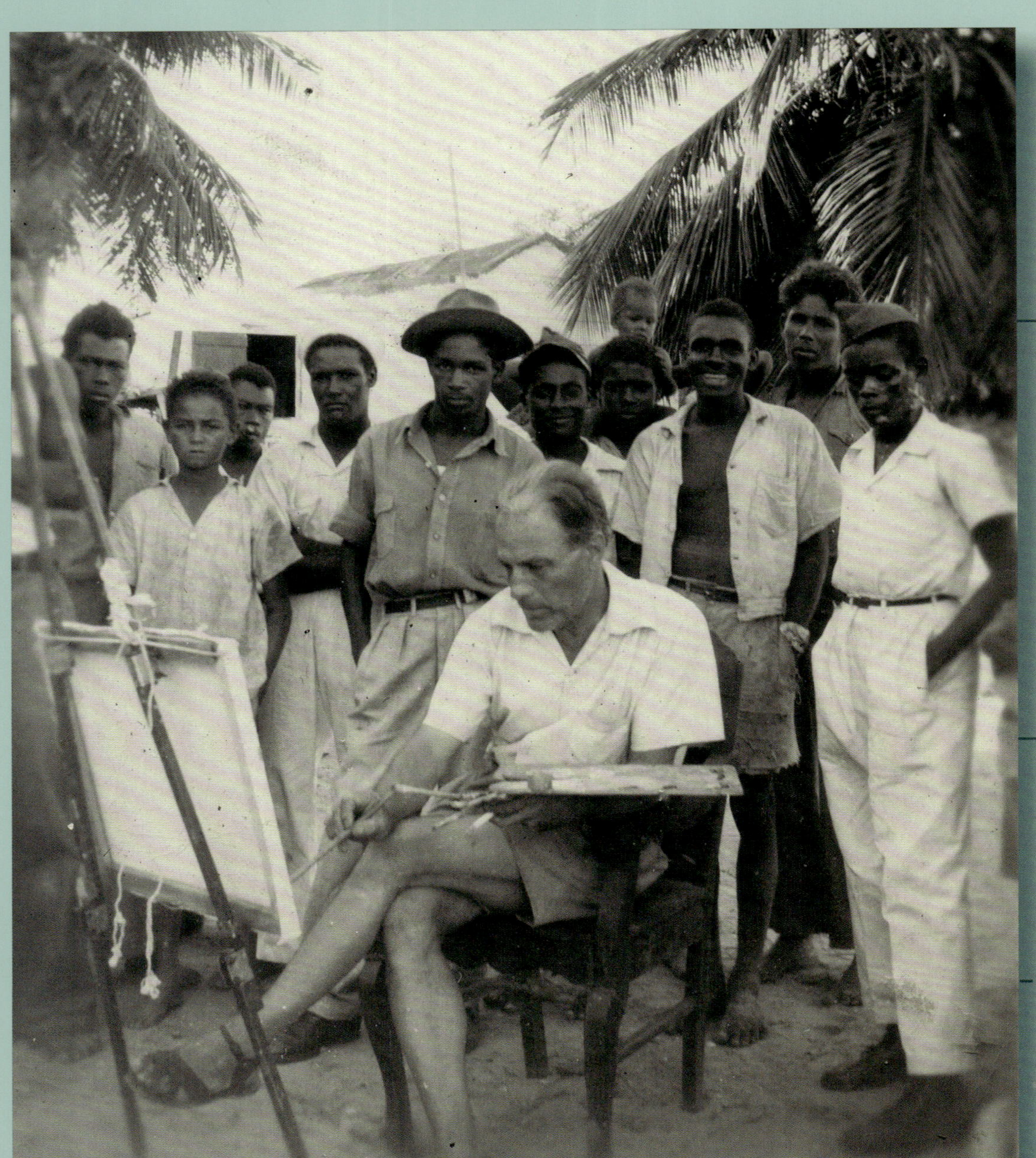

*I. Sola y Gómez (Chile)*

**Paap in the Dominican Republic c. 1948**

OCEAN

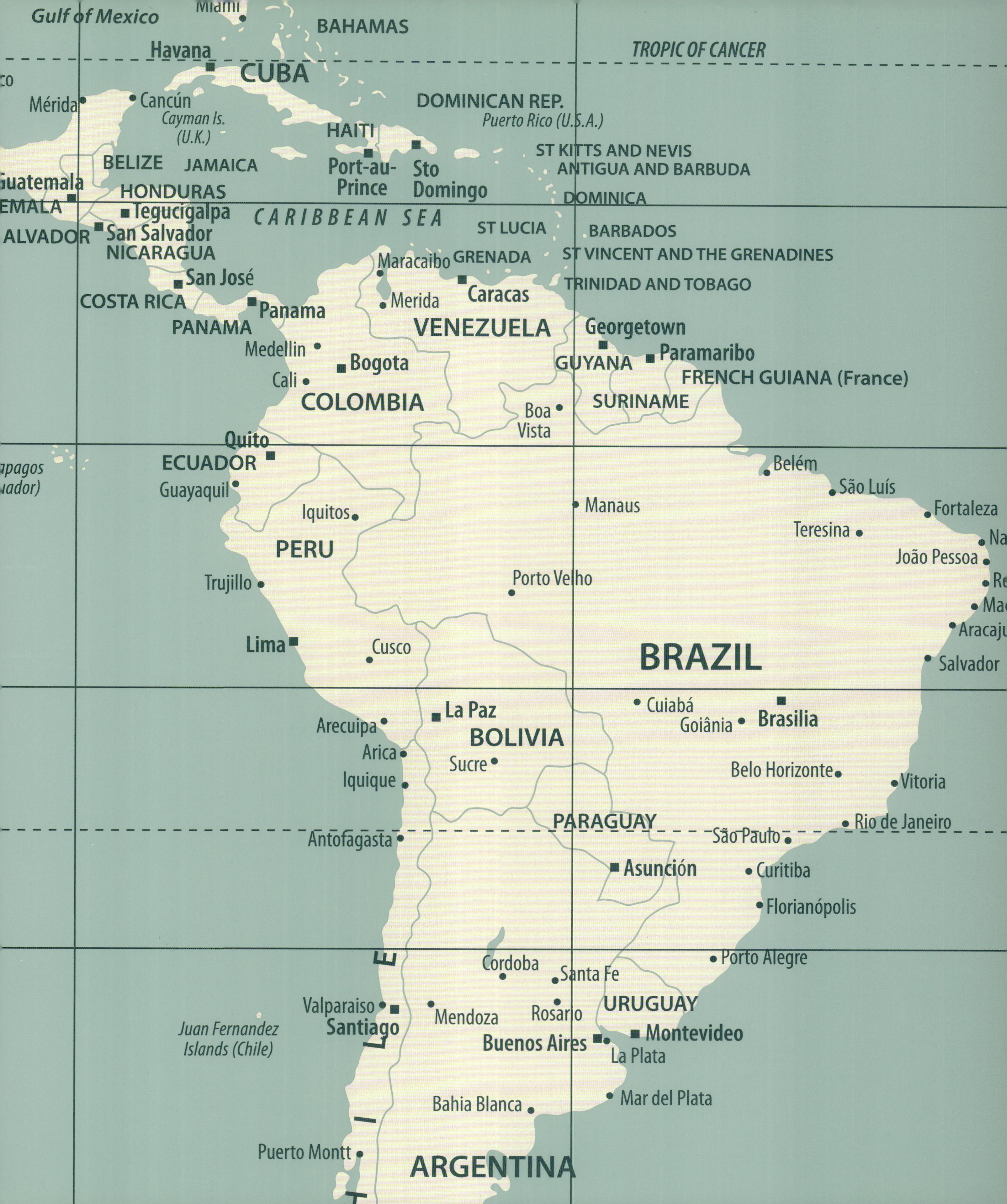

Gulf of Mexico
Miami
BAHAMAS
Havana
CUBA
TROPIC OF CANCER
Mérida
Cancún
Cayman Is.
(U.K.)
DOMINICAN REP.
Puerto Rico (U.S.A.)
HAITI
BELIZE
JAMAICA
Port-au-Prince
Sto Domingo
ST KITTS AND NEVIS
ANTIGUA AND BARBUDA
DOMINICA
HONDURAS
Tegucigalpa
CARIBBEAN SEA
ST LUCIA
BARBADOS
San Salvador
NICARAGUA
Maracaibo
GRENADA
ST VINCENT AND THE GRENADINES
San José
Caracas
TRINIDAD AND TOBAGO
COSTA RICA
Panama
Merida
PANAMA
VENEZUELA
Georgetown
Medellin
Bogota
GUYANA
Paramaribo
FRENCH GUIANA (France)
Cali
COLOMBIA
SURINAME
Boa Vista
Quito
ECUADOR
Belém
Guayaquil
São Luís
Iquitos
Manaus
Fortaleza
Teresina
PERU
João Pessoa
Trujillo
Porto Velho
Aracaju
Lima
Cusco
BRAZIL
Salvador
Cuiabá
Brasilia
La Paz
Goiânia
Arecuipa
BOLIVIA
Arica
Sucre
Belo Horizonte
Iquique
Vitoria
PARAGUAY
Rio de Janeiro
Antofagasta
São Paulo
Asunción
Curitiba
Florianópolis
Porto Alegre
Cordoba
Santa Fe
Valparaiso
URUGUAY
Mendoza
Rosario
Juan Fernandez
Islands (Chile)
Santiago
Buenos Aires
Montevideo
La Plata
Bahia Blanca
Mar del Plata
Puerto Montt
ARGENTINA

*The title is taken from the words Paap wrote on this painting of a Brazilian fisherman. Paap started every portrait by painting the subject's eyes. Taos sculptor Maye Torres remembers as a child being mesmerized by the eyes of the fisherman in this large portrait that hung in the living room of her grandparents. As owners of Tano's Bar in Taos, they took the painting in trade. It has now been in the family for three generations.*

***Brasil El Pescador***
***Valente de Inla***
***de Paqueta***
**oil on canvas**
**42 x 32 inches**
**Courtesy of Maye Torres**
**Taos, NM**

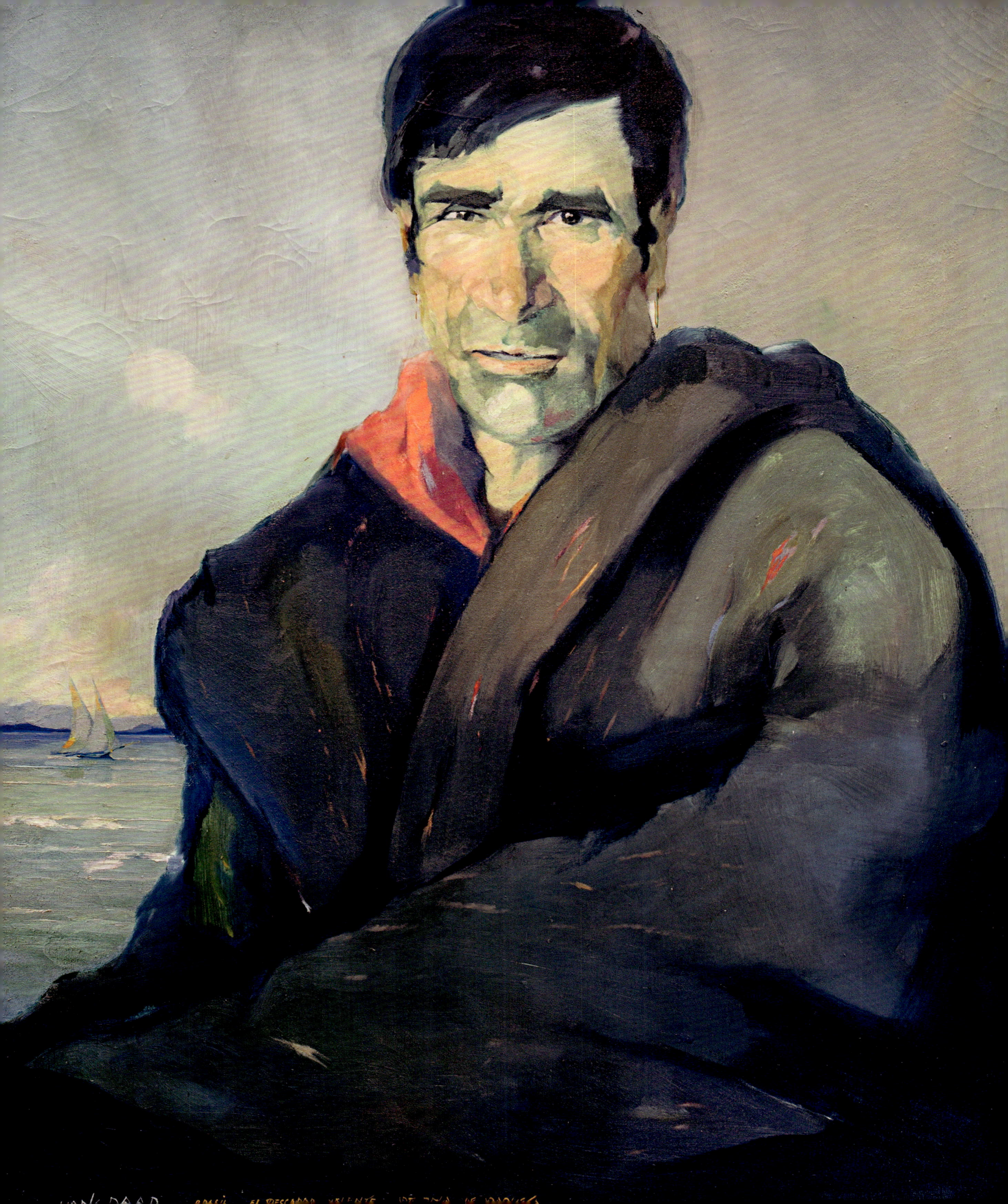

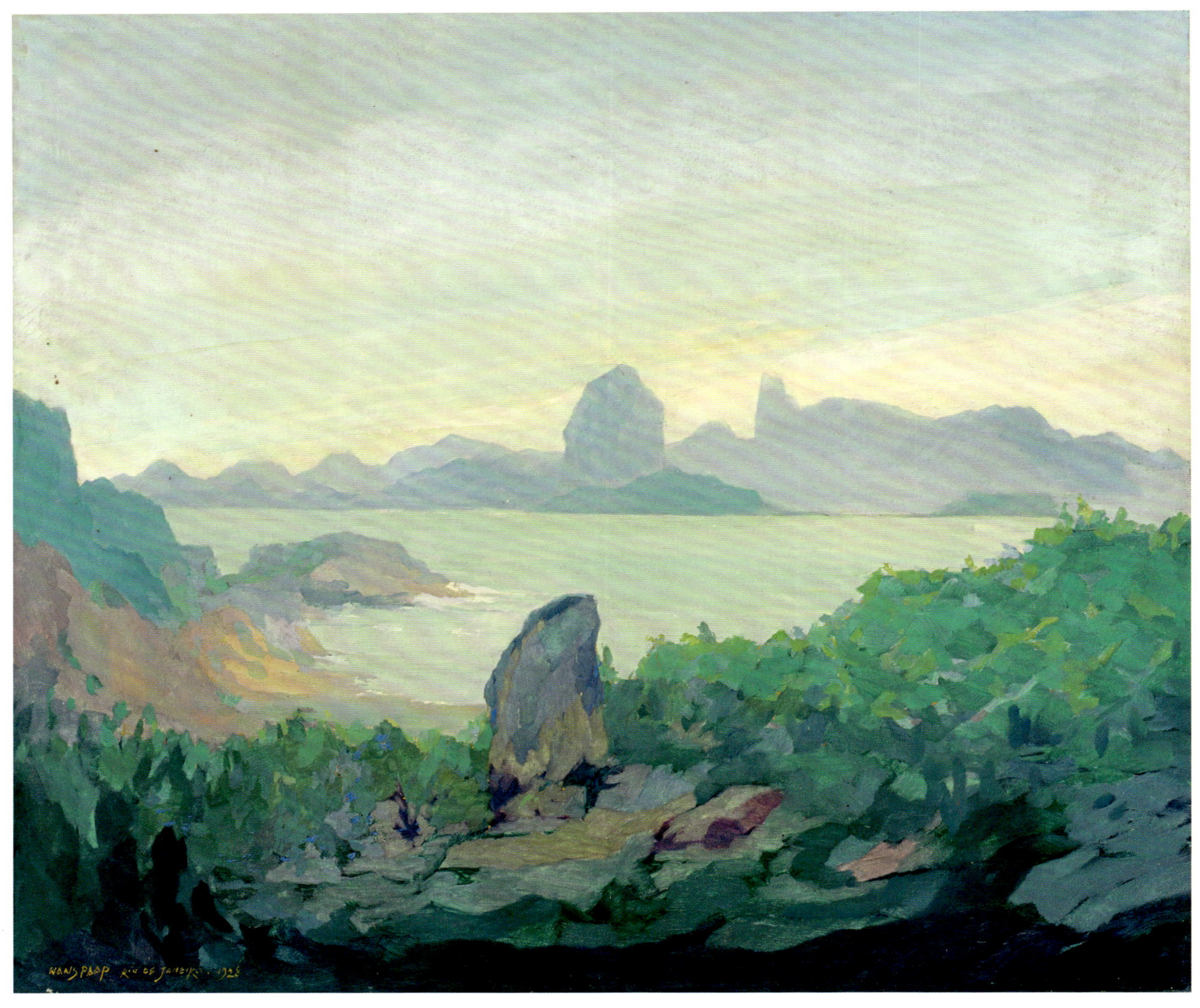

***Rio de Janeiro Harbor***
**oil on canvas**
**22 x 27 inches**
**1928**
**Courtesy of Nancy Paap**
**Tesuque, NM**

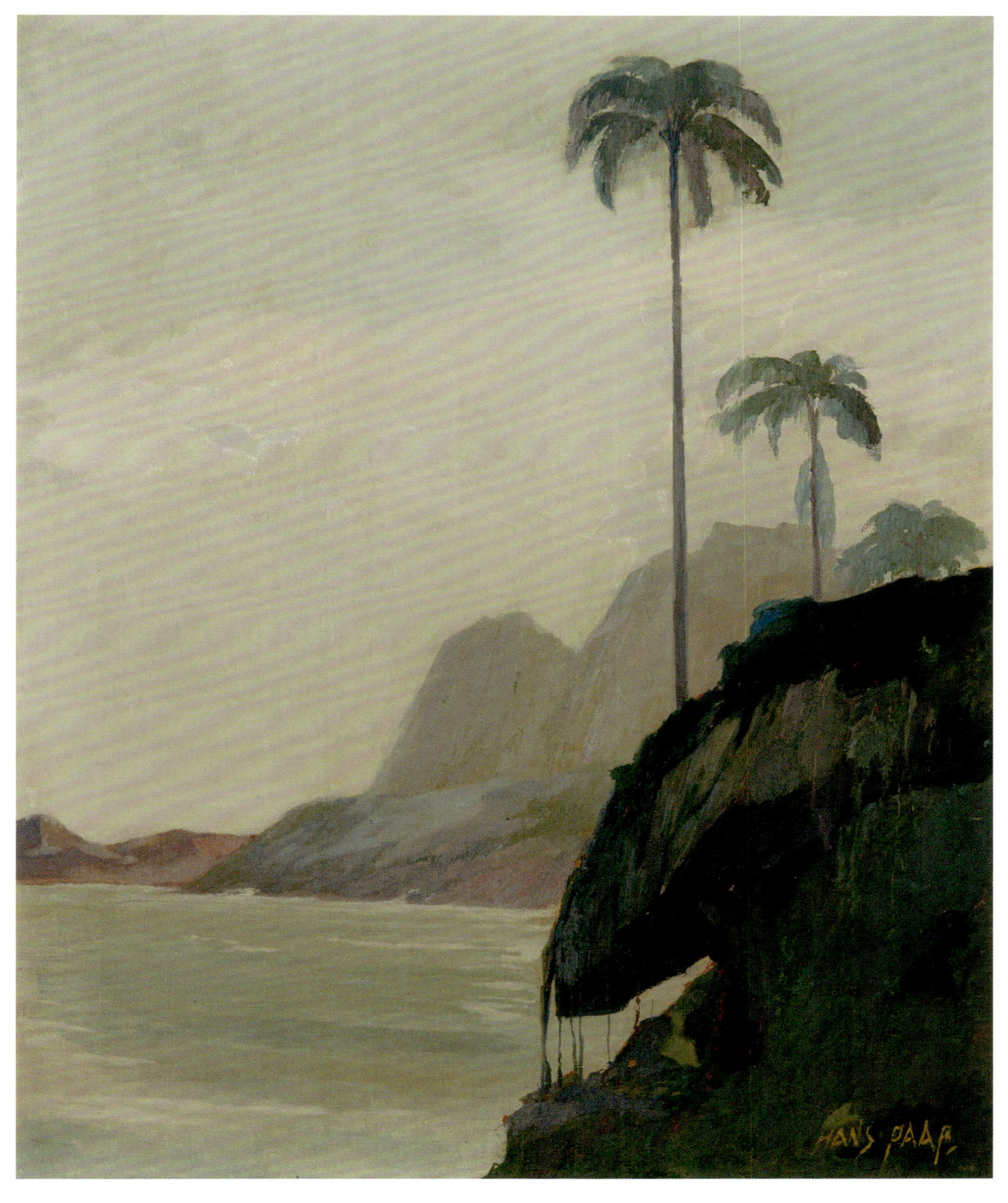


*Brazilian Seascape*
oil on canvas
24 x 19¼ inches
Courtesy of
Peter Boetsma
Havre de Grace, MD

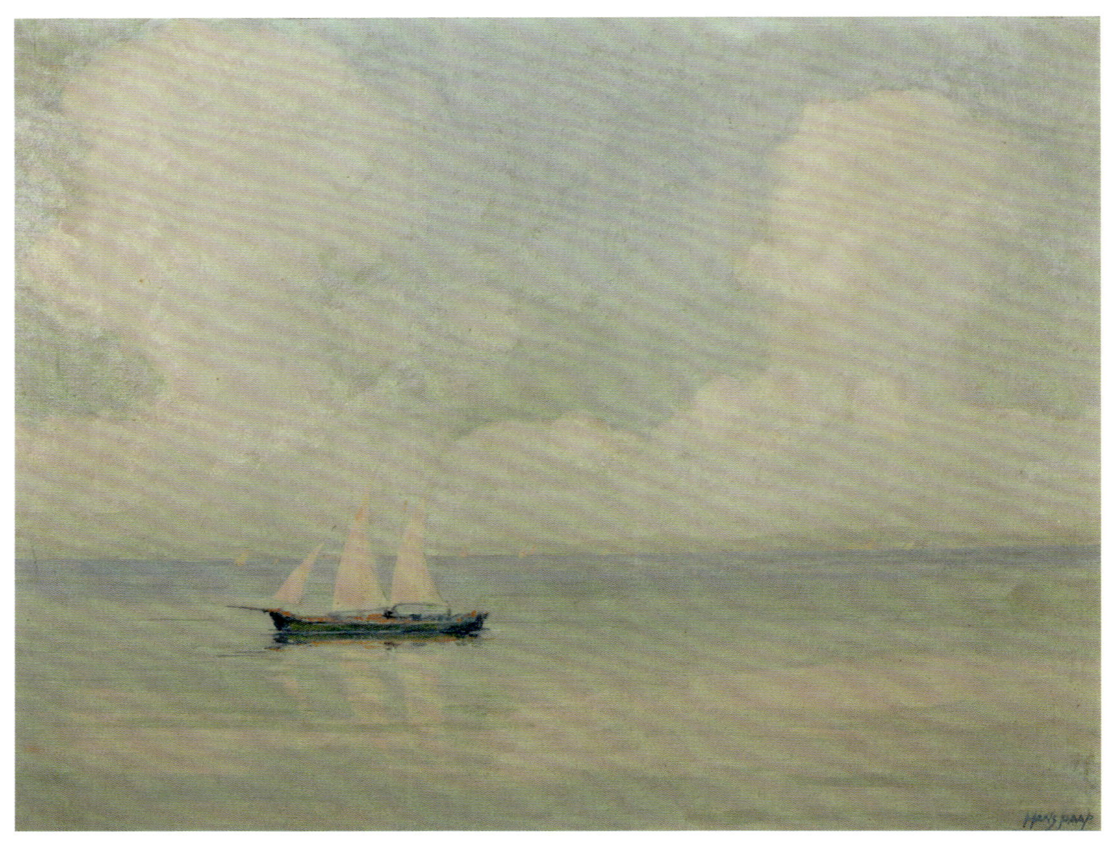

*In his early Brazilian landscapes, Paap used a softer, more muted palette than in his later landscape paintings. It is not known whether the more muted palette was a stylistic decision, or if he was accurately documenting the humid climate of the coast.*

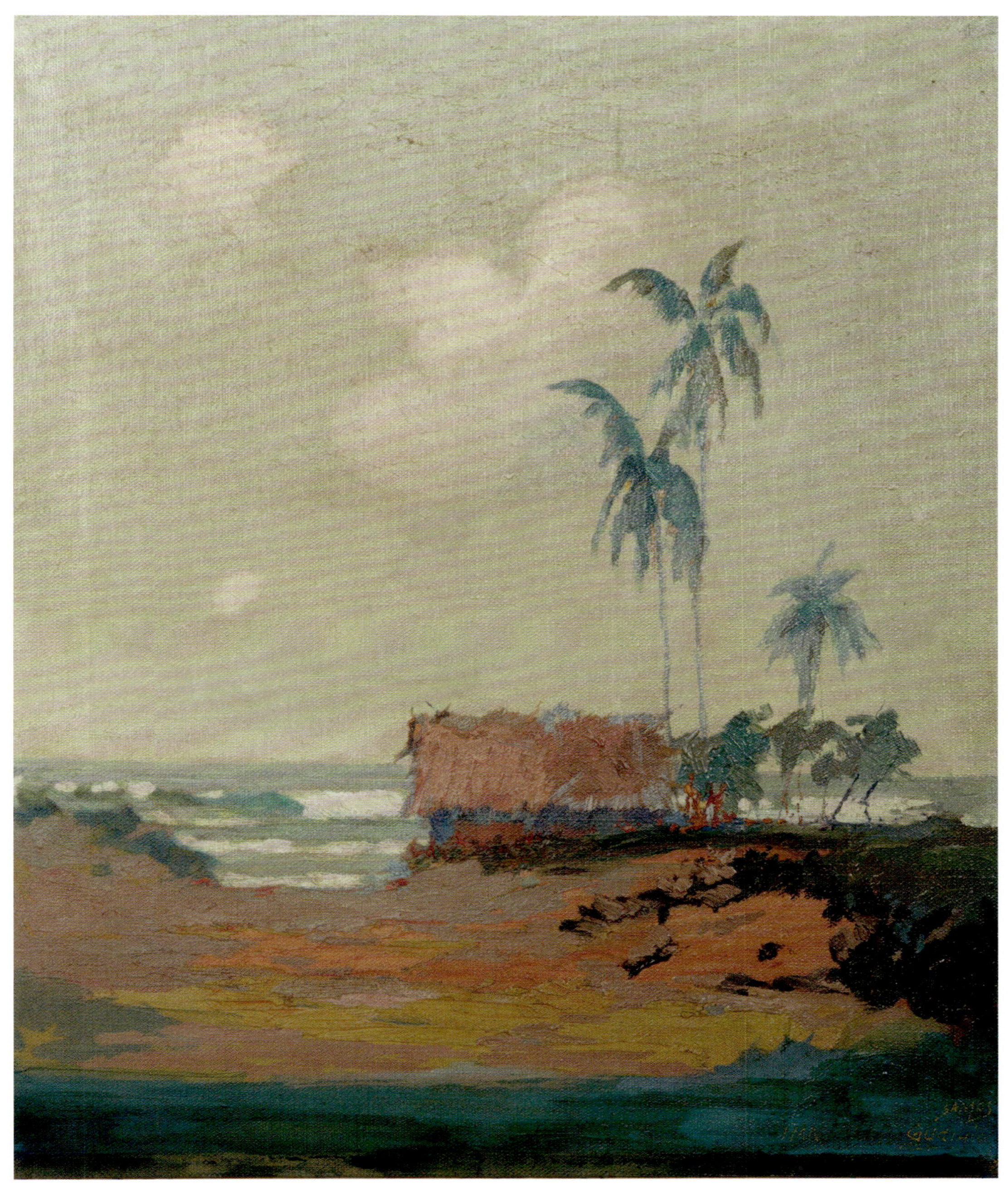

Far left:
***Sailing the Brazilian Coastline***
**oil on canvas**
**18 x 23 inches**
**Courtesy of**
**Peter Boetsma**
**Havre de Grace, MD**

Near left:
***Ocean Cottage, Santos, Brazil***
**oil on canvas**
**27 x 18½ inches**
**c. 1920-1924**
**Courtesy of**
**Peter Boetsma**
**Havre de Grace, MD**

*Paap's father, fearing his son could not making a living solely from painting, sent him to Mexico to learn a trade. There, Paap became proficient in textile printing, leather engraving and lithography.* Corcovado *is done on silk. It is the only piece in this book that showcases one of the skills Paap studied and mastered while in Mexico.*

*Corcovado* (Brazil)
black ink on silk
15 x 12 inches
1927
Courtesy of JoAnna Paap
Santa Fe, NM

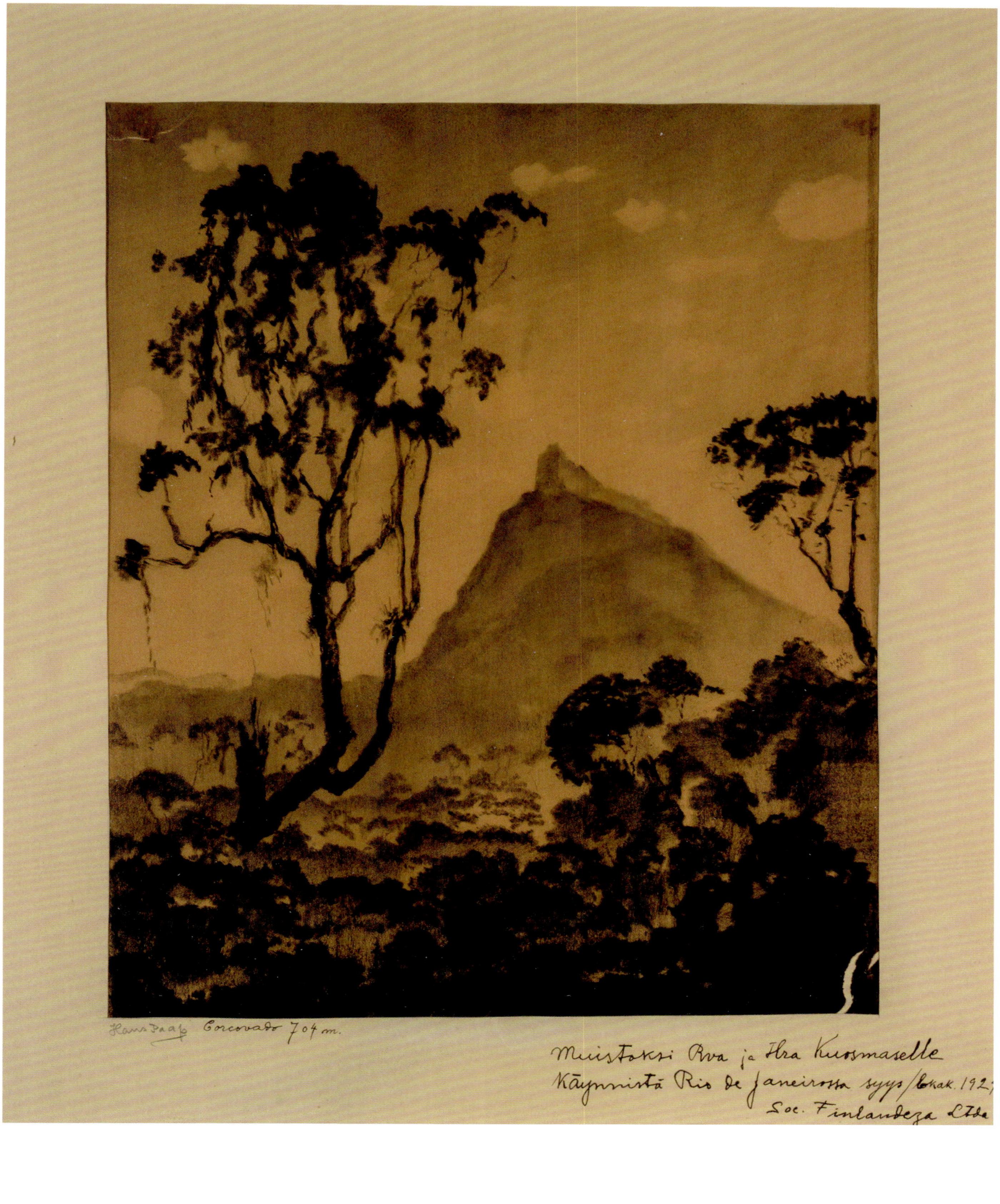
Corcovado 704 m.
Muistoksi Rva ja Hra Kuosmaselle
Käynnistä Rio de Janeirossa syys/lokak. 192
Soc. Finlandeza Ltda

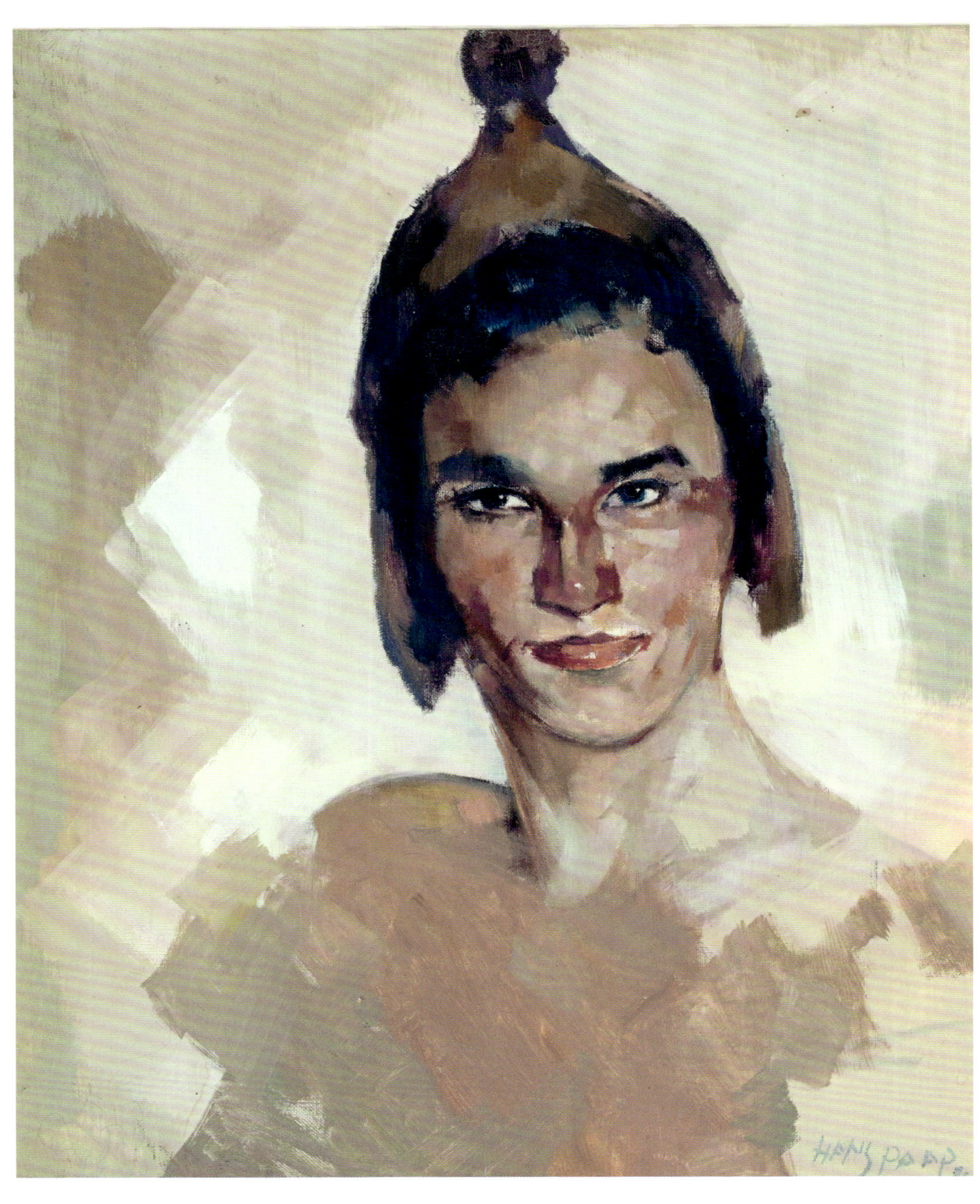
HANS PAAP

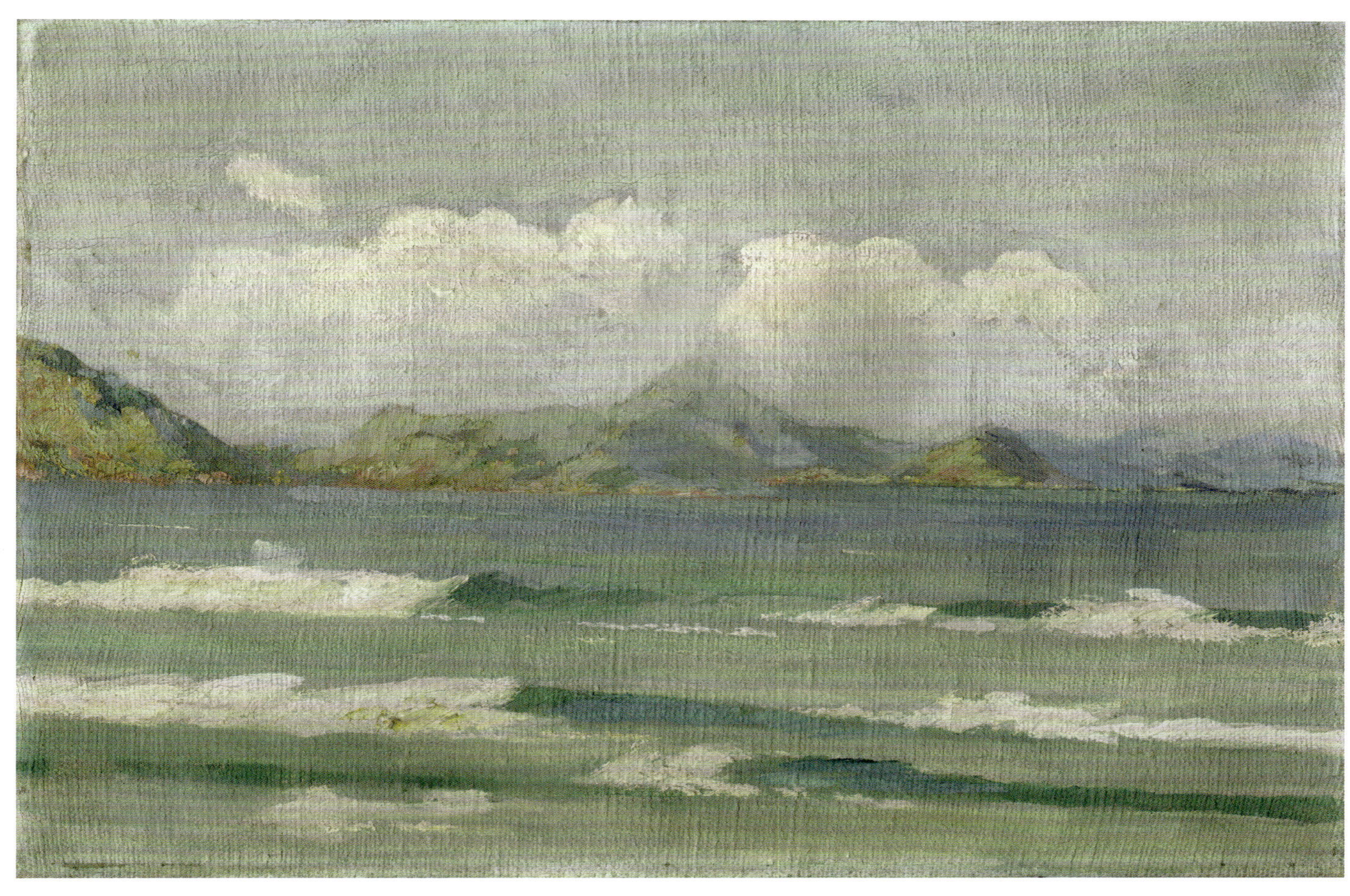

Left:
*Portrait of a Young Man*
oil on board
22 x 18 inches
Courtesy of JoAnna Paap
Santa Fe, NM

Above:
*Dusk Seascape*
oil on canvas
13 x 18½ inches
Courtesy of
Garrett W. Boetsma
and Renee G. Boetsma
Lawrenceville, NJ

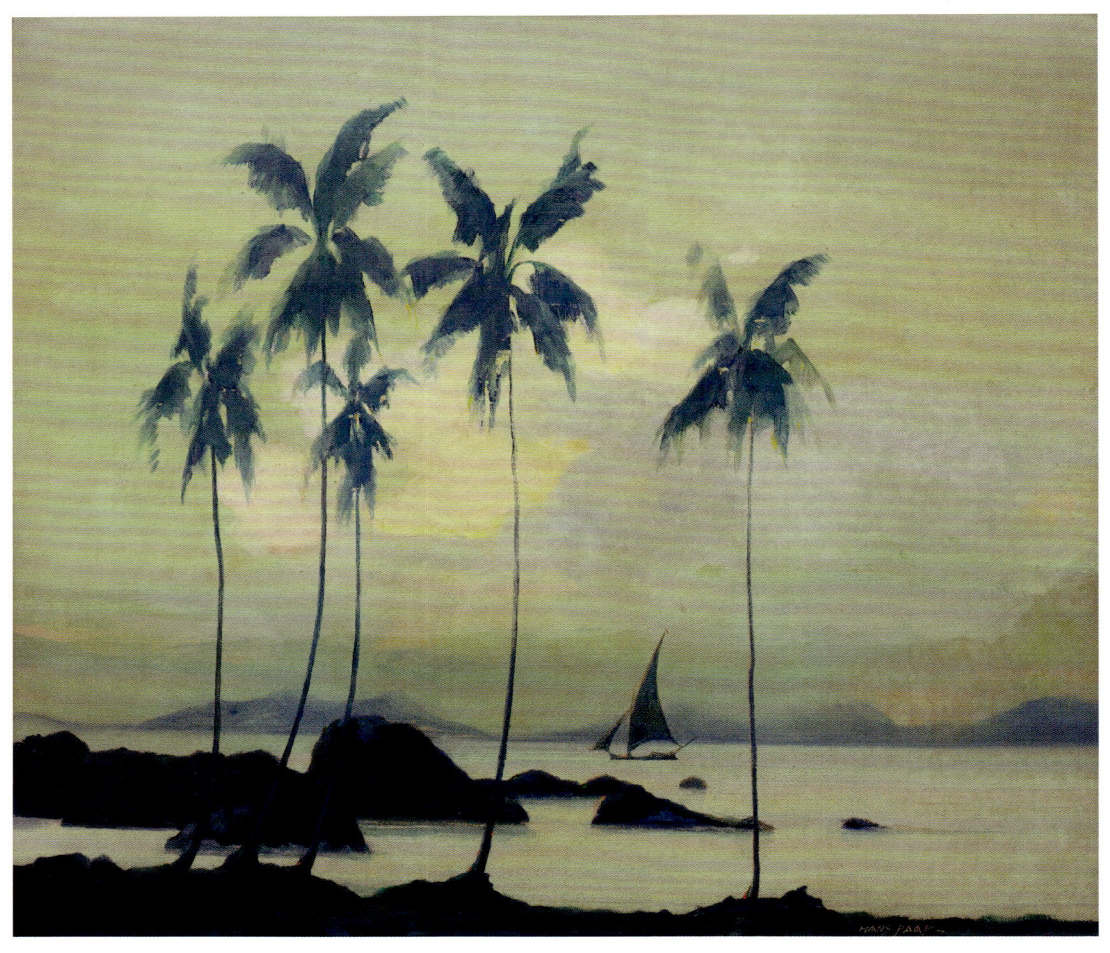

**Near right:**
***Dusk on Brazilian Coast***
**20 x 22 inches**
**oil on canvas**
**c. 1923**
**Courtesy of**
**Garrett W. Boetsma**
**and Renee G. Boetsma**
**Lawrenceville, NJ**

**Far right:**
***Paquito***
**oil on canvas**
**13 x 11¼ inches**
**1921**
**Courtesy of**
**Peter Boetsma**
**Havre de Grace, MD**

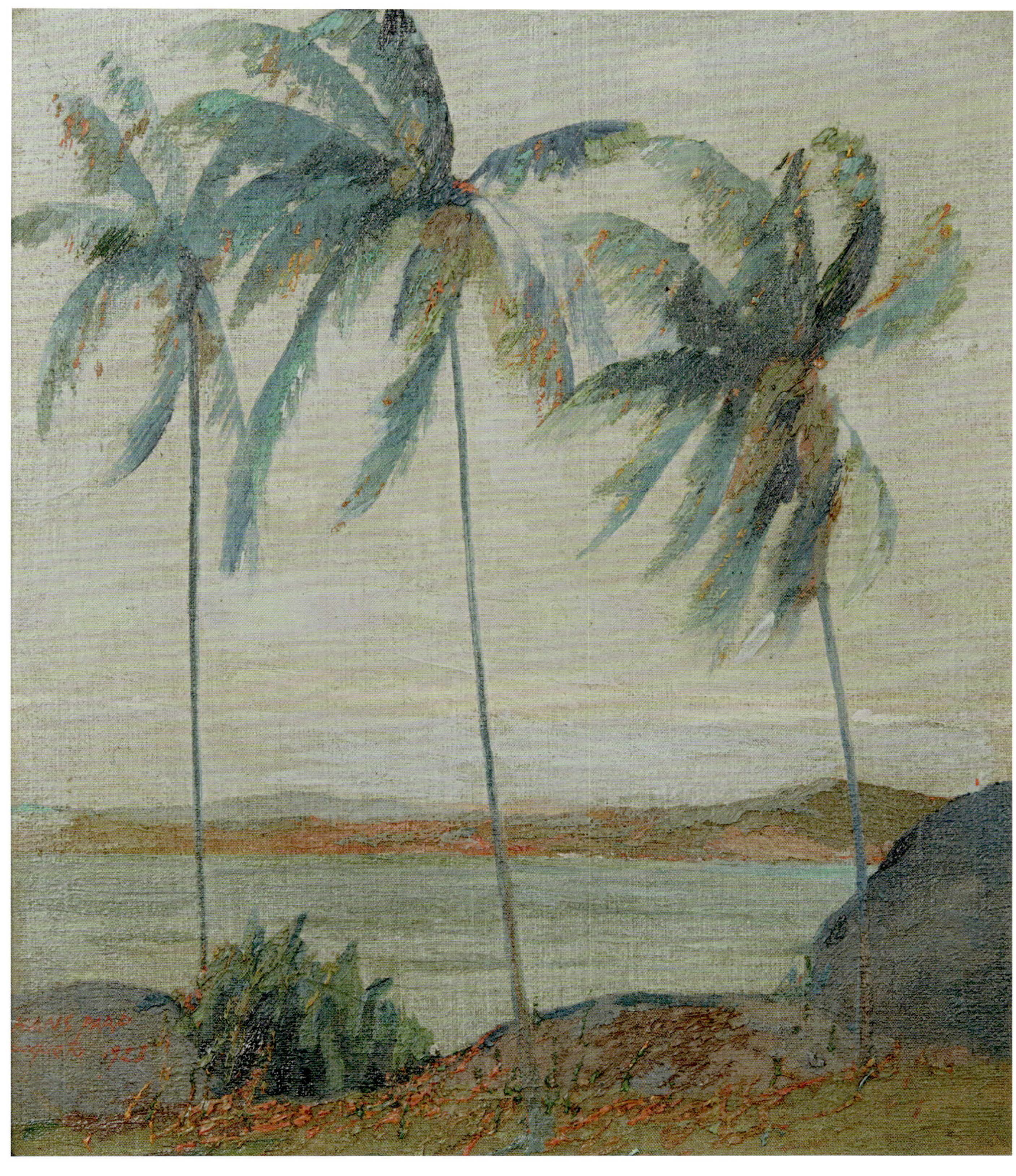

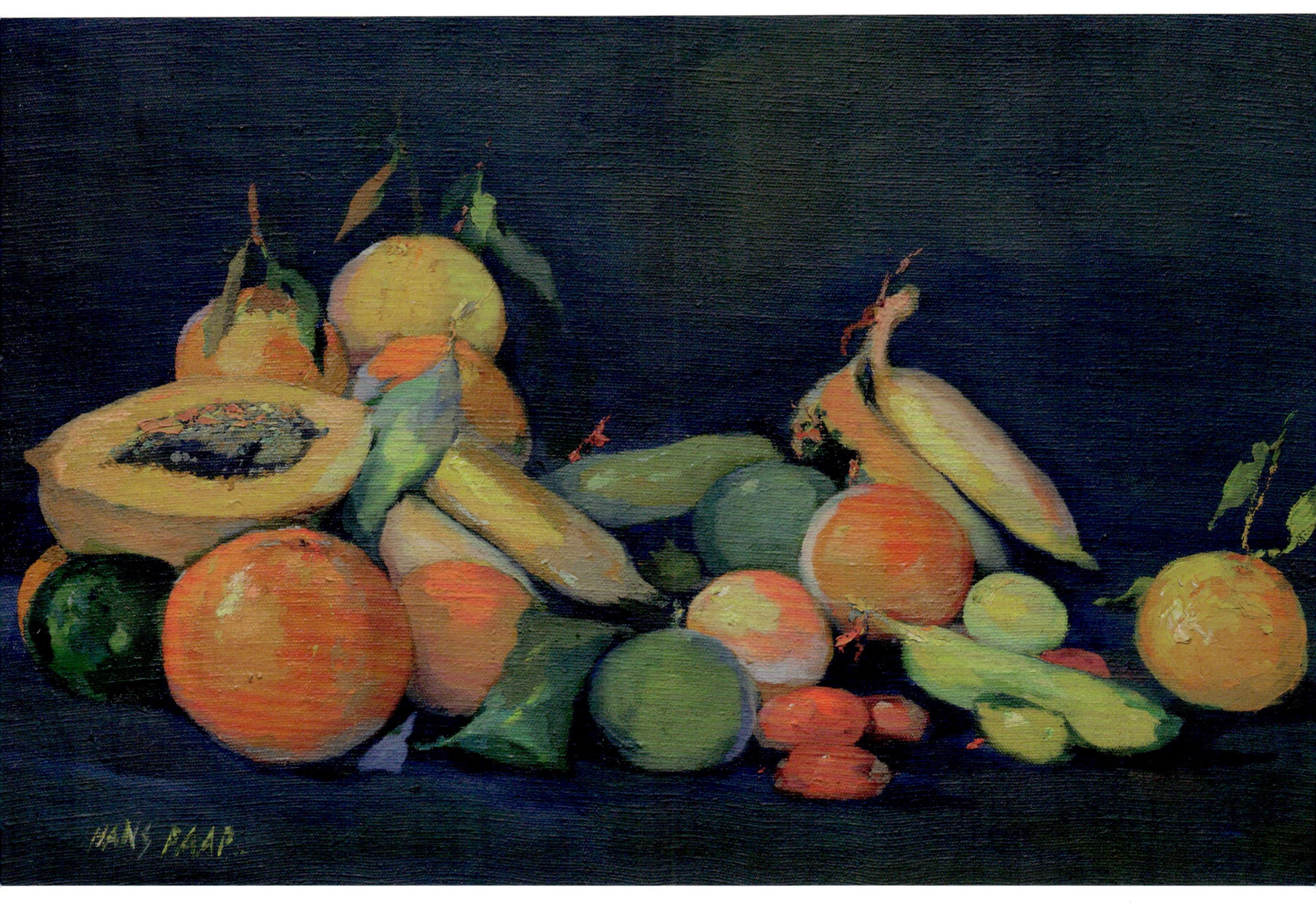
HANS PAAP.

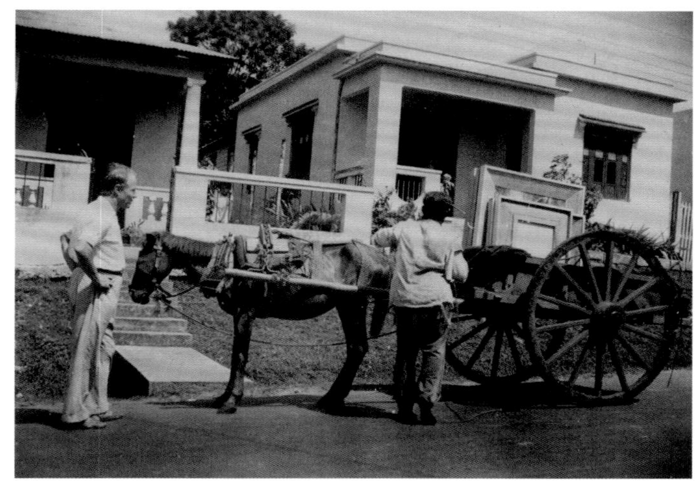

Left:
*Tropical Fruit Still Life*
oil on canvas
18½ x 27 inches
c. 1923
Courtesy of
Garrett W. Boetsma
and Renee G. Boetsma
Lawrenceville, NJ

Above:
Paap supervises the
loading of paintings in
front of his house,
Villa Duarte,
the Dominican Republic
c. 1947–1949

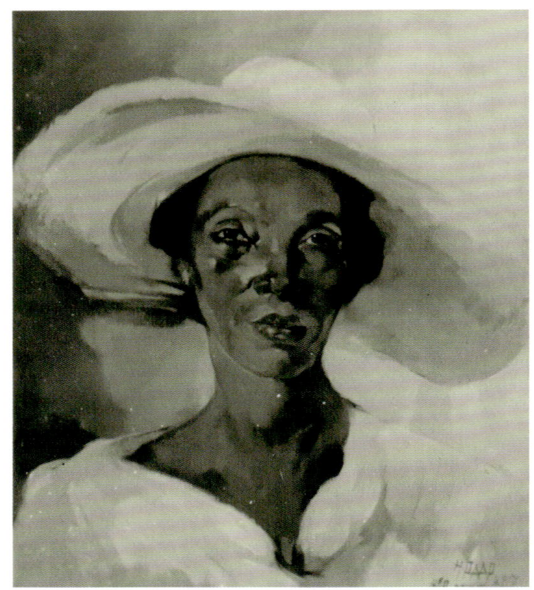

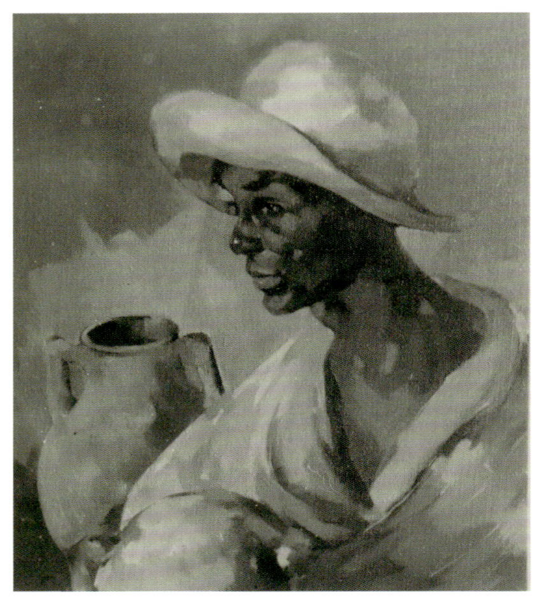

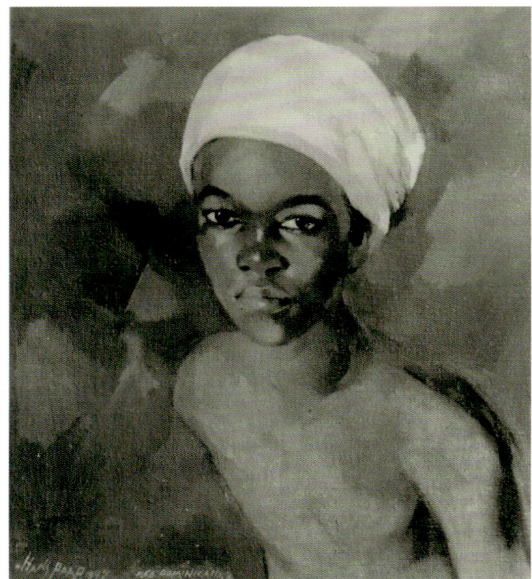

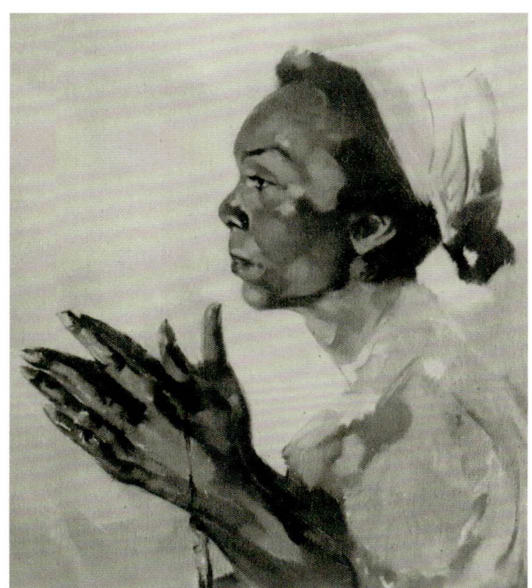

**Portraits by Hans Paap, photographed by Ilse Paap, The Dominican Republic c. 1948**

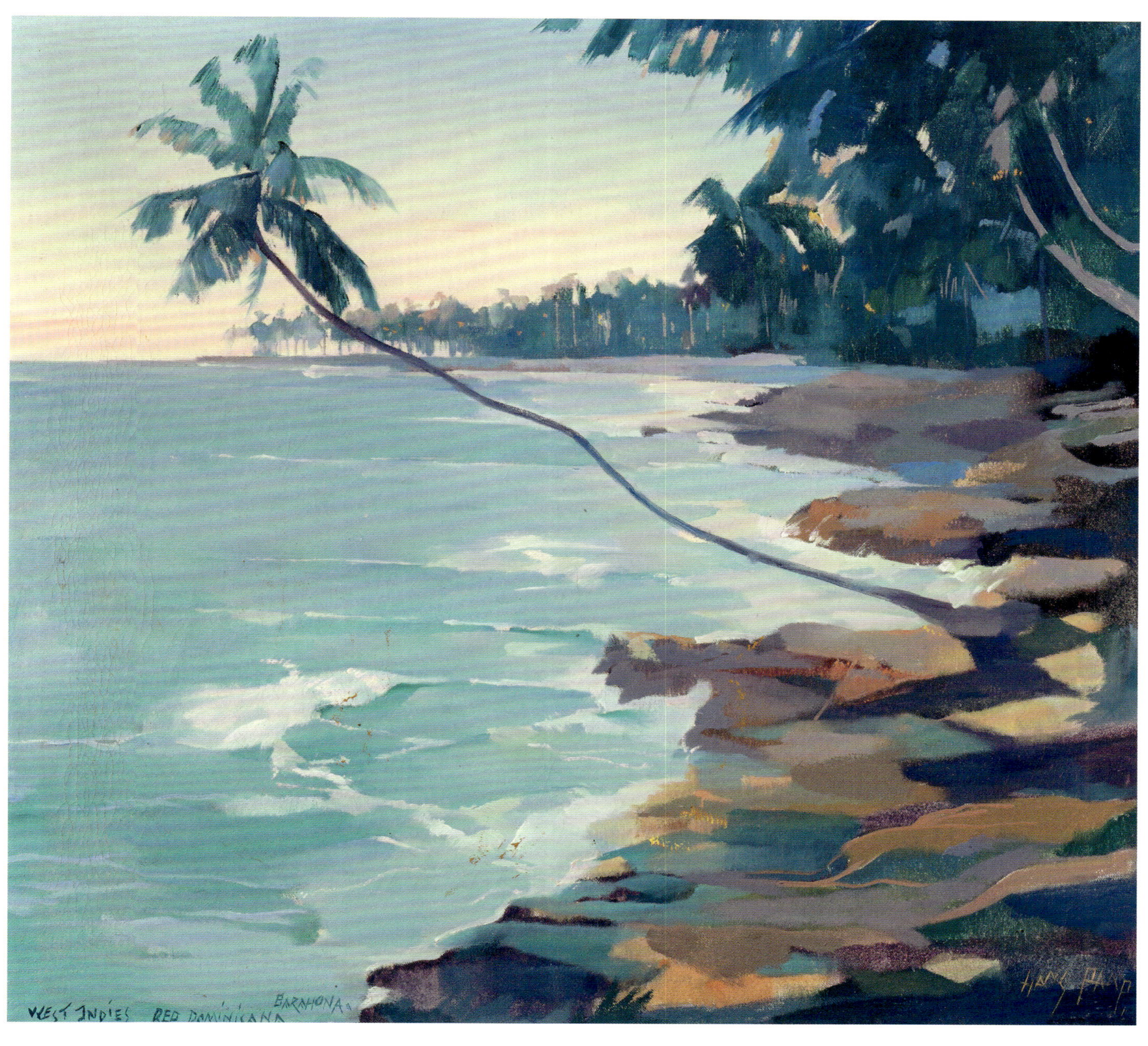


***West Indies,***
***Red Dominicana Barahona***
**oil on canvas**
**19 x 20 inches**
**Courtesy of Nancy Paap**
**Tesuque, NM**

Portlar

## Taos, New Mexico

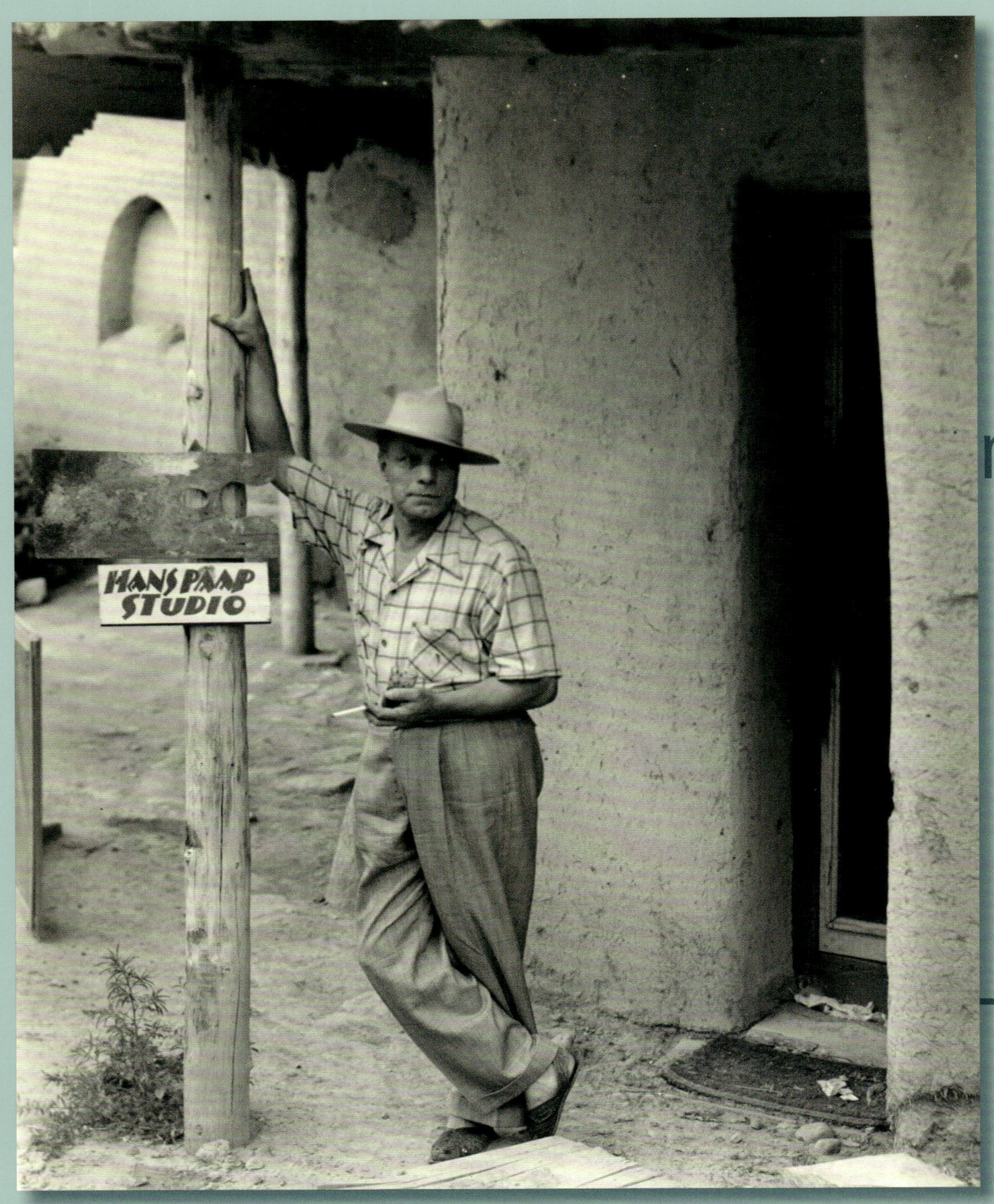


n Francis

L

**Paap in front of his studio on Quesnel Street, Taos, New Mexico c. 1950**

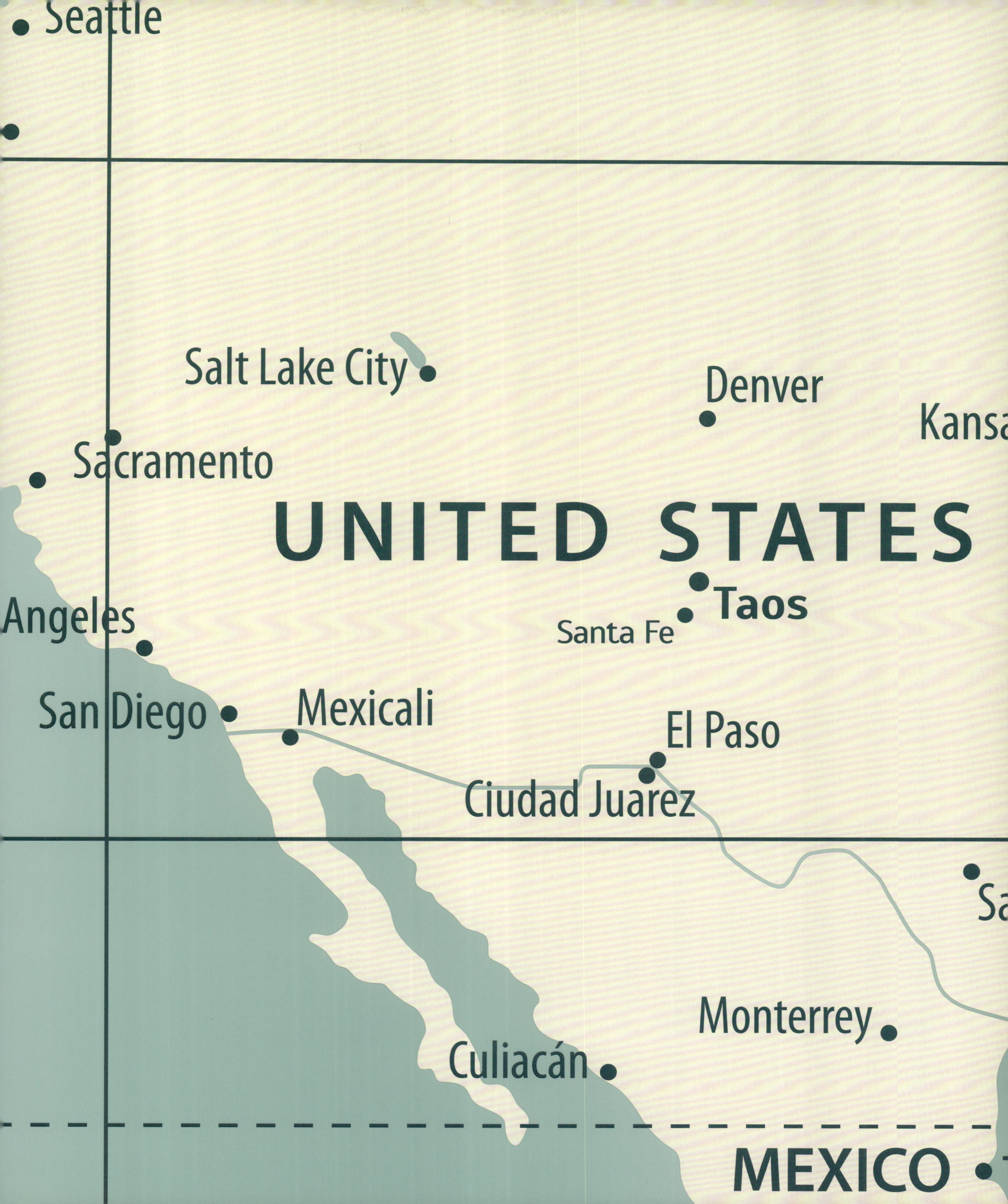
Seattle
Salt Lake City
Denver
Kansa
Sacramento
UNITED STATES
Taos
Santa Fe
Angeles
San Diego
Mexicali
El Paso
Ciudad Juarez
Sa
Monterrey
Culiacán
MEXICO

*Indian Man, Taos Pueblo*
oil on canvas
20 x 18 inches
Courtesy of JoAnna Paap
Santa Fe, NM

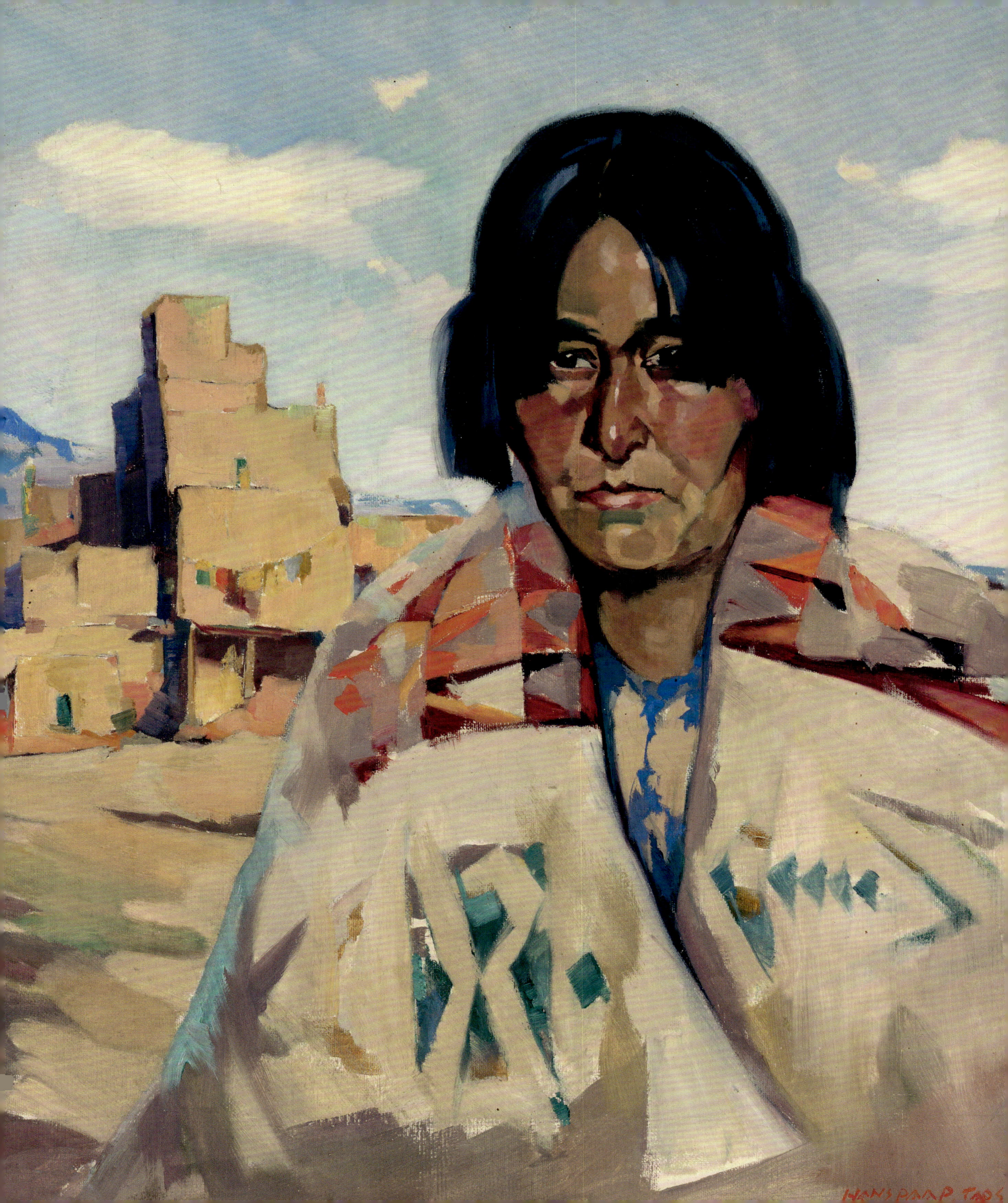
HANS PAAP

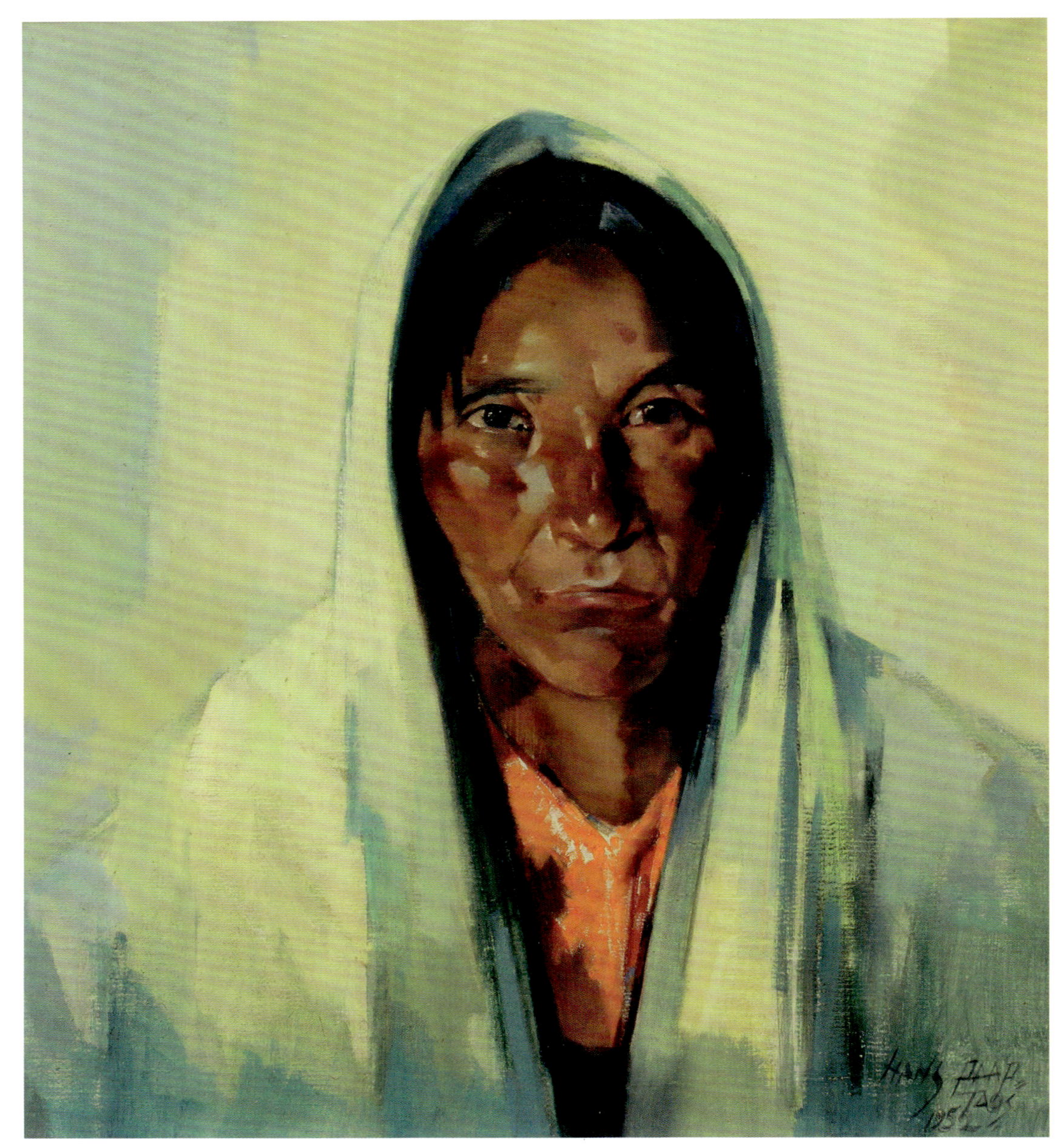

**Near right:**
***Untitled Taos Portrait***
**oil on canvas**
**19½ x 17½ inches**
**1952**
**Courtesy of**
**Addison Rowe Gallery**
**Santa Fe, NM**

**Far right:**
***Church, Talpa, New Mexico***
**oil on canvas**
**15 x 16 inches**
**1924**
**Courtesy of Clarence Vigil**
**Santa Fe, NM**

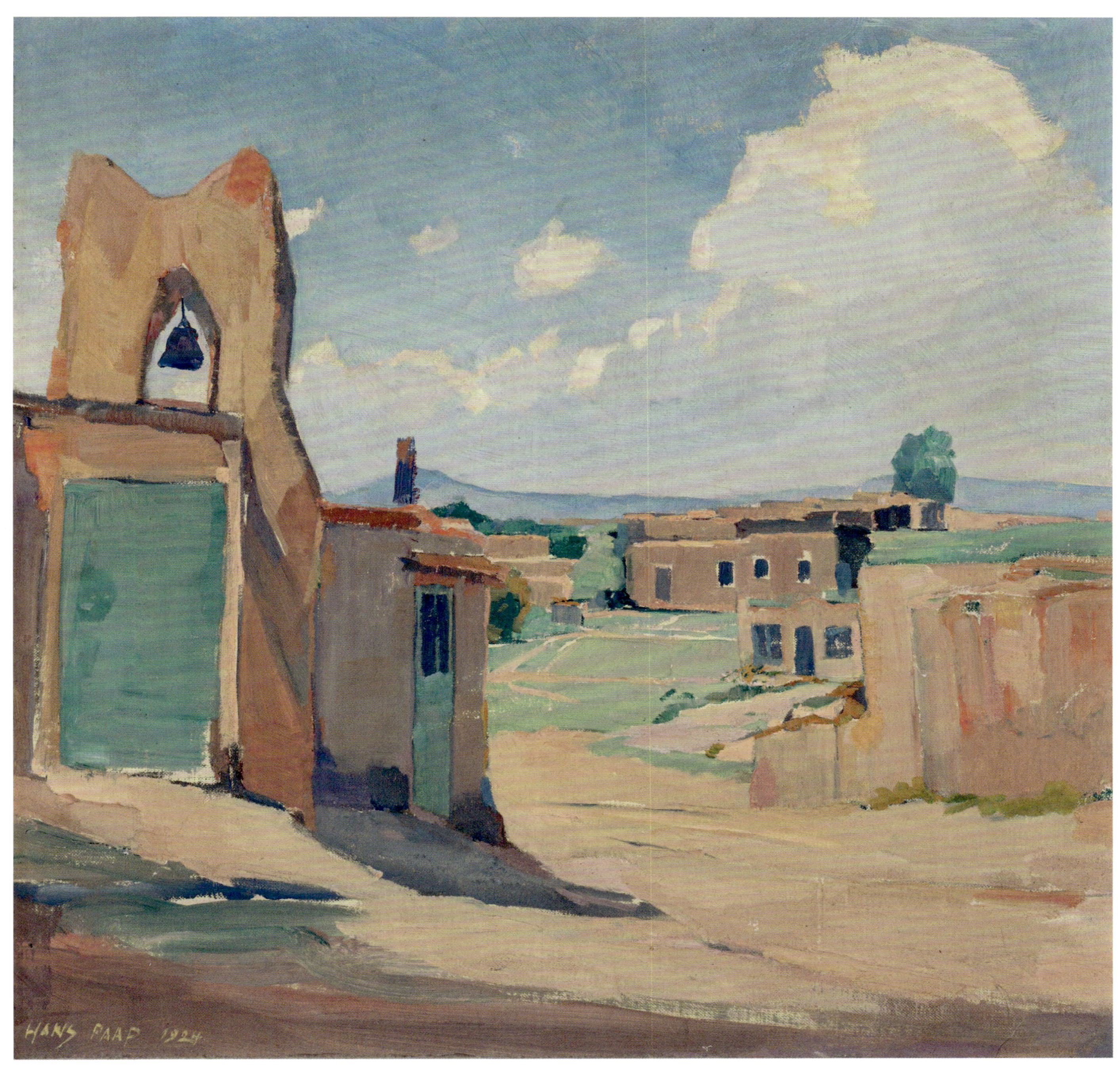
HANS PAAP 1924

*Indian with Headdress*
oil on board
18 x 15 inches
1929
Courtesy of Nancy Paap
Tesuque, NM

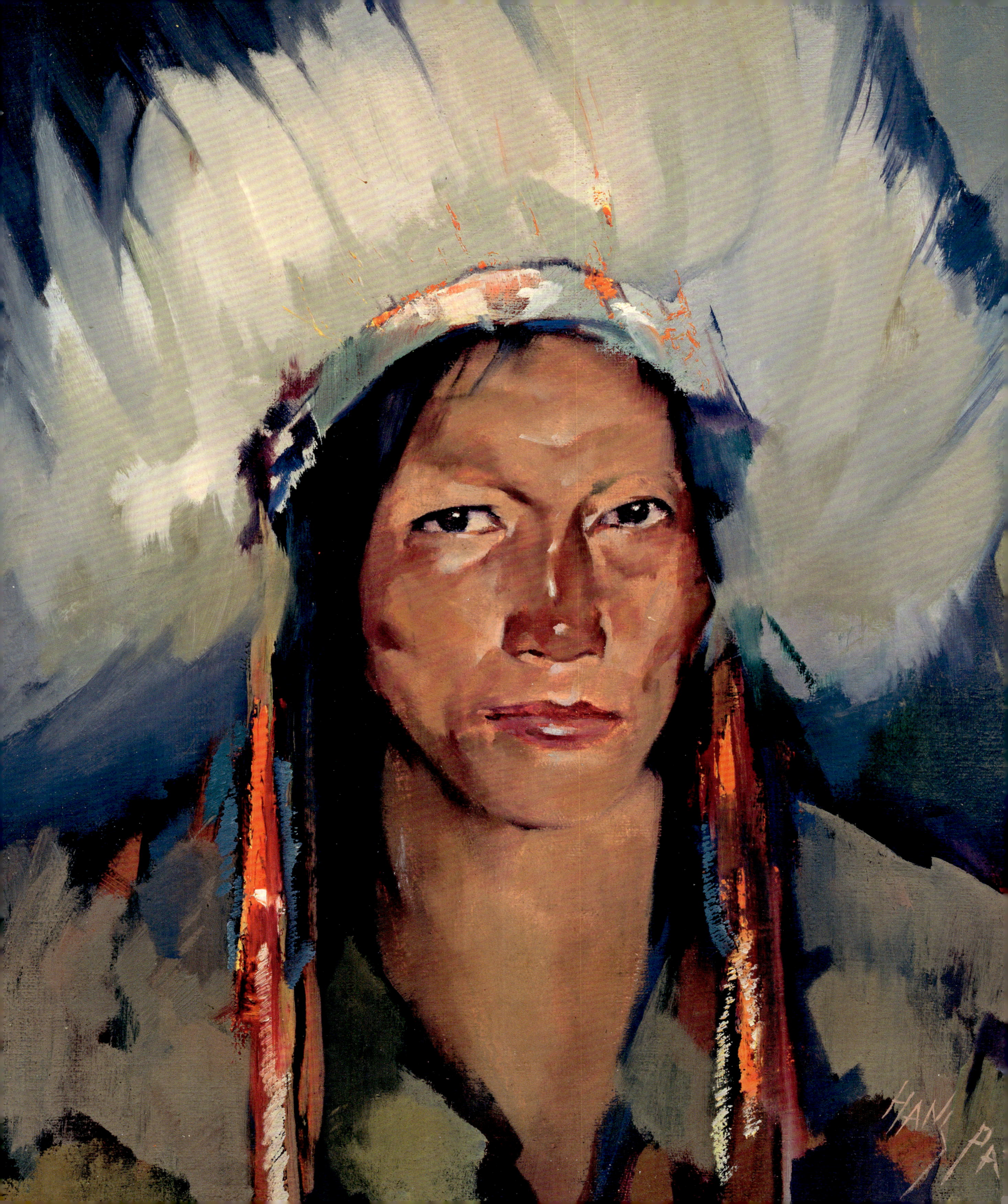

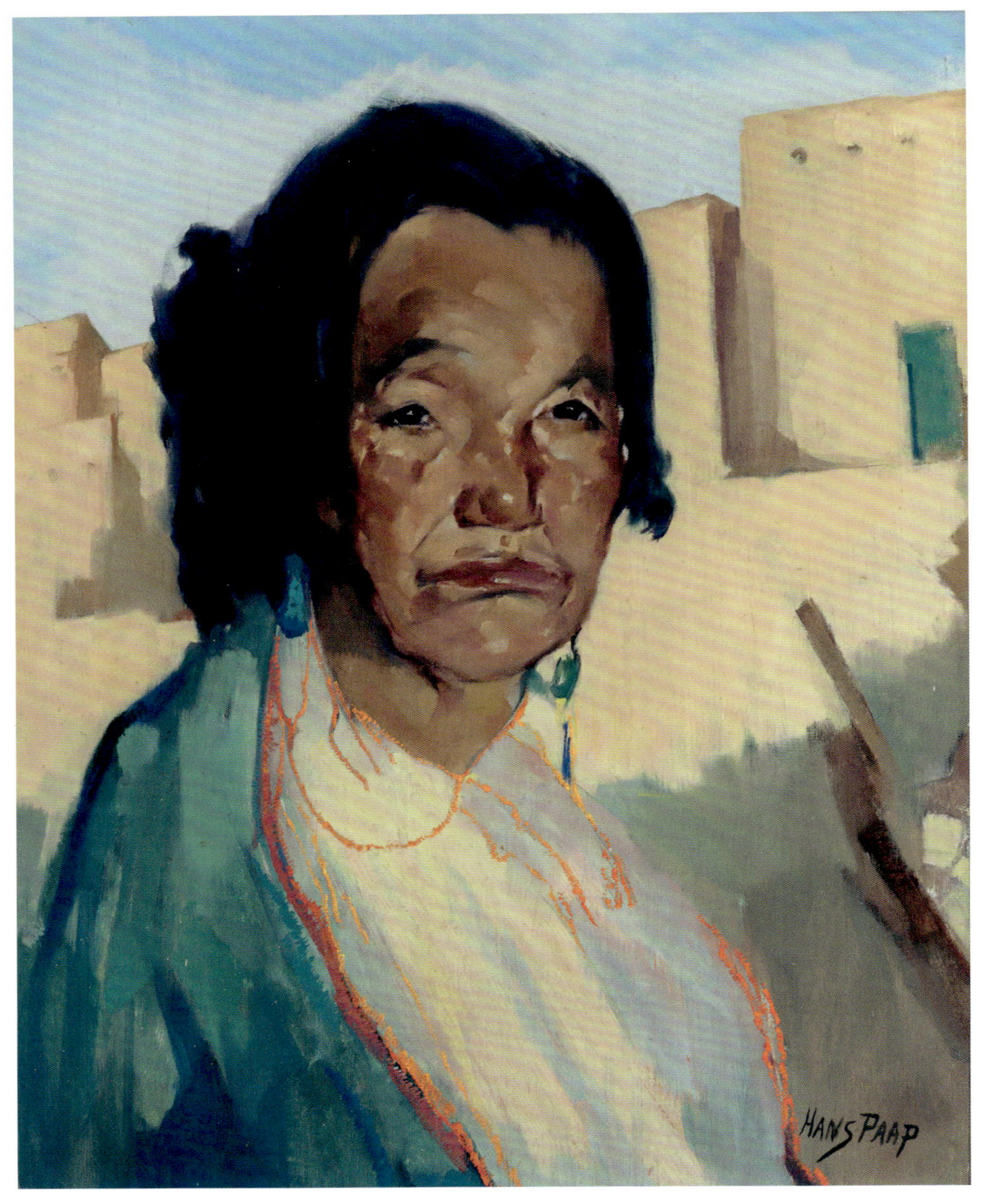


**Near Right:**
***Indian Woman,***
***Taos Pueblo***
**oil on canvas**
**20 x 16 inches**
**c. 1956**
**Courtesy of Roy Paap**
**Albuquerque, NM**

**Far Right:**
***Indian in Profile,***
***Taos, New Mexico***
**oil on linen**
**18 x 20 inches**
**1928**
**Courtesy of Nancy Paap**
**Tesuque, NM**

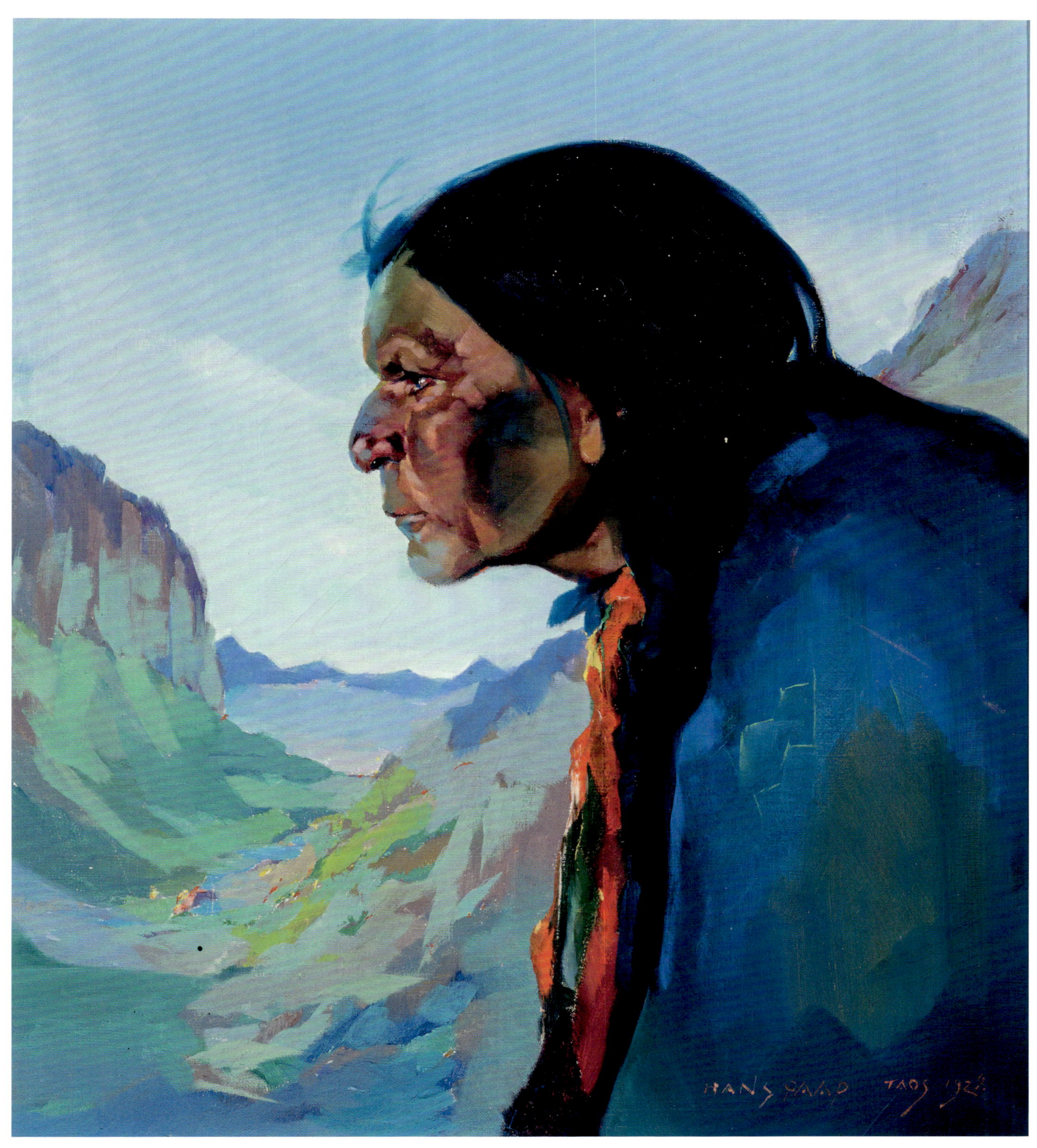

*Paap socialized with and painted the portraits of several Taos luminaries, including Antonio (Tony) and Mabel Dodge Luhan. Tony was a Tiwa Indian from Taos Pueblo. Mabel Luhan was a wealthy socialite and arts patron who made their Taos home a gathering place for many of the country's most acclaimed writers, artists and intellectuals. She embraced Taos and its people, even bobbing her hair to look more like a Pueblo woman.*

***Mable Dodge & Tony Lujan***
**oil on canvas**
**23 x 24 inches**
**1956**
**Courtesy of Nancy Paap**
**Tesuque, NM**

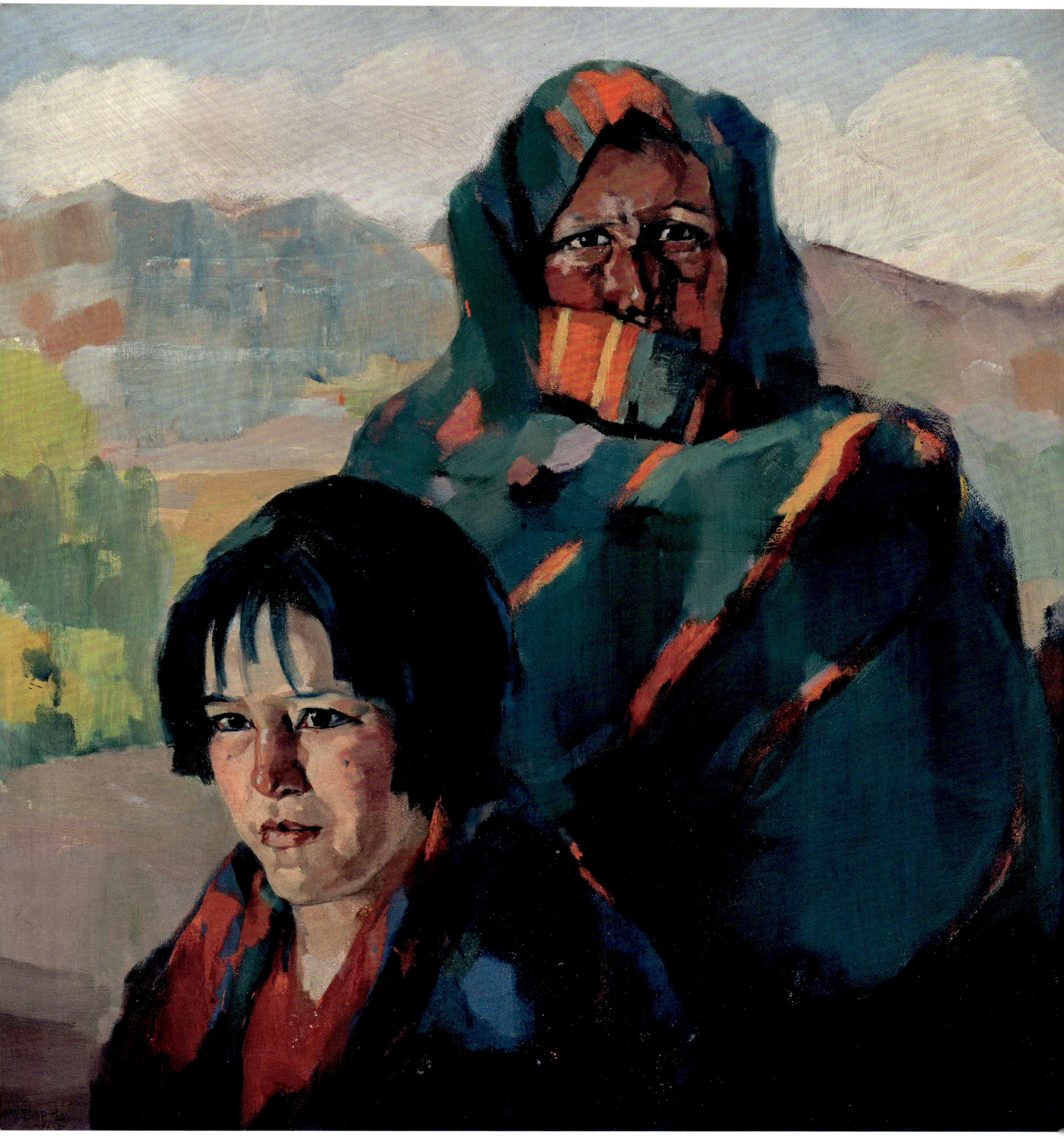

*The ruins depicted in the painting are in the Taos Pueblo. Paap was one of the few outsiders who was allowed to visit any part of the pueblo he liked. Because the Taos Indians liked and trusted him, they invited him to the sacred Blue Lake ceremonial site in the Sangre de Cristo Mountains, a rare honor. Moreover, as a sign of their acceptance and respect, they gave him the name "Arcoiris ("Rainbow") because of the beautiful colors in his paintings.*

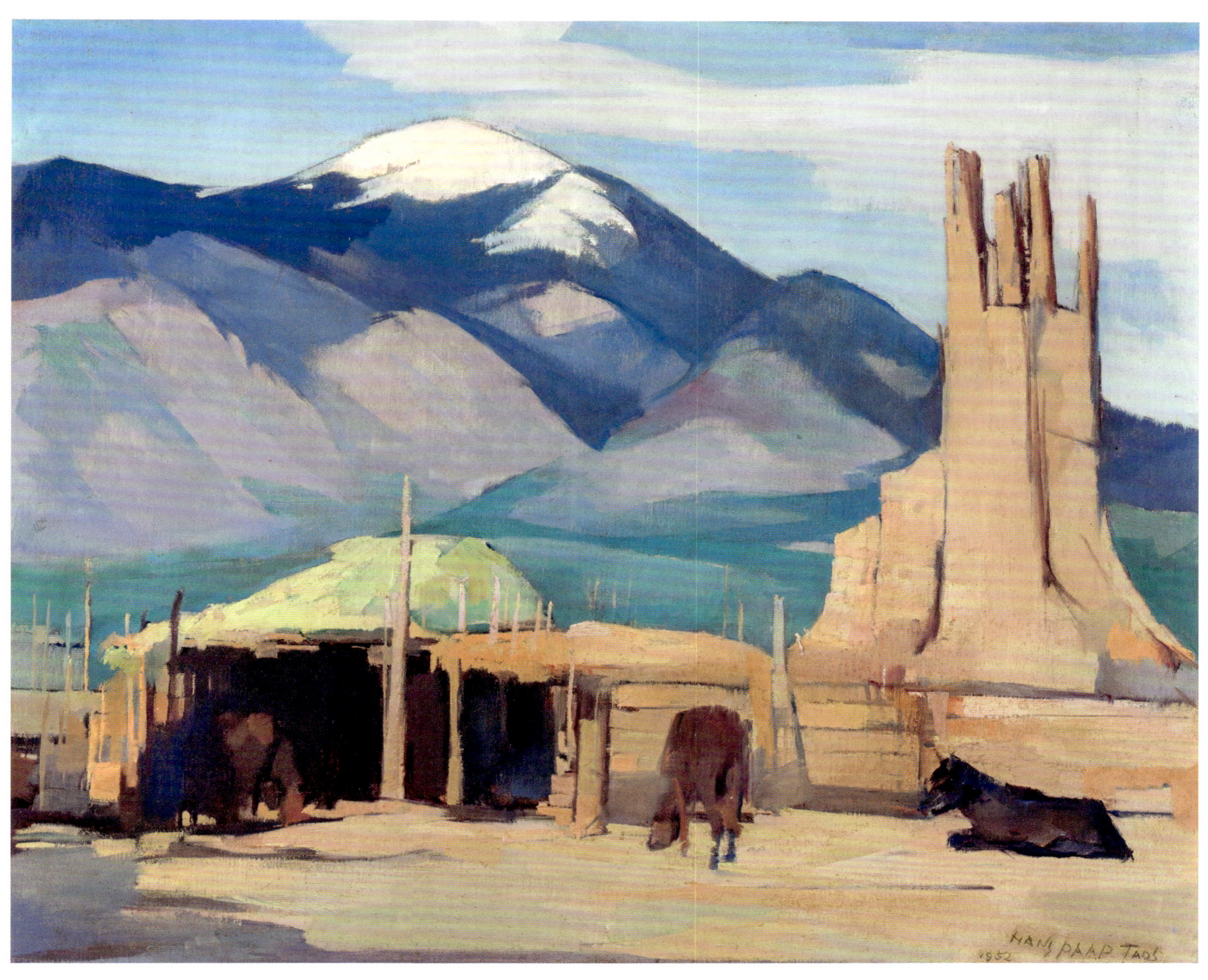


***Taos Pueblo Church Ruin Behind Stables***
**oil on canvas**
**18 x 22 inches**
**1952**
**Courtesy of Nancy Paap, Tesuque, NM**

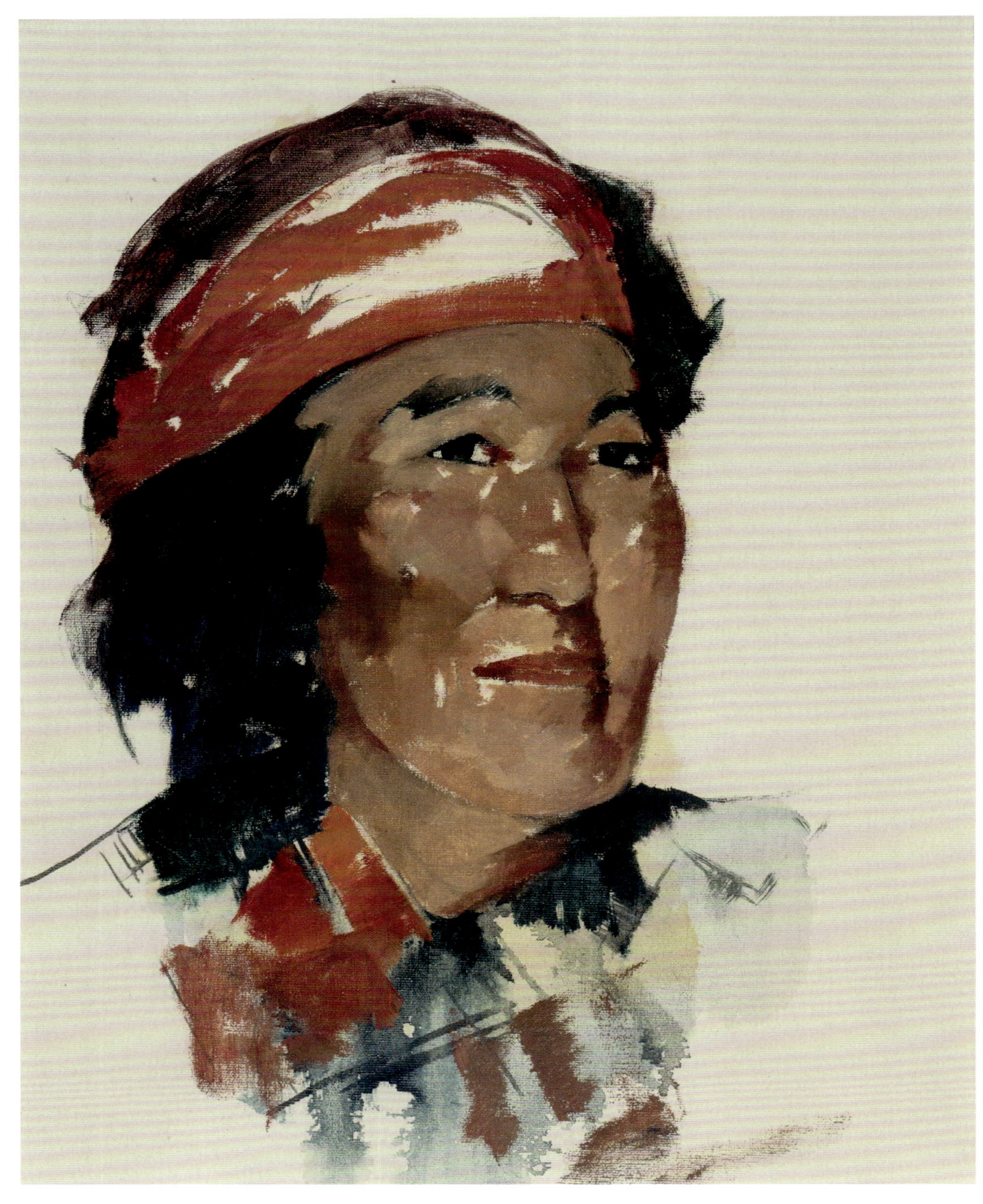

**Near Right:**
***Indian Portrait***
**18 x 14 inches**
**oil on canvas**
**Courtesy of Nancy Paap**
**Tesuque, NM**

**Far Right:**
***Taos Indian***
***Wrapped in Blanket***
**19 x 16 inches**
**oil on canvas**
**1956**
**Courtesy of Nancy Paap**
**Tesuque, NM**

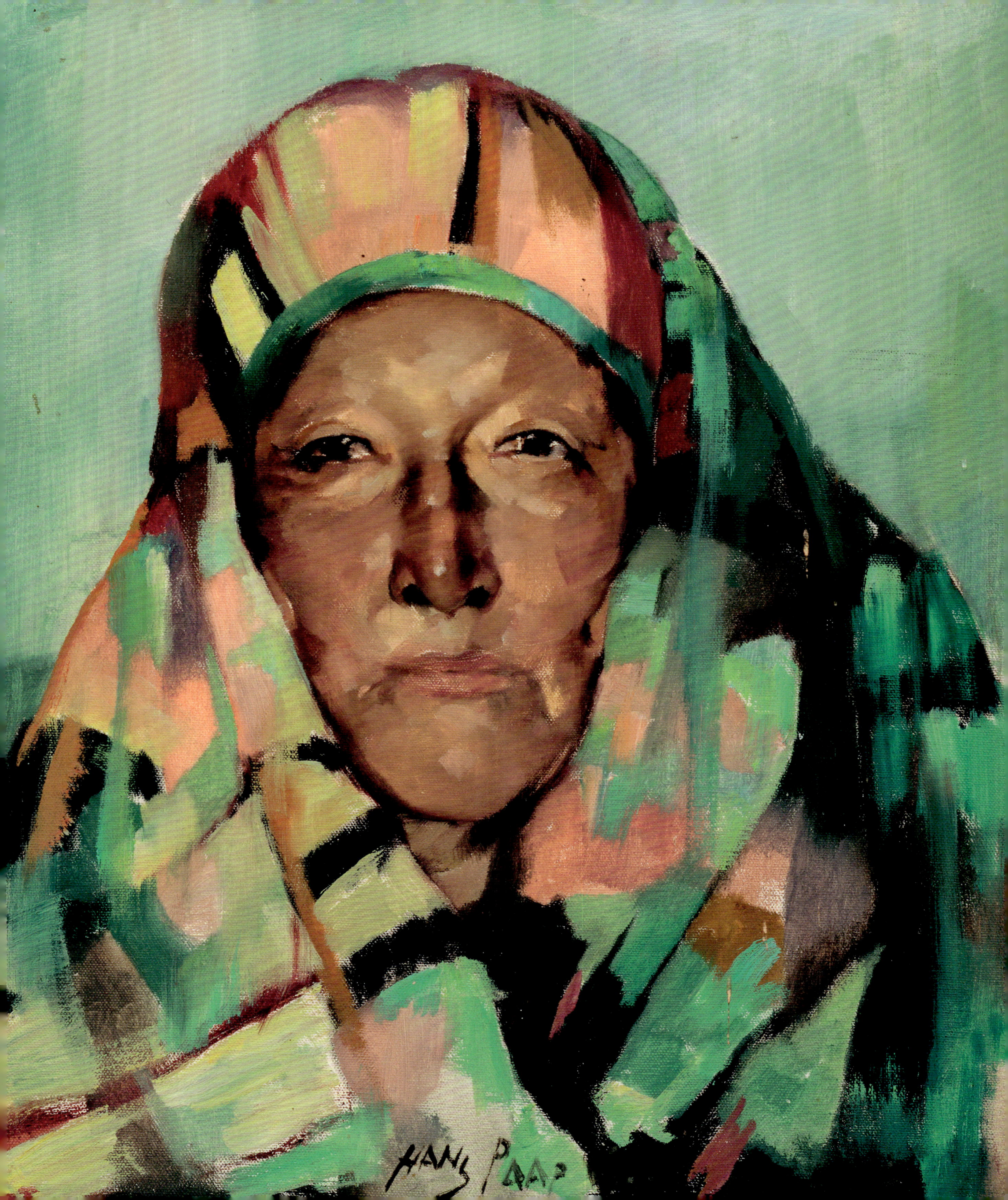
HANS PAAP

*At some point, Paap spent a year living near Acoma Pueblo, 60 miles west of Albuquerque, painting landscapes and portraits. Situated atop of 367-foot high mesa, "Sky City" is the oldest continuously inhabited settlement in North America.*

***Acoma Cliffs***
**oil on canvas**
**19 x 17 inches**
**1930**
**Courtesy of Nancy Paap**
**Tesuque, NM**

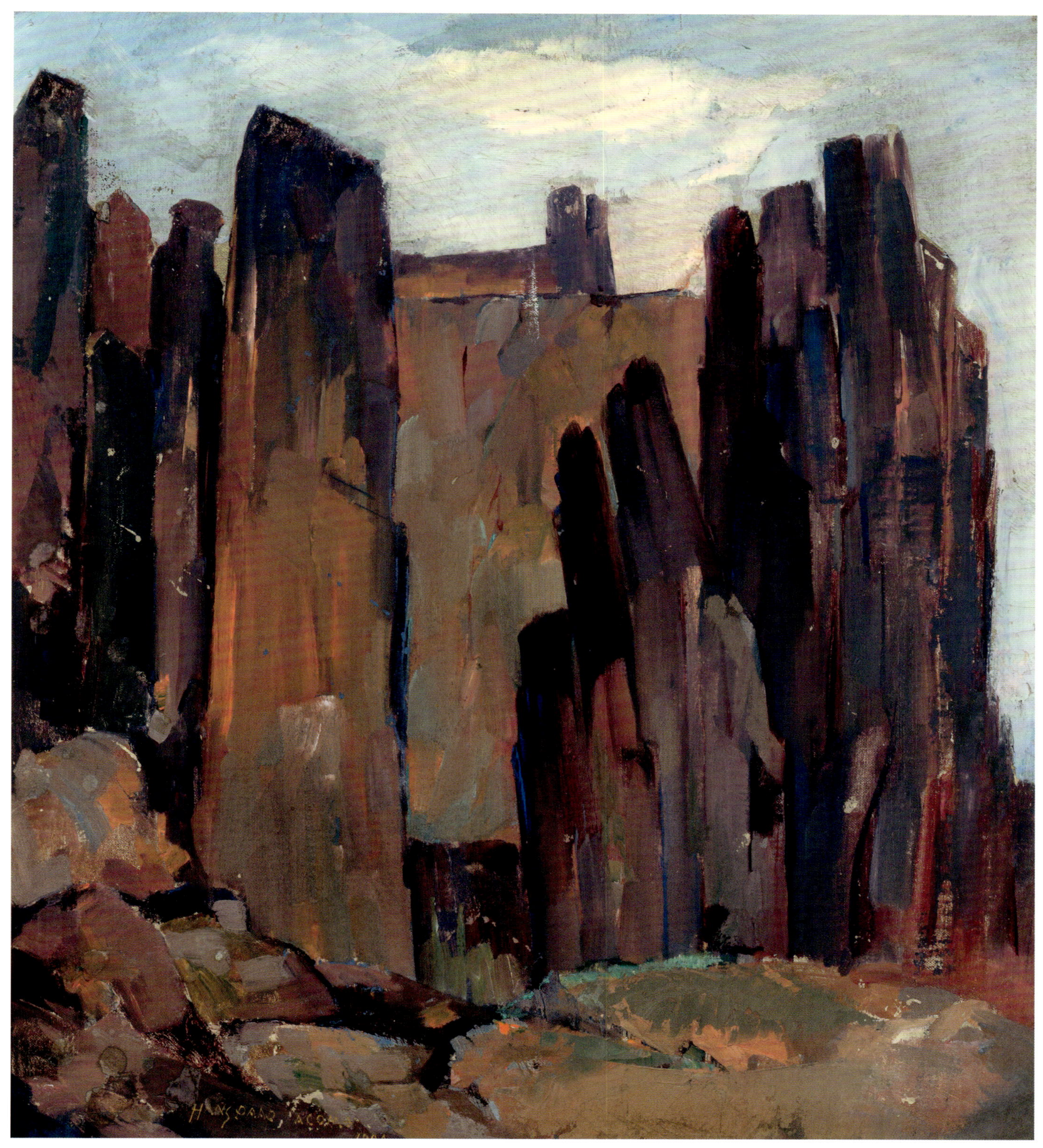

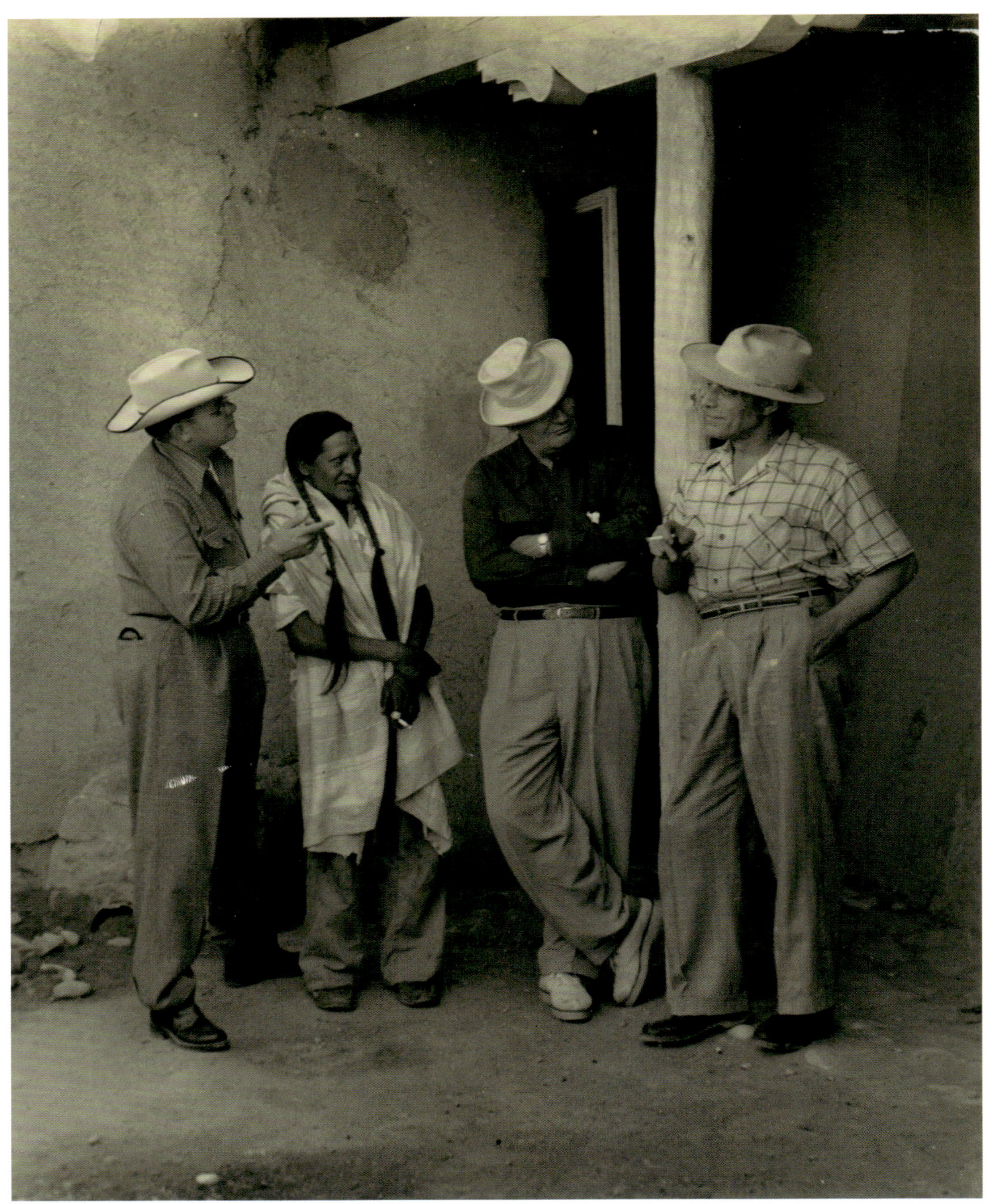

**Near right:**
**Paap and friends**
**in front of his studio**
**Taos, New Mexico**
**c. 1950**

**Far right:**
***Taos Indian Portrait***
**oil on canvas**
**21 x 19 inches**
**Courtesy of**
**Tucson Museum of Art**
**Tucson, AZ**

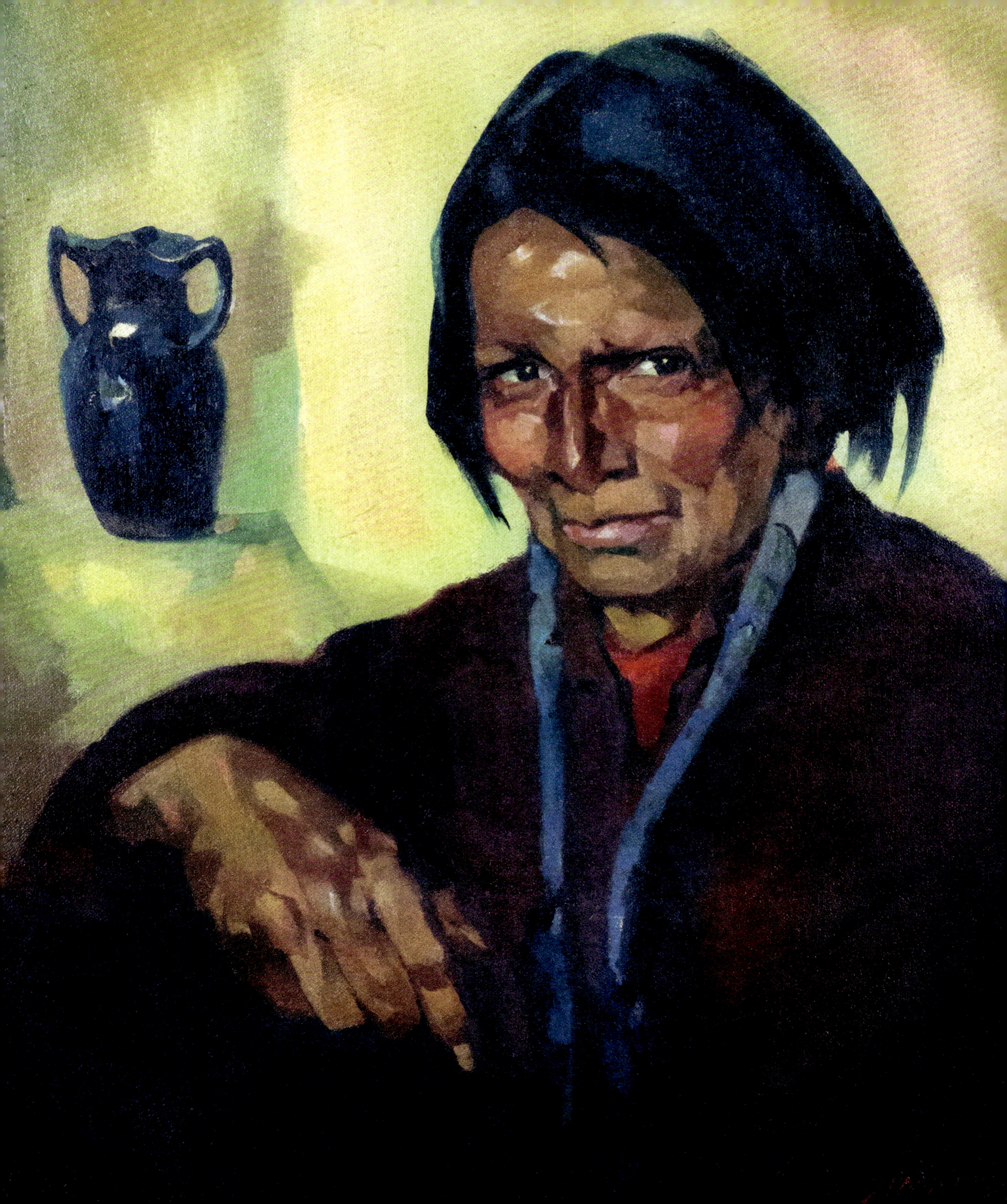

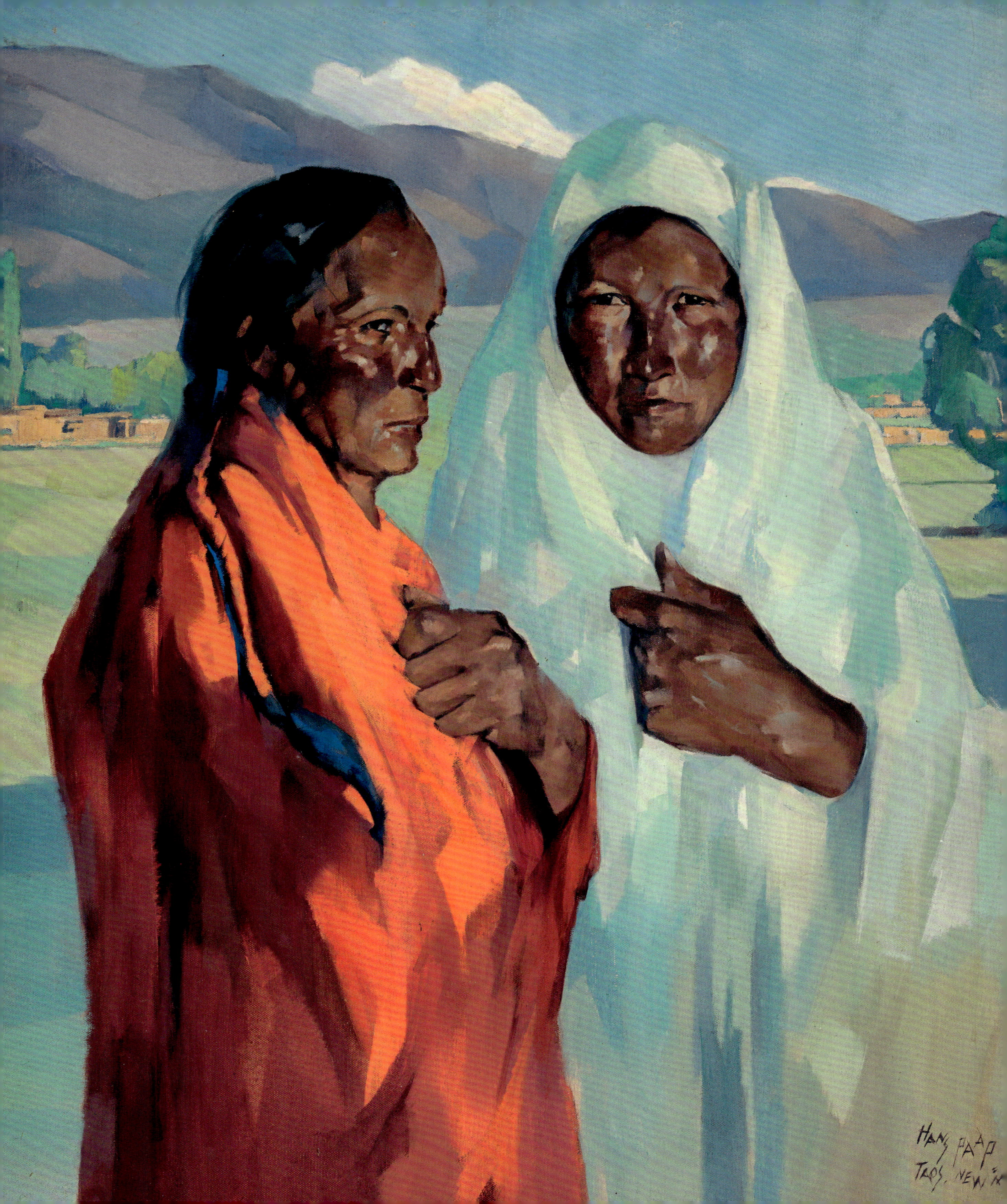
HANS PAAP
TAOS, NEW

*Also shown on the front cover, this beautiful rendering combines portraiture and a Southwest landscape. It was discovered in Santa Fe at the end of the author's year-long, worldwide search for Hans Paap paintings.*

**Untitled**
**(Two Indians,**
**Taos, New Mexico)**
**oil on canvas**
**29¼ x 24¼ inches**
**Courtesy of**
**Buffalo Tracks Gallery**
**Santa Fe, NM**

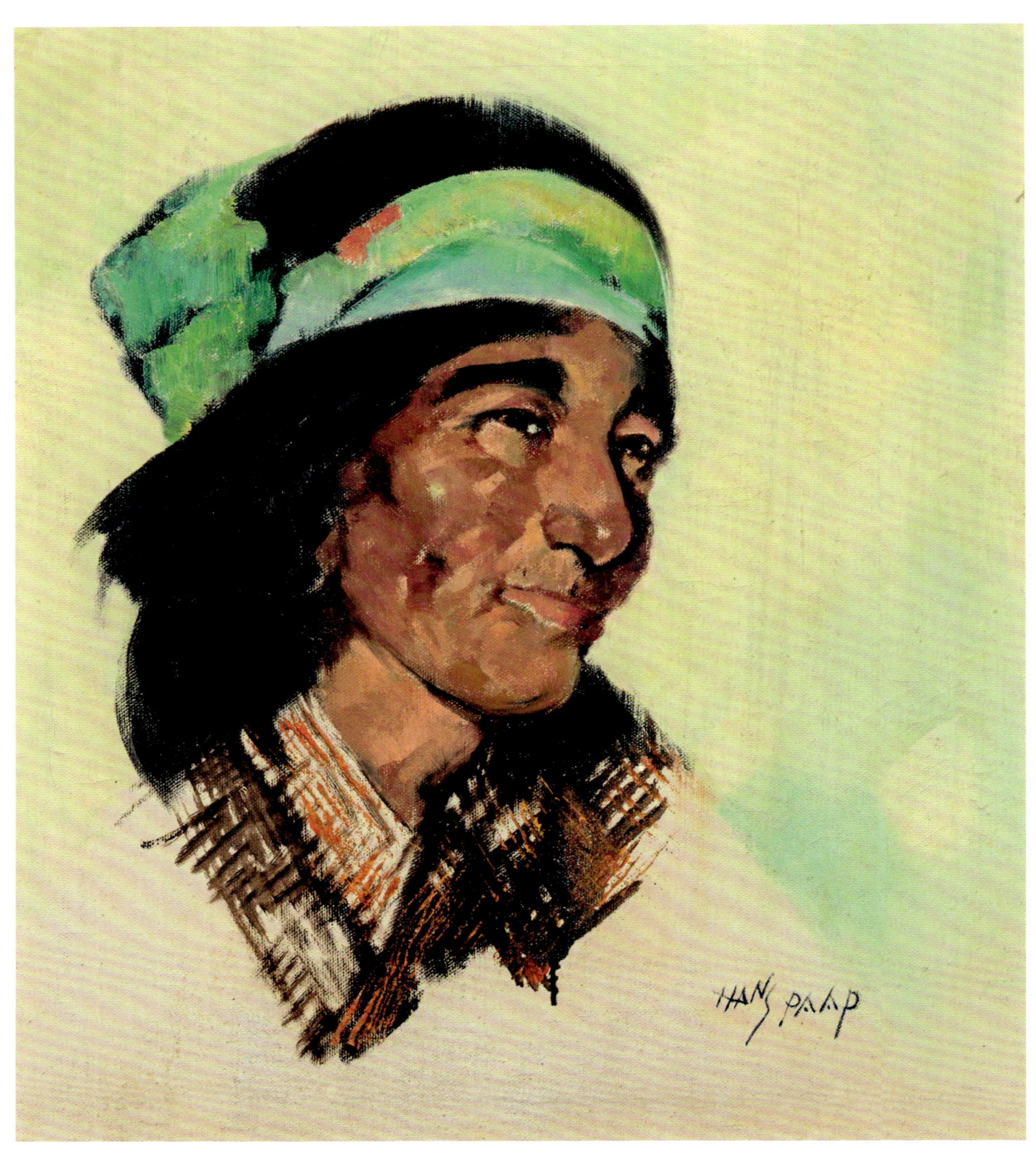


*Navaho Indian,*
*Green Headband*
oil on canvas
17 x 15 inches
Courtesy of Nancy Paap
Tesuque, NM

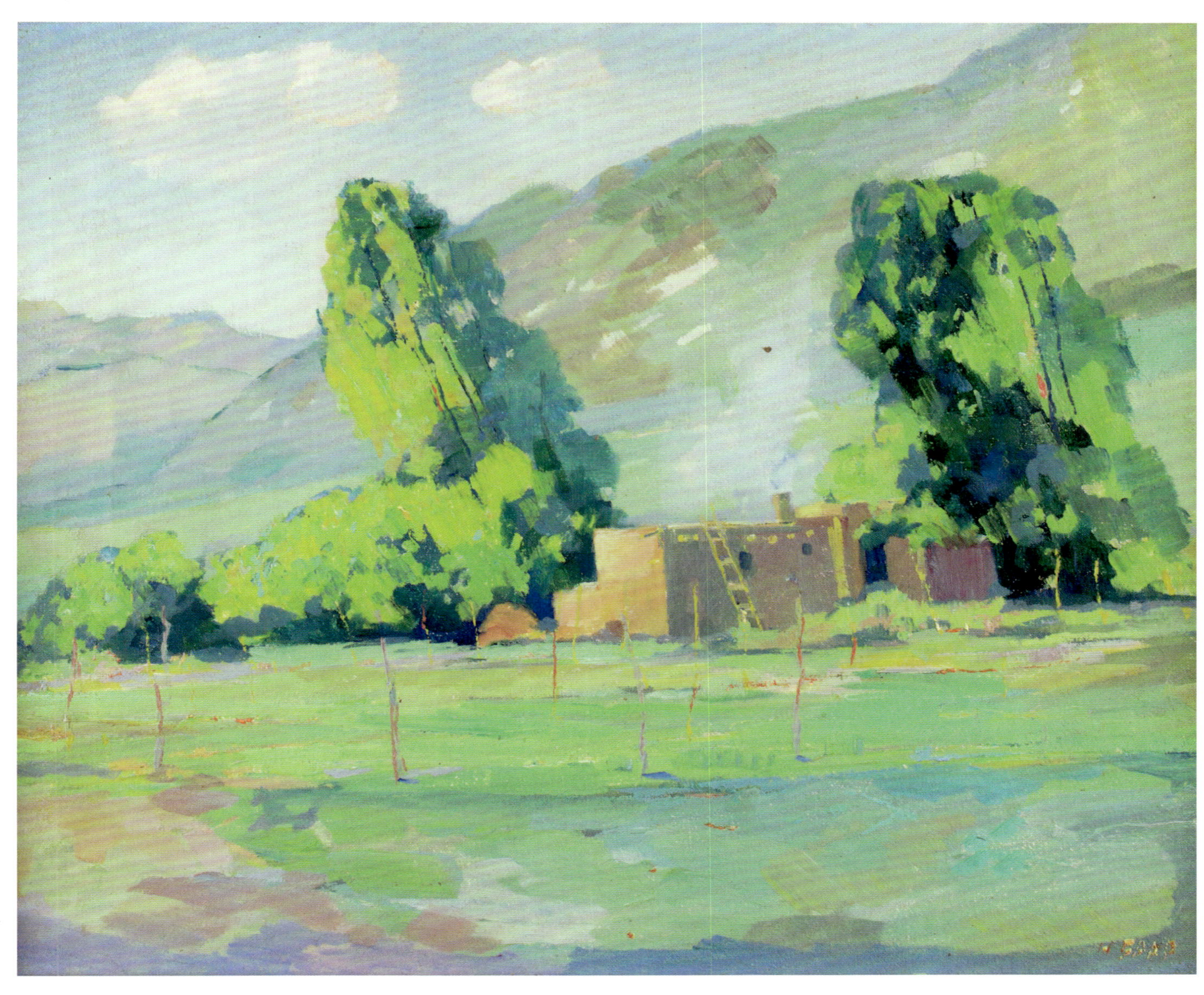

*Pueblo Scene*
**oil on canvas**
**12 x 15 inches**
**Courtesy of**
**Jackson Hole Art Auction**
**Jackson, WY**

*Portrait of Indian Chief*
oil on canvas
20 x 18 inches
1929
Courtesy of Nancy Paap
Tesuque, NM

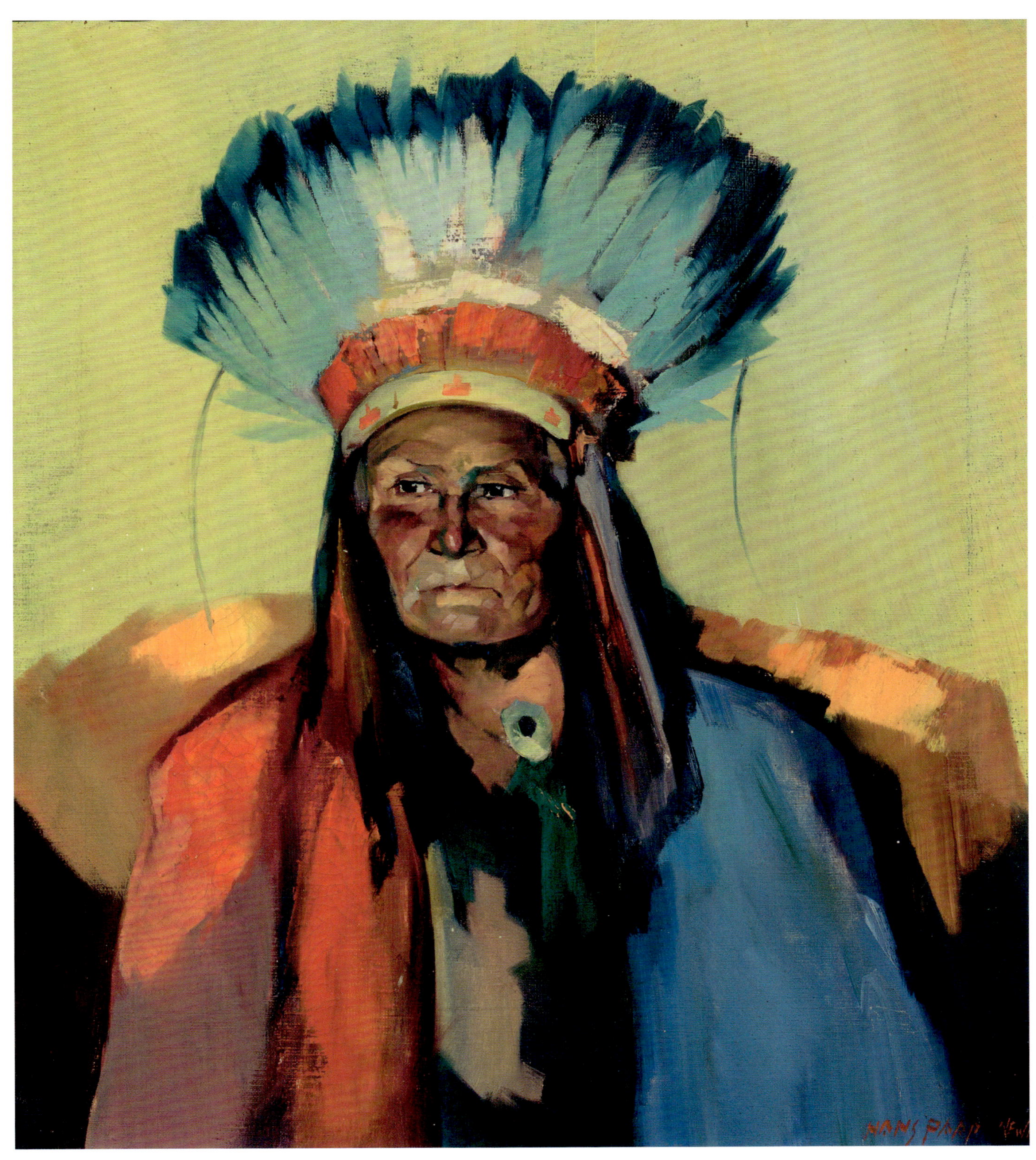

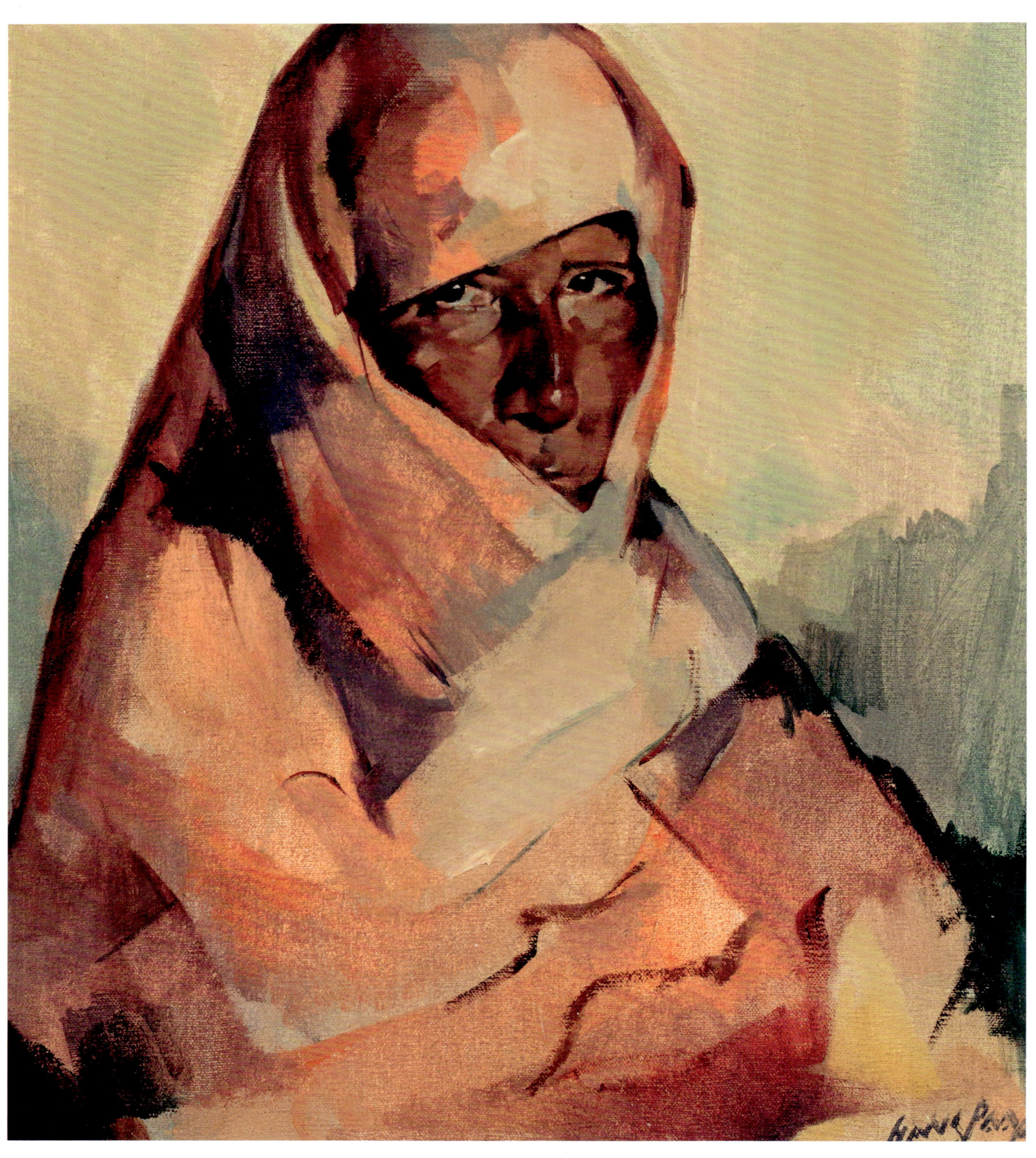

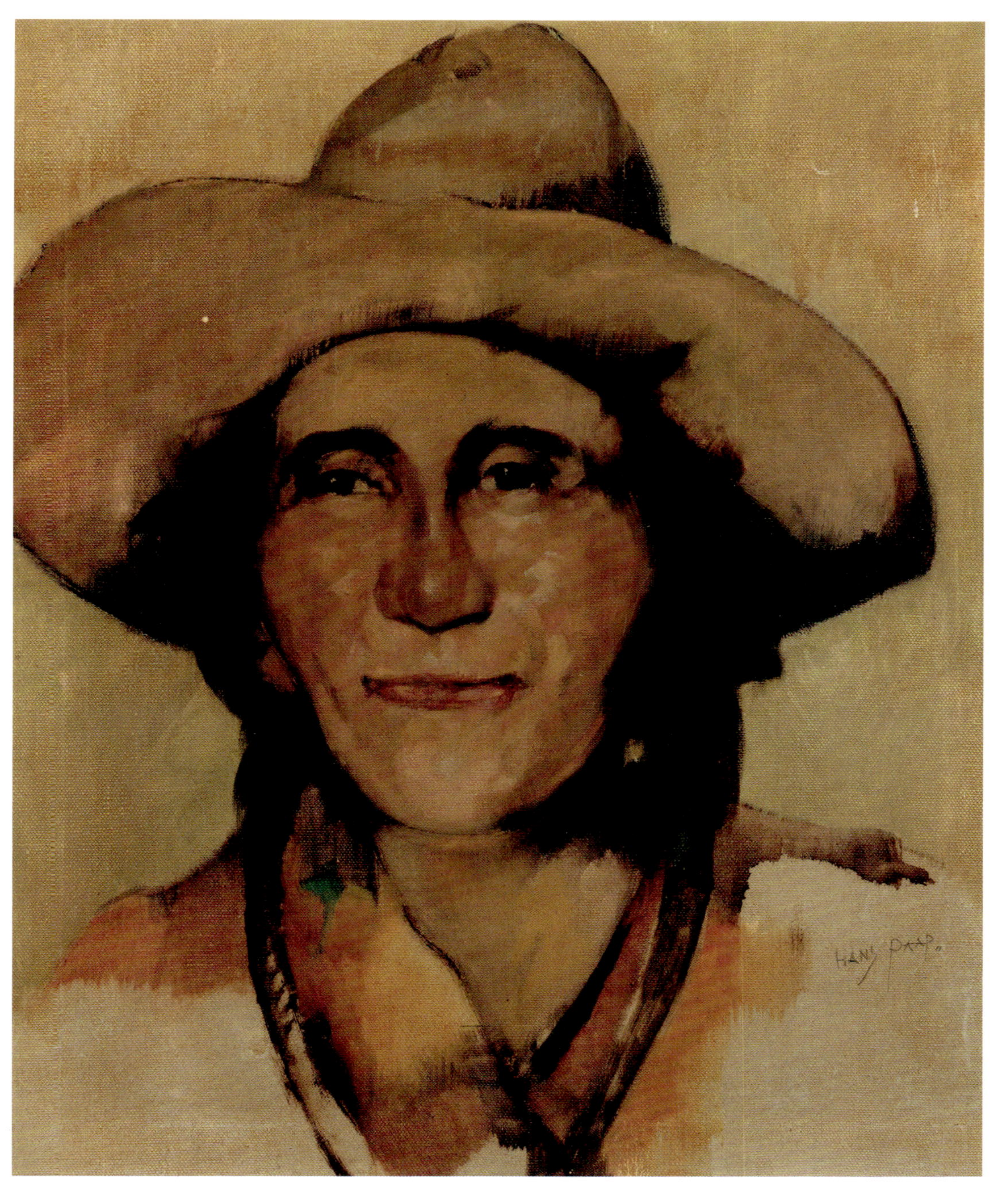


Far left:
*Taos Indian Wrapped in Salmon-Colored Blanket*
oil on canvas
18 x 16 inches
1956
Courtesy of Nancy Paap
Tesuque, NM

Near left:
*Navaho Indian*
oil on canvas
17 x 14 inches
Courtesy of Nancy Paap
Tesuque, NM

*Dry-docked Boat*
*in Taos*
oil on canvas
15 x 15 inches
Courtesy of Nancy Paap
Tesuque, NM

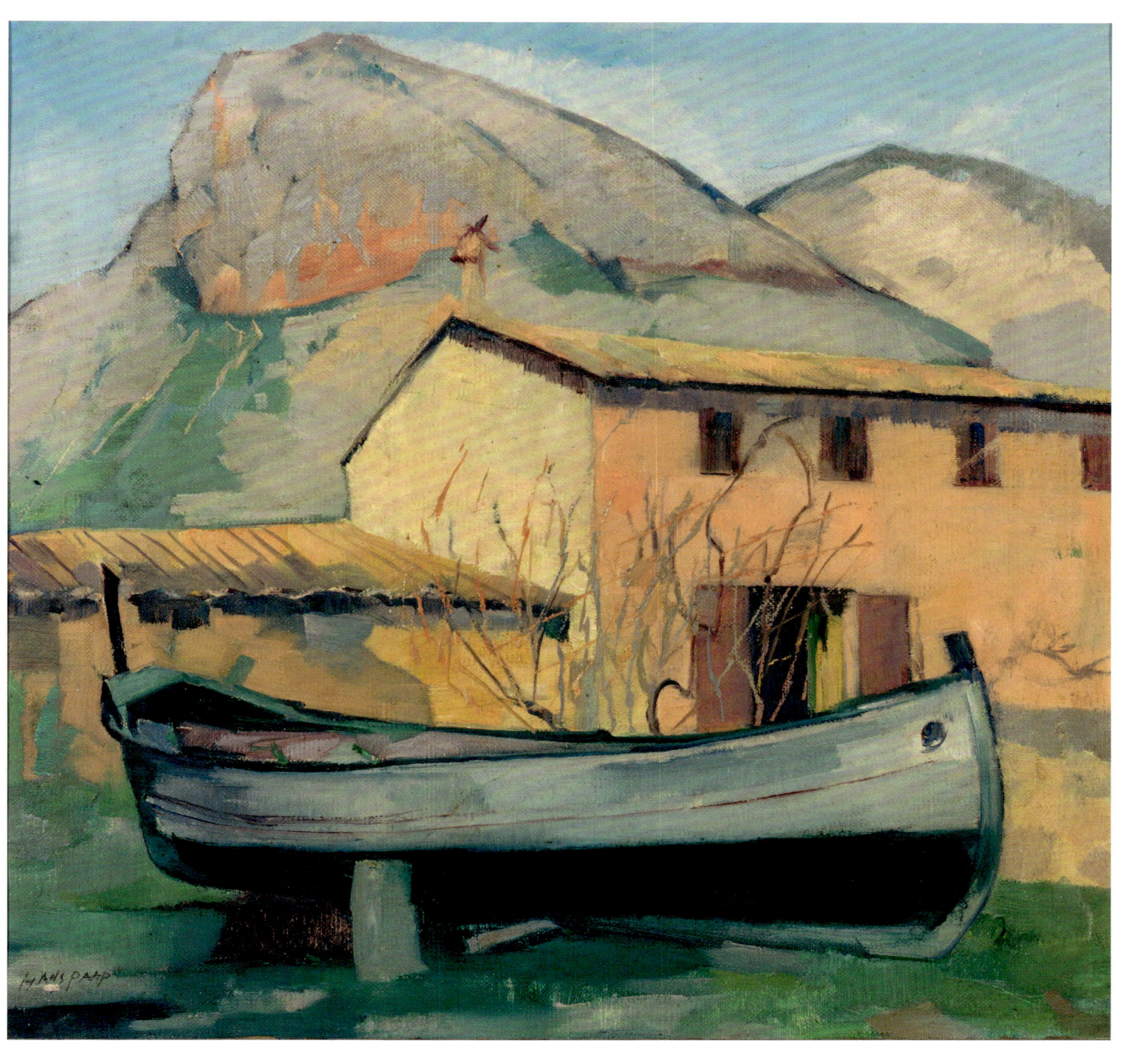
HANS PAAP

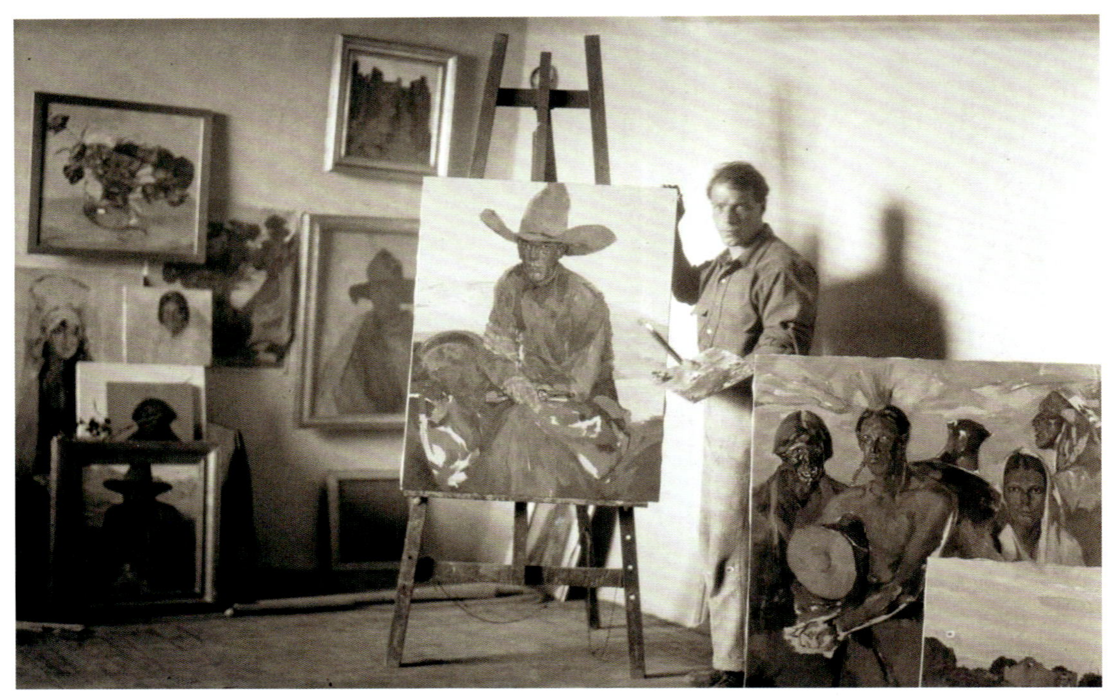

*The Colorado Springs Fine Arts Center included this painting in its 2010 exhibition,* The American West: Cowboys from the Collection. The Colorado Springs Independent, *a newsweekly, selected it for their "Best of 2010" feature, writing: "Though subtle at first, with time, everything about this work grows wonderfully strange. It's both colorful and dimly cast. Its composition is simple but strikingly immediate; a half-imposing character sitting right in front of you, likely on a rock over on a high vantage point. In contrast, the background is oddly indistinct, pastel hills and blotchy clouds. For such a ho-hum moment, the work feels incredibly dramatic. And mysterious — no one knows who this cowboy is." (Courtesy of Edie Adelstein,* The Colorado Springs Independent*)*

**Above:**
**Hans Paap in his studio,**
**Taos, NM**
**c. 1930**

**Far right:**
***Portrait of a Cowboy***
**oil on canvas**
**42 x 33 inches**
**1930**
**Courtesy of Colorado Springs Fine Arts Center at Colorado College, Colorado Springs, CO, Gift of Mrs. Helen E. Britzman**

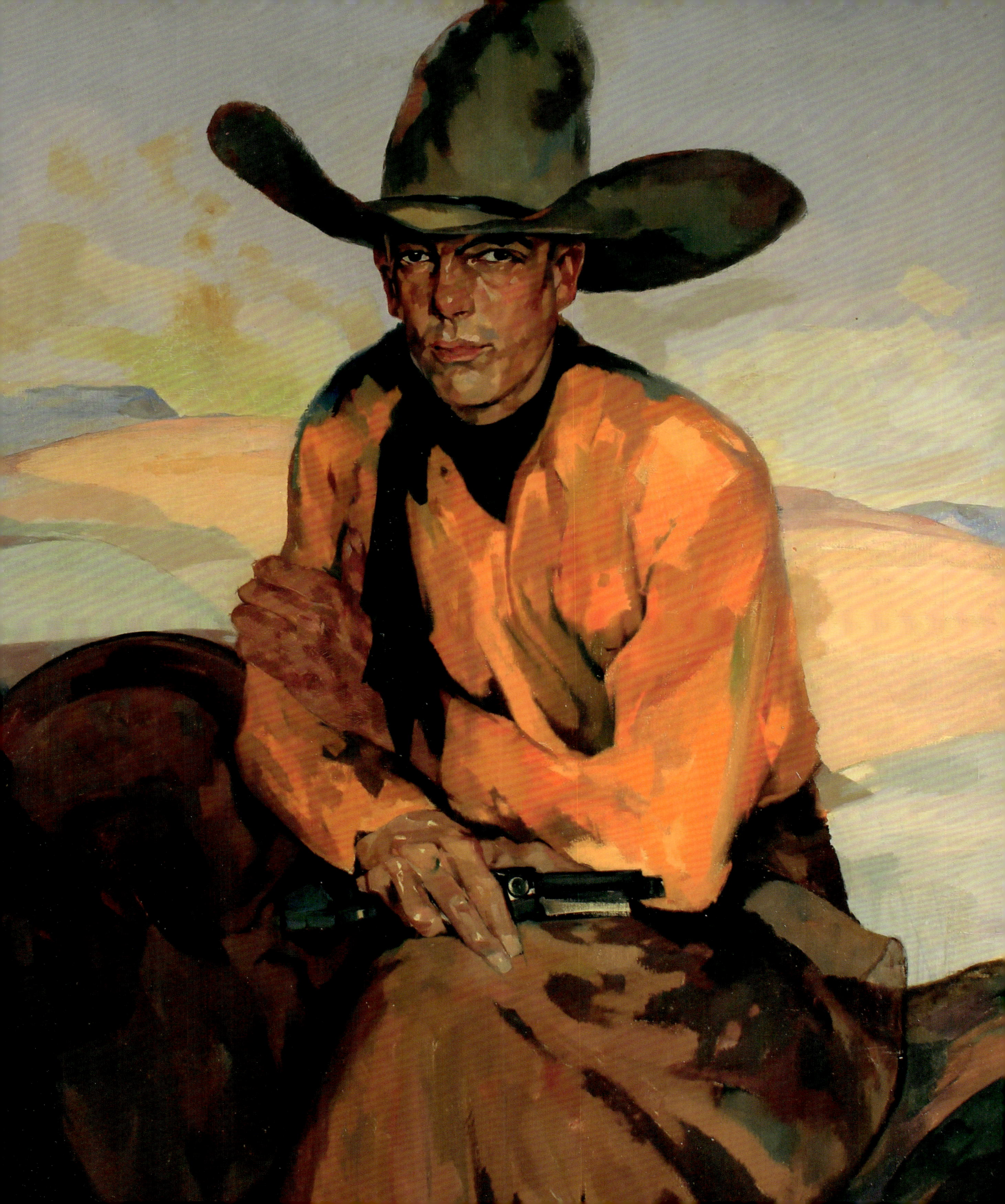

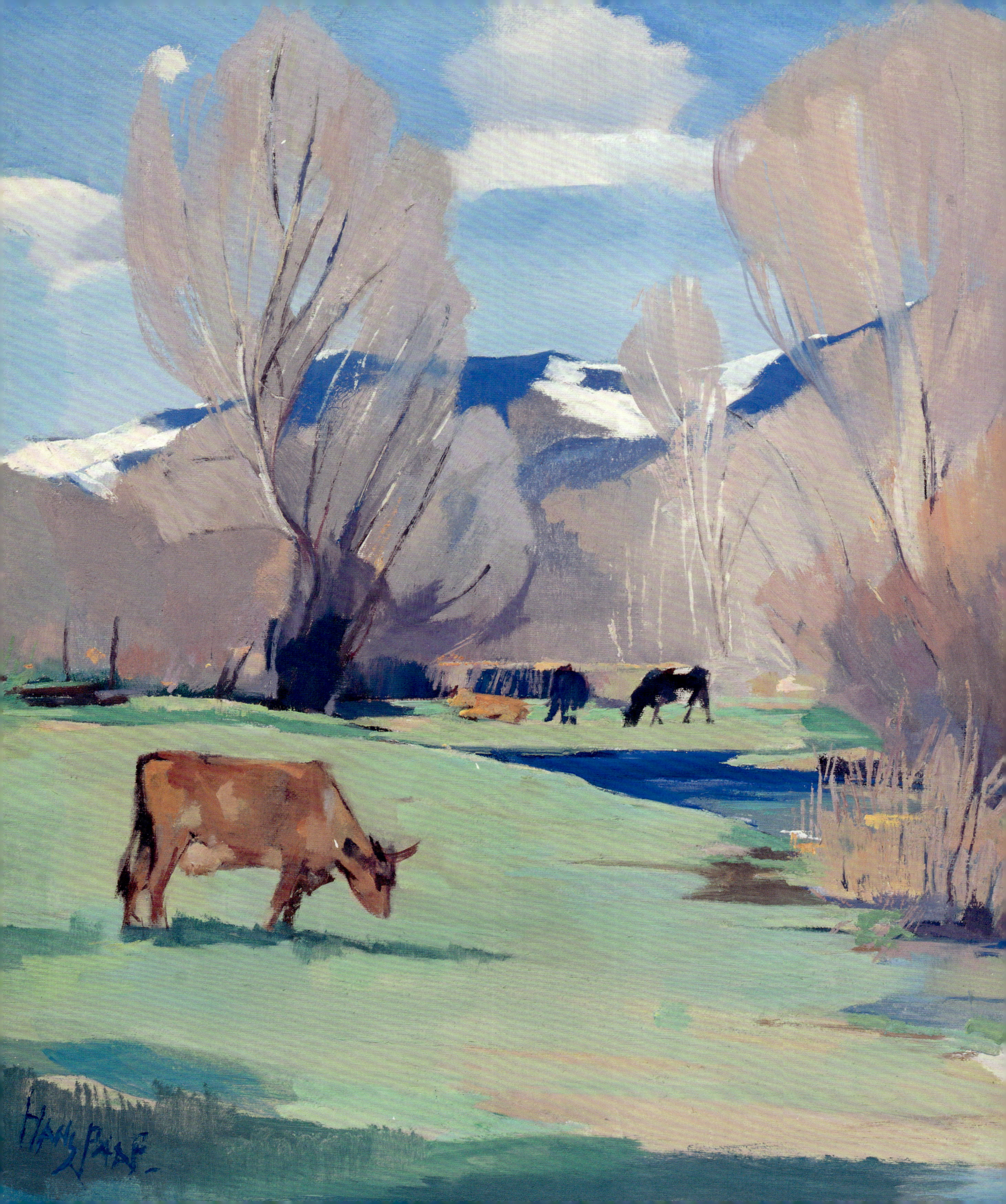
HANS PAAP

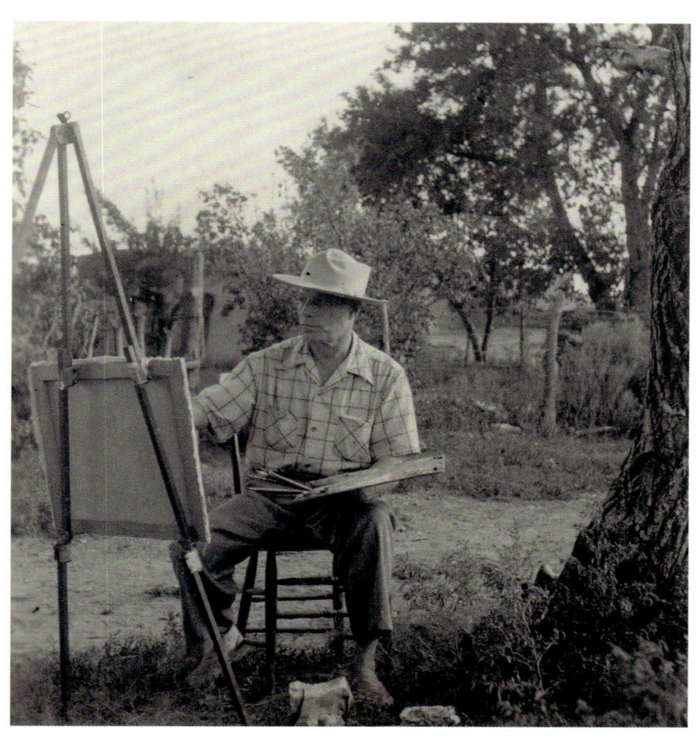

**Left:**
***Peñasco, New Mexico***
**oil on canvas**
**17 x 17 inches**
**Courtesy of Roy Paap**
**Albuquerque, NM**

**Above:**
**Paap painting en plein air**
**in Taos**

*Taos Indian Sheep Herder*
oil on board
22 x 19 inches
Courtesy of Nancy Paap
Tesuque, NM

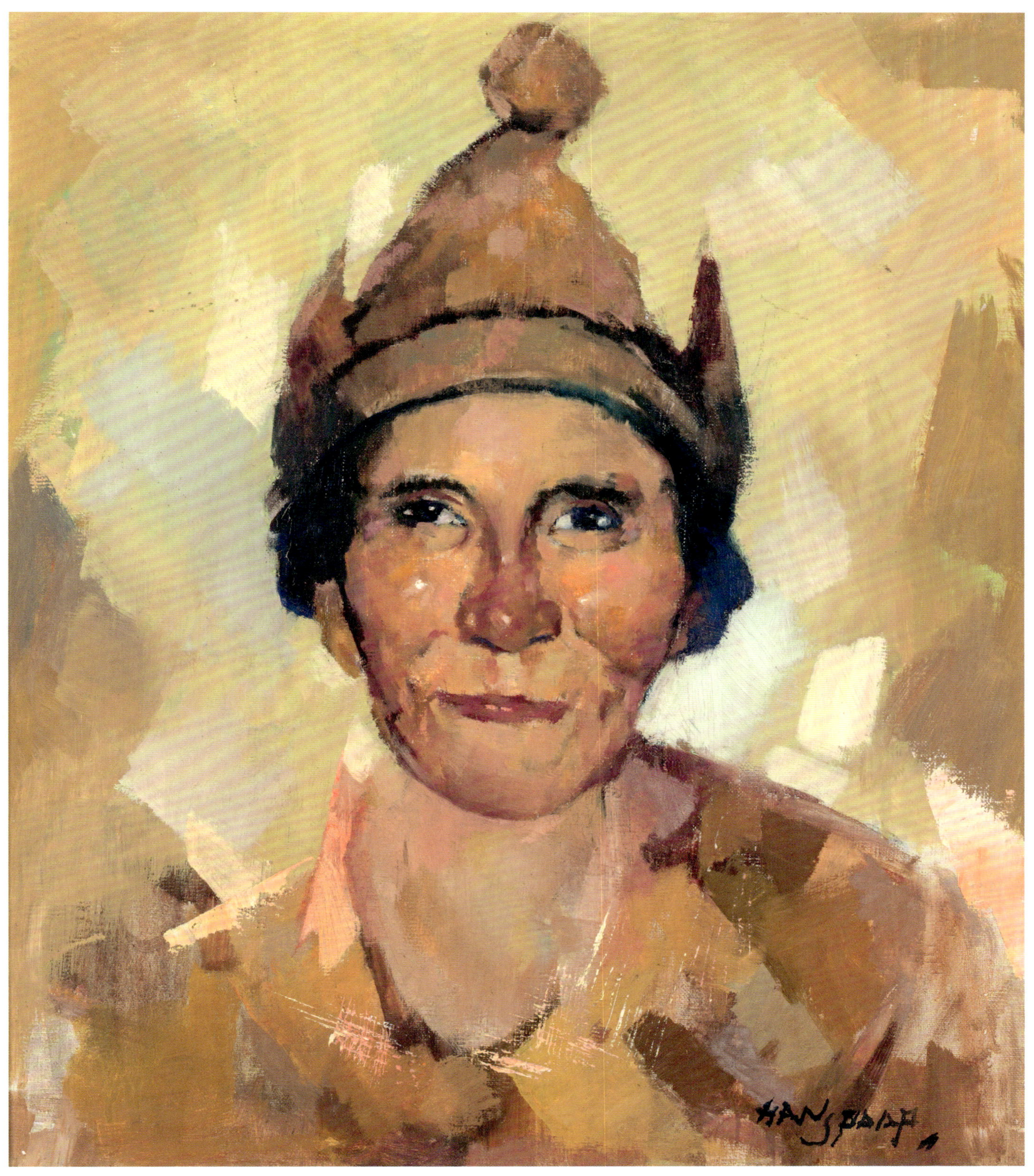

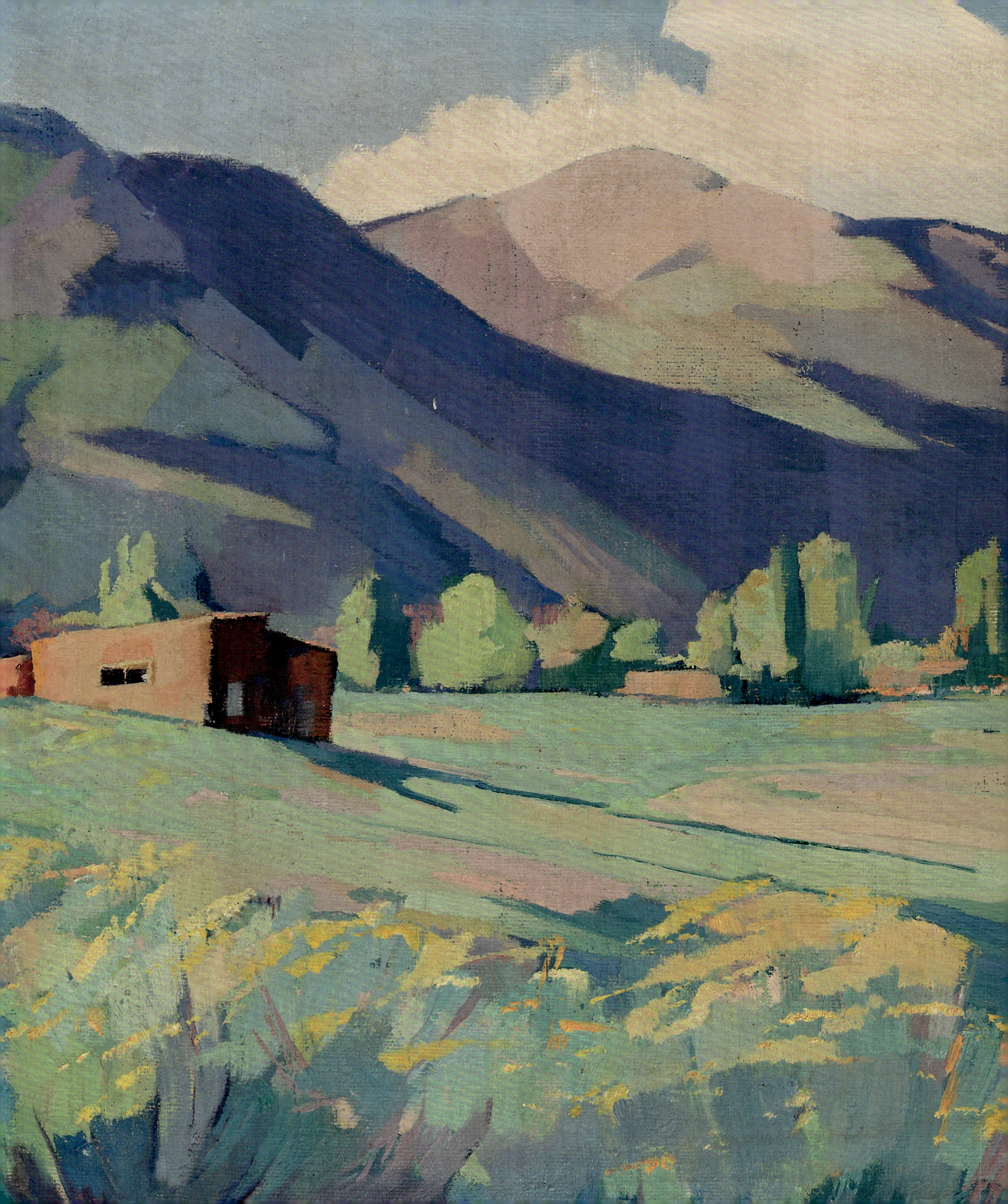

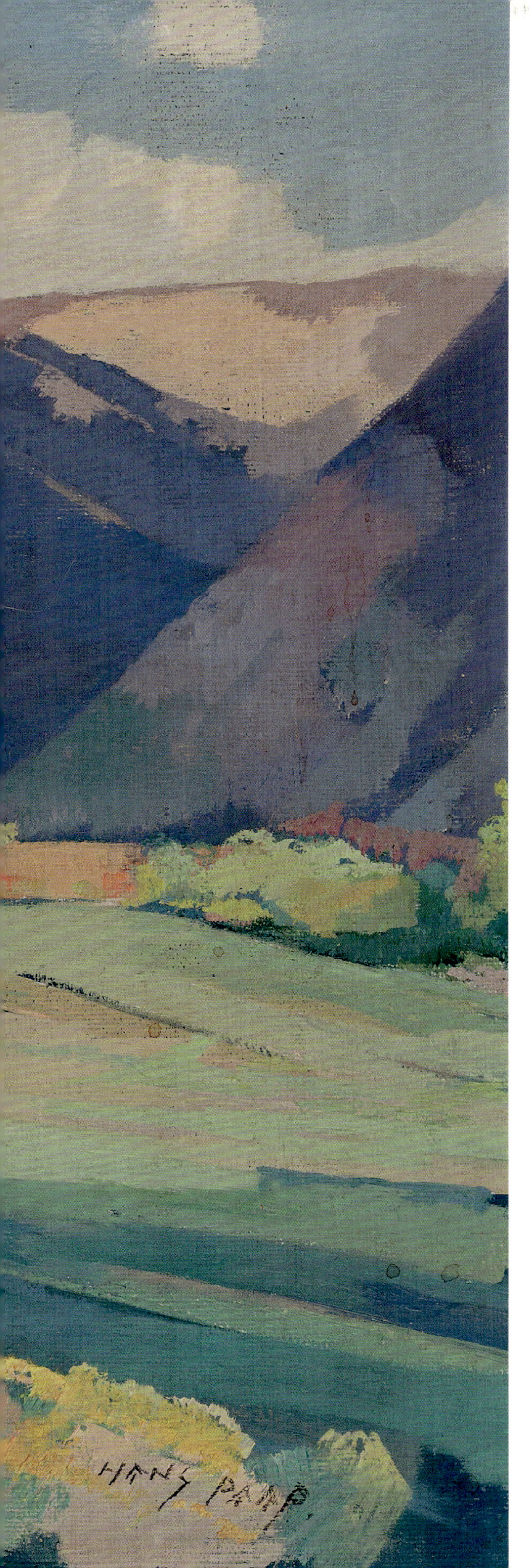


*Adobe and Mountains*
15 x 17 inches
oil on canvas
Courtesy of Nancy Paap
Tesuque, NM

***Portrait of Man in front of San Francisco de Asis Mission Church, Rancho de Taos, New Mexico***
**oil on canvas**
**20 x 16 inches**
**Courtesy of Nancy Paap**
**Tesuque, NM**

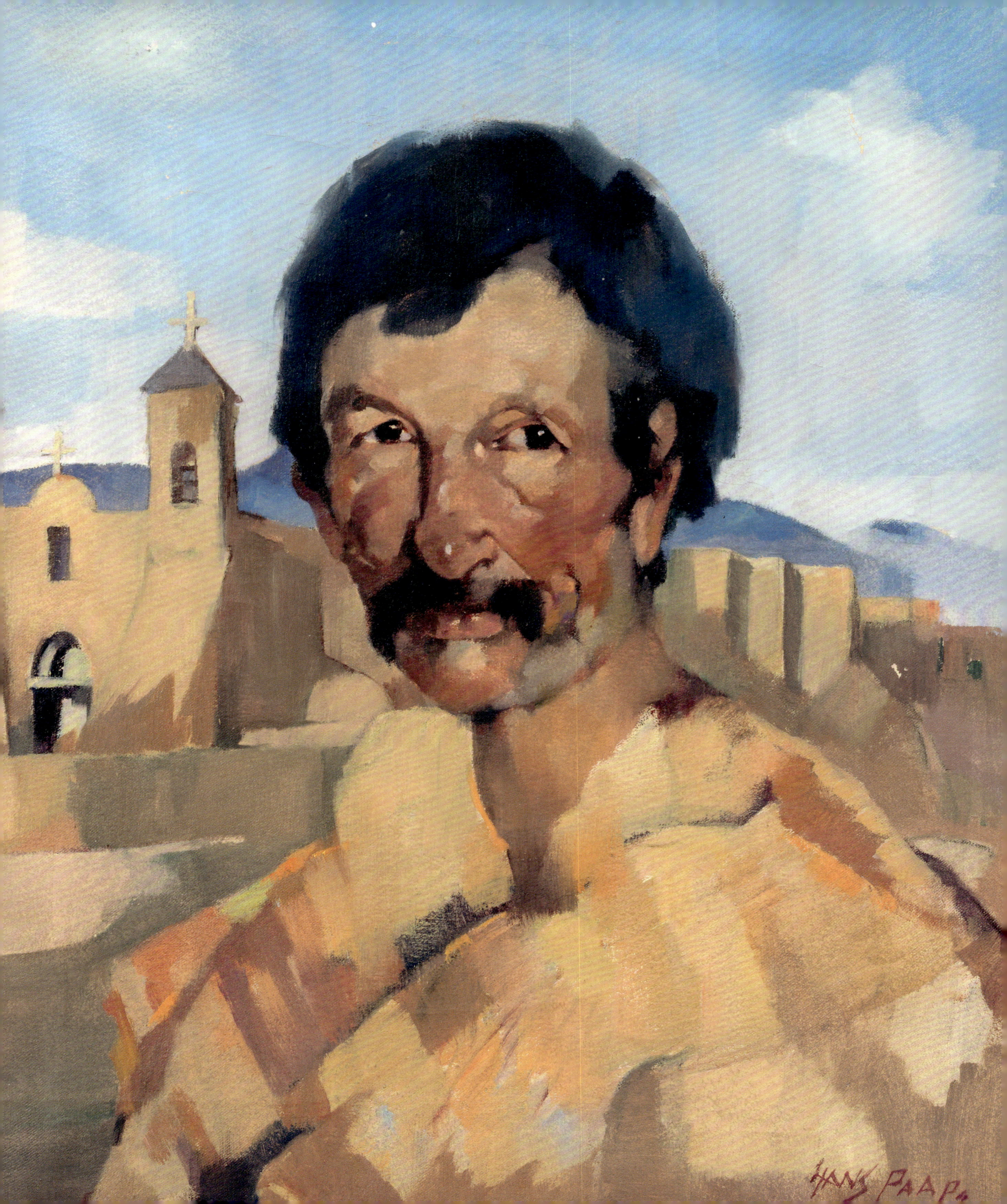
HANS PAAP

*The Westerner*
oil on canvas
20 x 18 inches
c. 1925
Courtesy of Panhandle-Plains Historical Museum, Canyon, TX
James D. Hamlin Collection

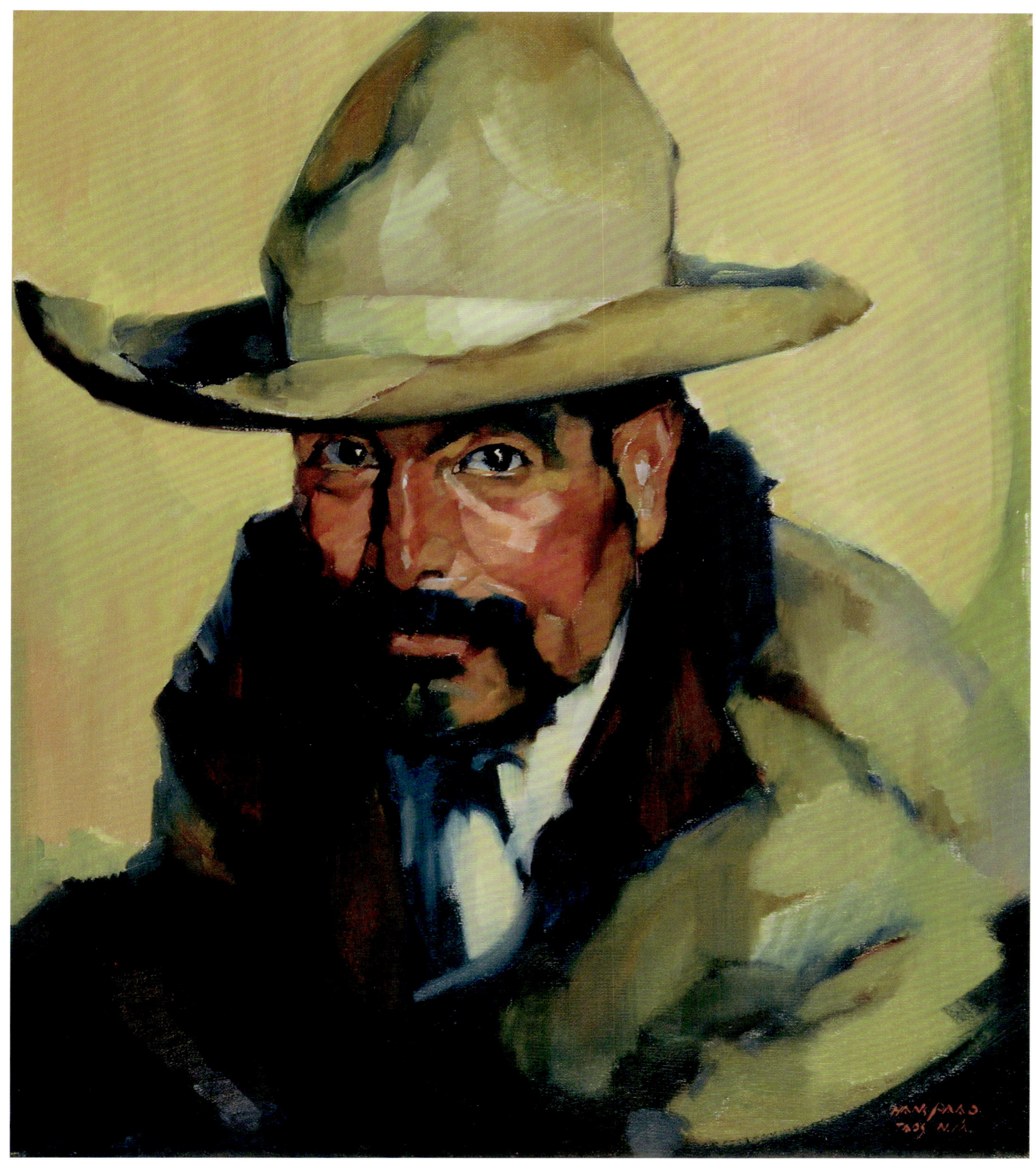

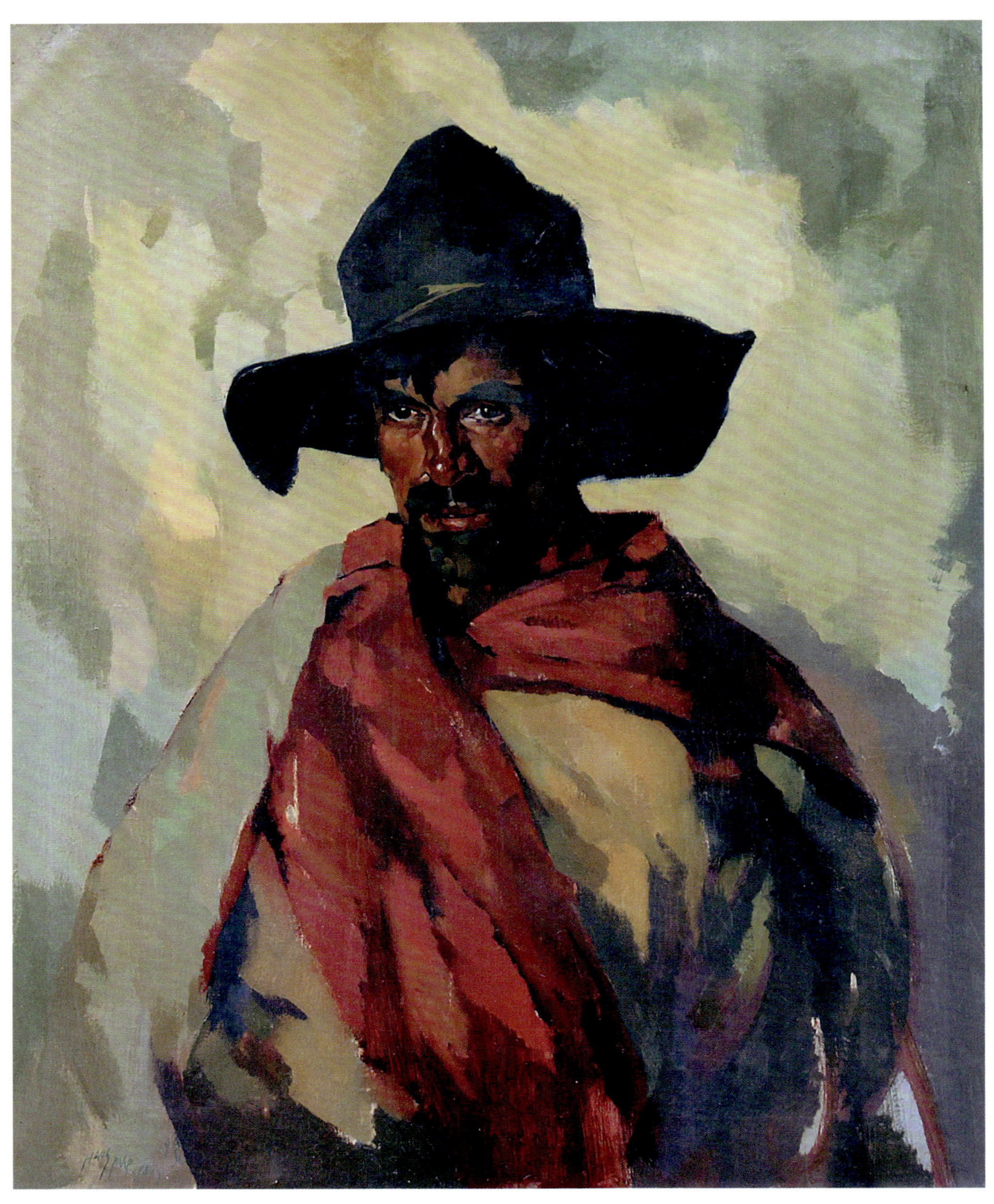

*Taos Sheep Herder*
34 x 28 inches
oil on canvas
1930
Courtesy of
Clars Auction Gallery
Oakland, CA

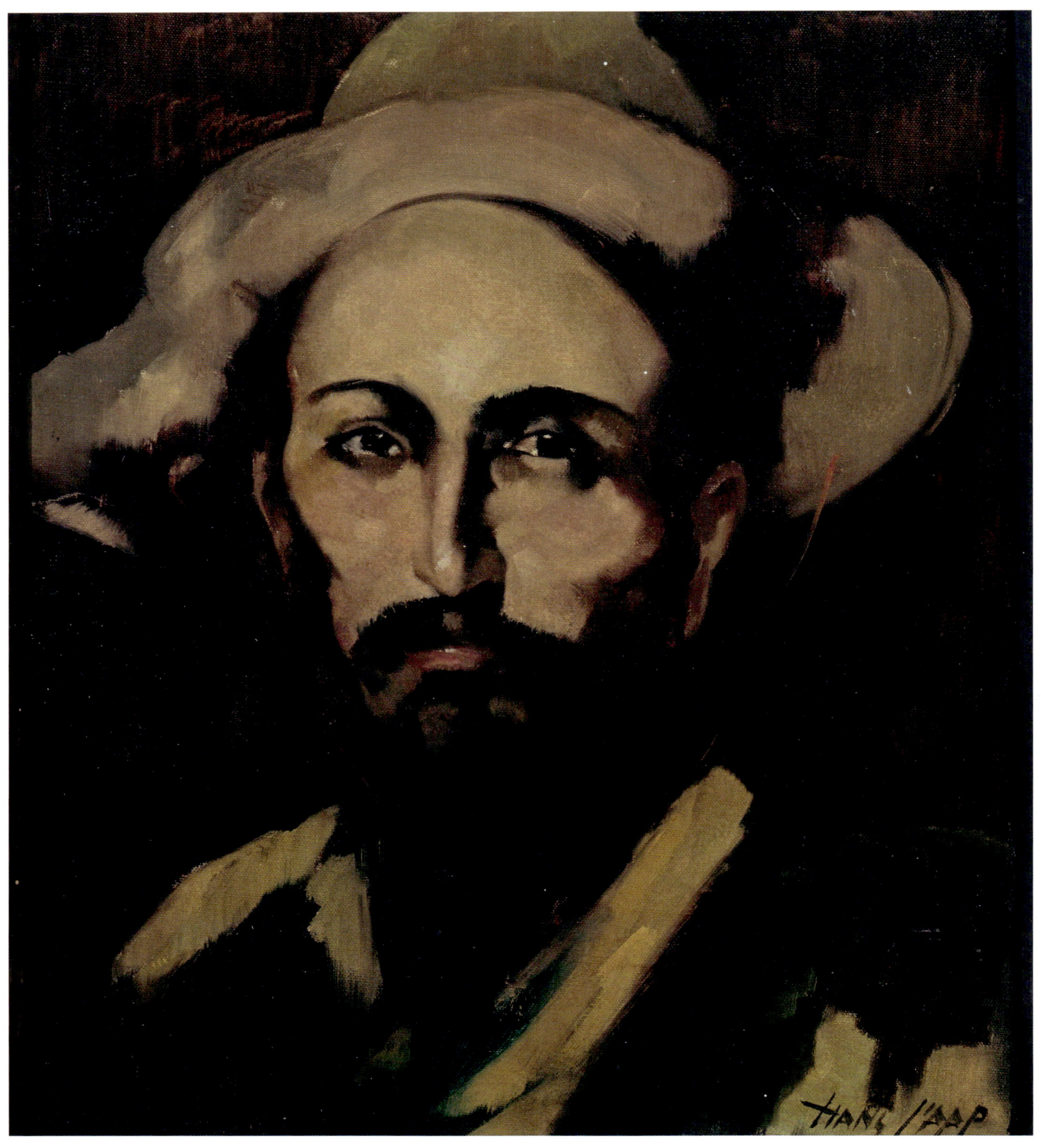

*In Spanish-speaking parts of the country,* vaquero *is the word for "cowboy" or "cattle driver." The two portraits were most likely painted within hours of each other, with* Vaquero 1 – Yellow *painted first. However, it was not until several decades later that the family learned of and acquired* Vaquero 2 – Orange.

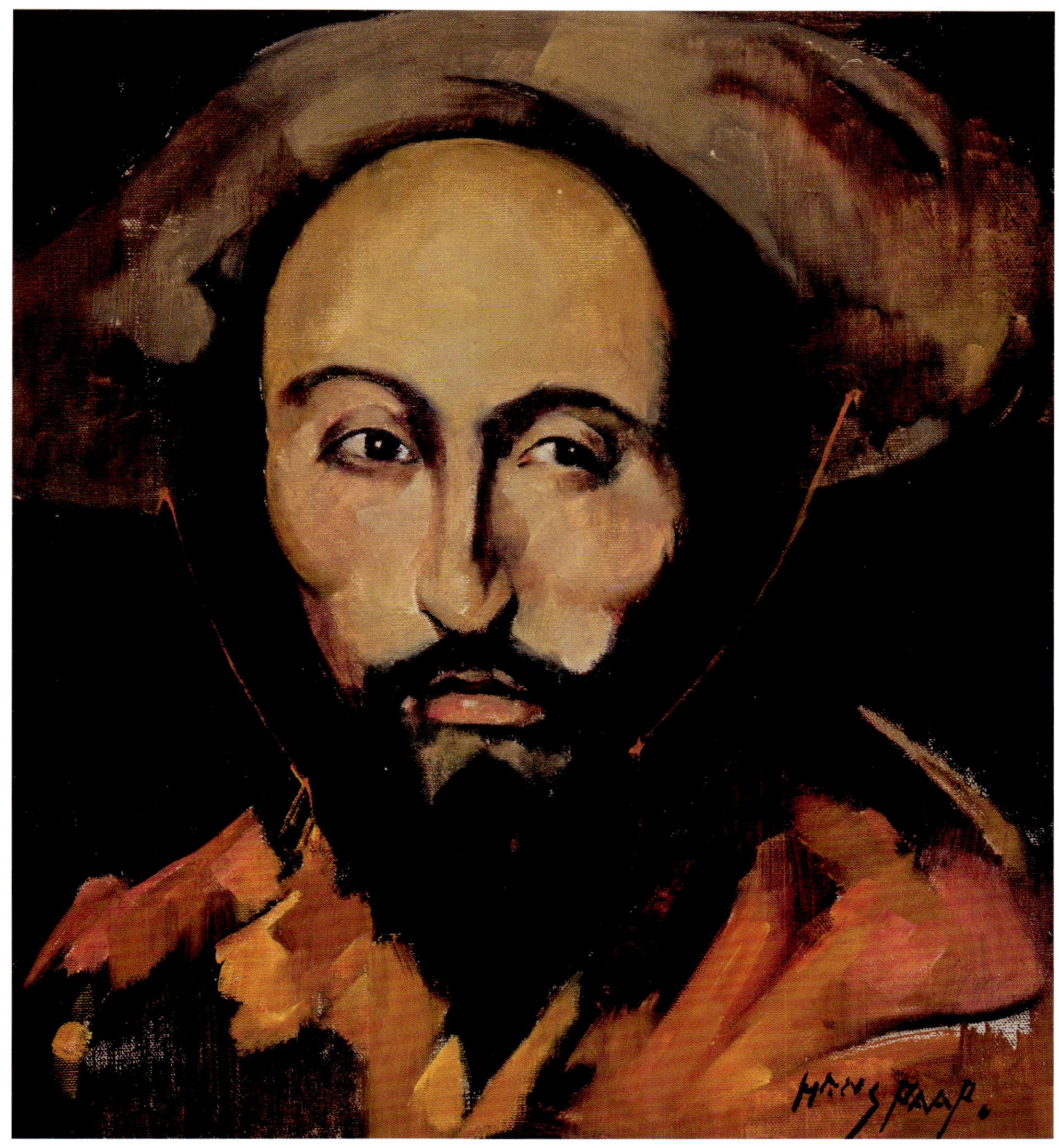


Far left:
*Vaquero 1 - Yellow*
oil on canvas
19 x 16 inches
Courtesy of Roy Paap
Albuquerque, NM

Near left:
*Vaquero 2 - Orange*
oil on canvas
17 x 15 inches
Courtesy of Nancy Paap
Tesuque, NM

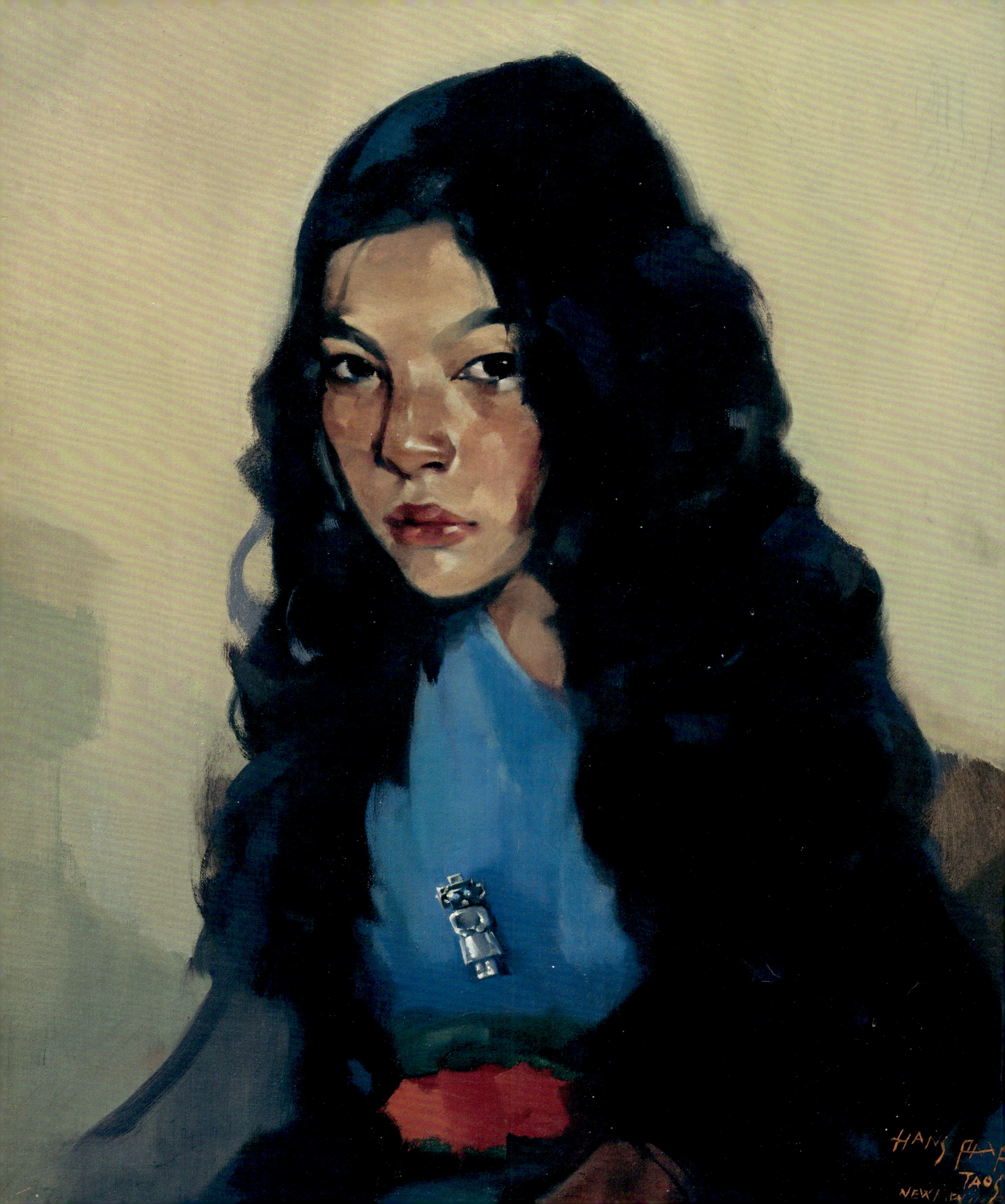
HANS
TAOS
NEW

*In the 1990s, an Oklahoma woman who owned several Paap paintings contacted Nancy Paap. Nancy recognized the sterling silver pin worn by the girl in this painting: it belonged to her mother, Ilse. Hans Paap often styled his models with objects from his collection. It is likely this sterling silver Mudhead katsina (kachina, or ancestral spirit) pin was given to him by a Taos Pueblo jeweler. In the 2018 photo on the jacket flap, Nancy is wearing the same pin.*

***Girl with Katsina Pin***
**oil on board**
**21 x 18 inches**
**Courtesy of Roy Paap**
**Albuquerque, NM**

***Portrait of Ilse Paap with Mantilla and Hibiscus Flower***
**oil on canvas**
**20 x 16 inches**
**Courtesy of Brendon Paap**
**Albuquerque, NM**

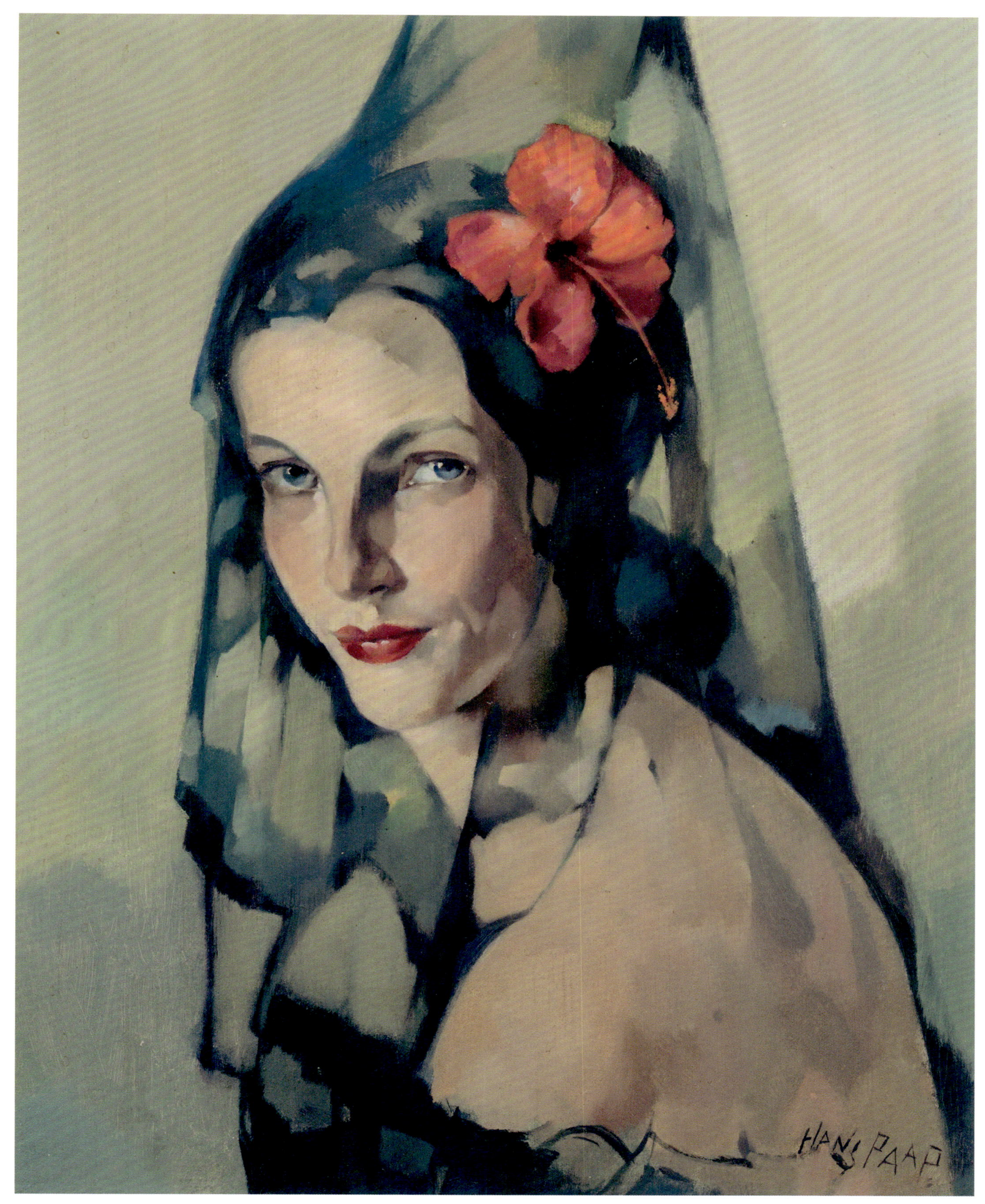
HANS PAAP

*"I only exist because the wagon wheel broke," quipped Margo Beutler Gins, great-granddaughter of Bert Geer Phillips, a founding member of the Taos Society of Artists. She was referring to the mishap on the way to Mexico that caused him and fellow painter E.L. Blumenschein to stay in Taos. Paap gifted the painting to Gins' grandmother, Margo Phillips Beutler. It has been treasured and displayed prominently by three generations, with family tradition dictating that it always be hung in the dining room.*

***Still Life***
**oil on canvas**
**19 x 25**
**Courtesy of**
**The Beutler**
**Family Collection**
**Taos, NM**

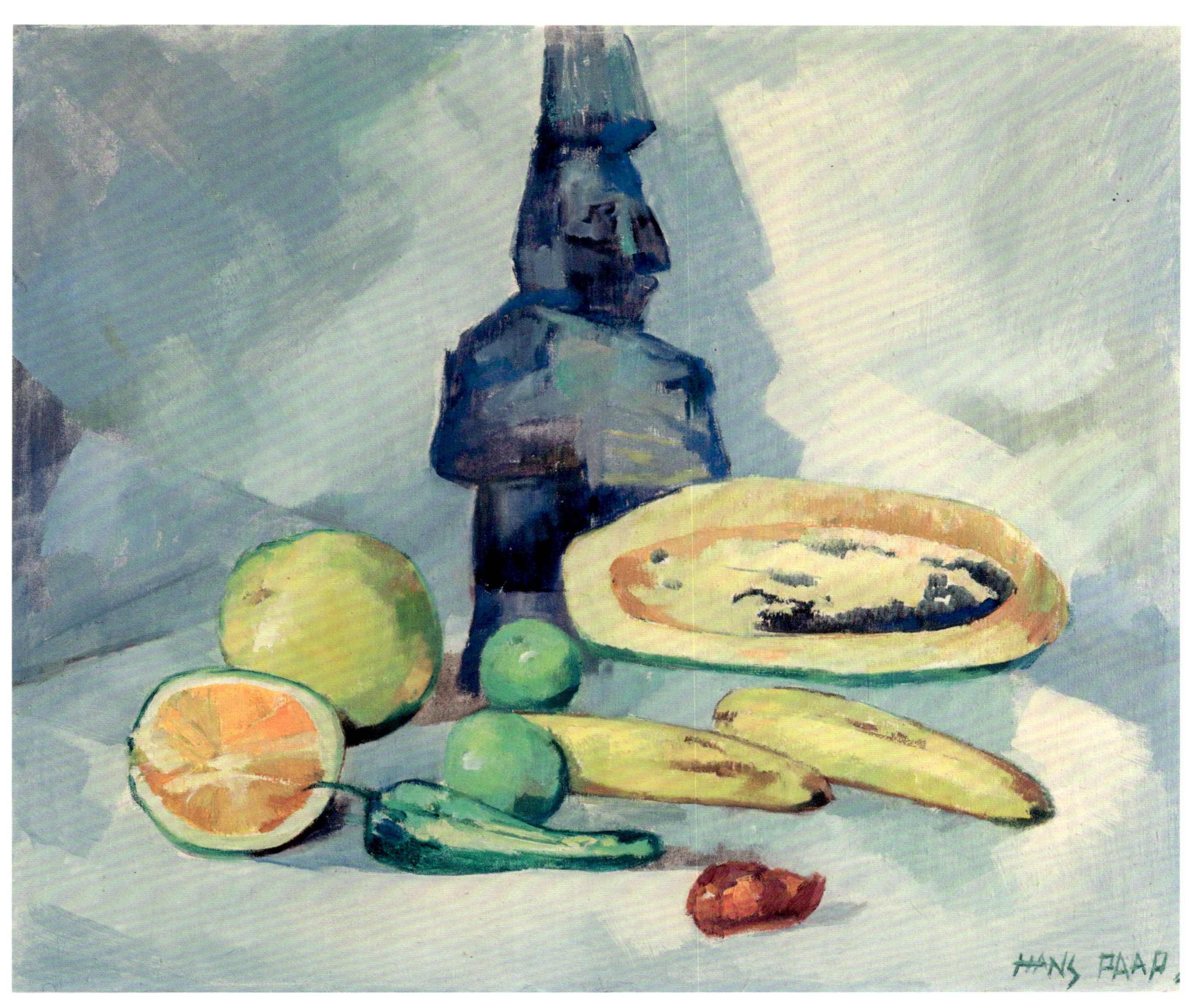
HANS PAAP

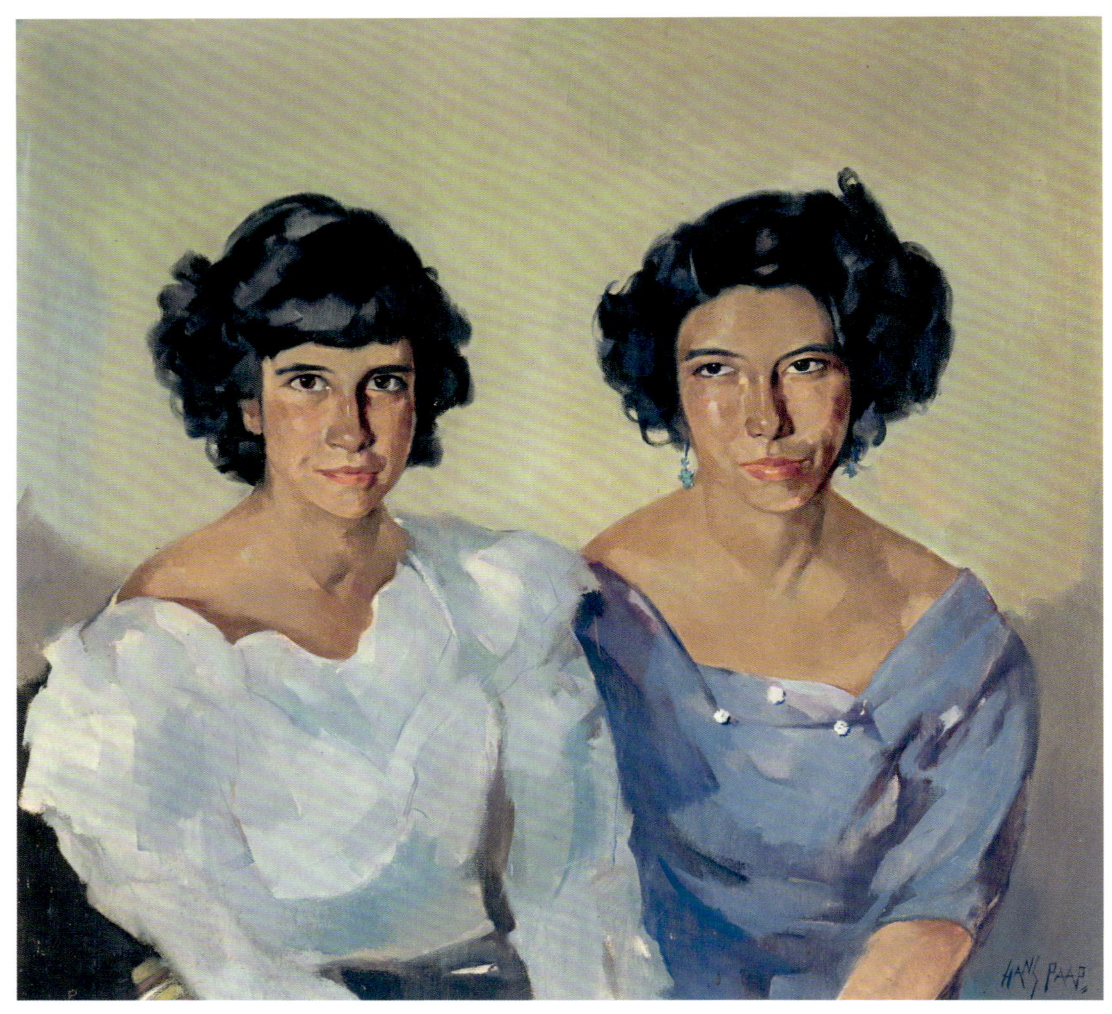


*Paap often painted the people around him. Carmen D. Medina and her cousin Alice (above) lived in the same Taos neighborhood as the Paaps. Deanna Luciani (far right) and her family lived across the street from the Paap family, on Quesnel Street. Fourteen years old when she had her portrait painted, Luciani worked for thirty-five cents a day to repay her mother for the ten-dollar sitting fee. Now eighty years old, she treasures this portrait of herself.*

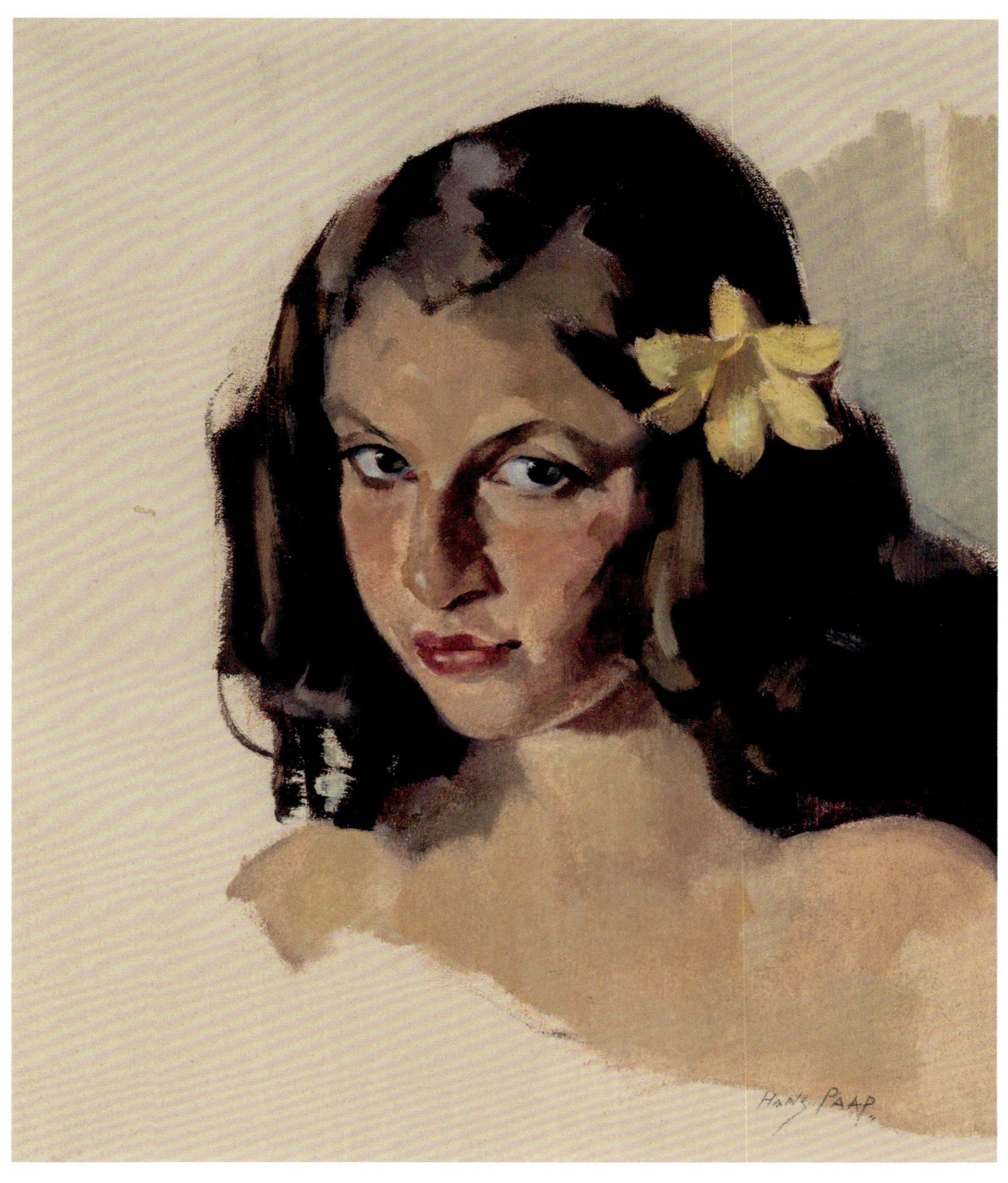


Far left:
*Taos Ladies*
*(Carmen Medina*
*and Cousin Alice)*
oil on canvas
30 x 28 inches
c. 1950s
Courtesy of Nancy Paap
Tesuque, NM

Near left:
*Portrait of Deanna Luciani*
oil on board
24 x 17 inches
1951
Courtesy of
Deanna Luciani
Albuquerque, NM

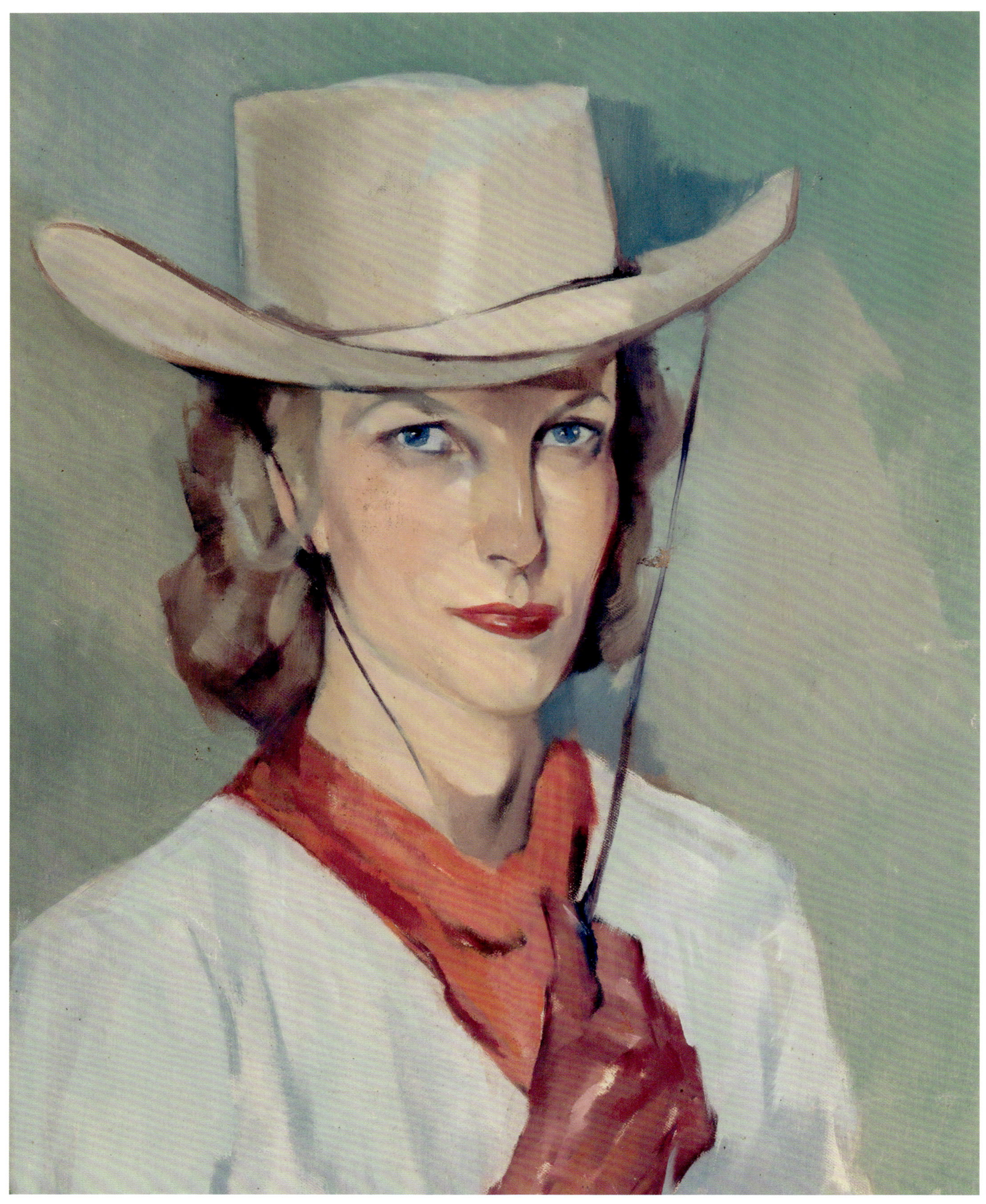

*Portrait of Ilse Paap in Western Attire*
oil on canvas
20 x 16 inches
c. 1950
Courtesy of Roy Paap
Albuquerque, NM

***Blue Madonna***
**oil on canvas**
**24¾ x 21¼**
**Courtesy of**
**Betsy Wall**
**Salt Lake City, UT**

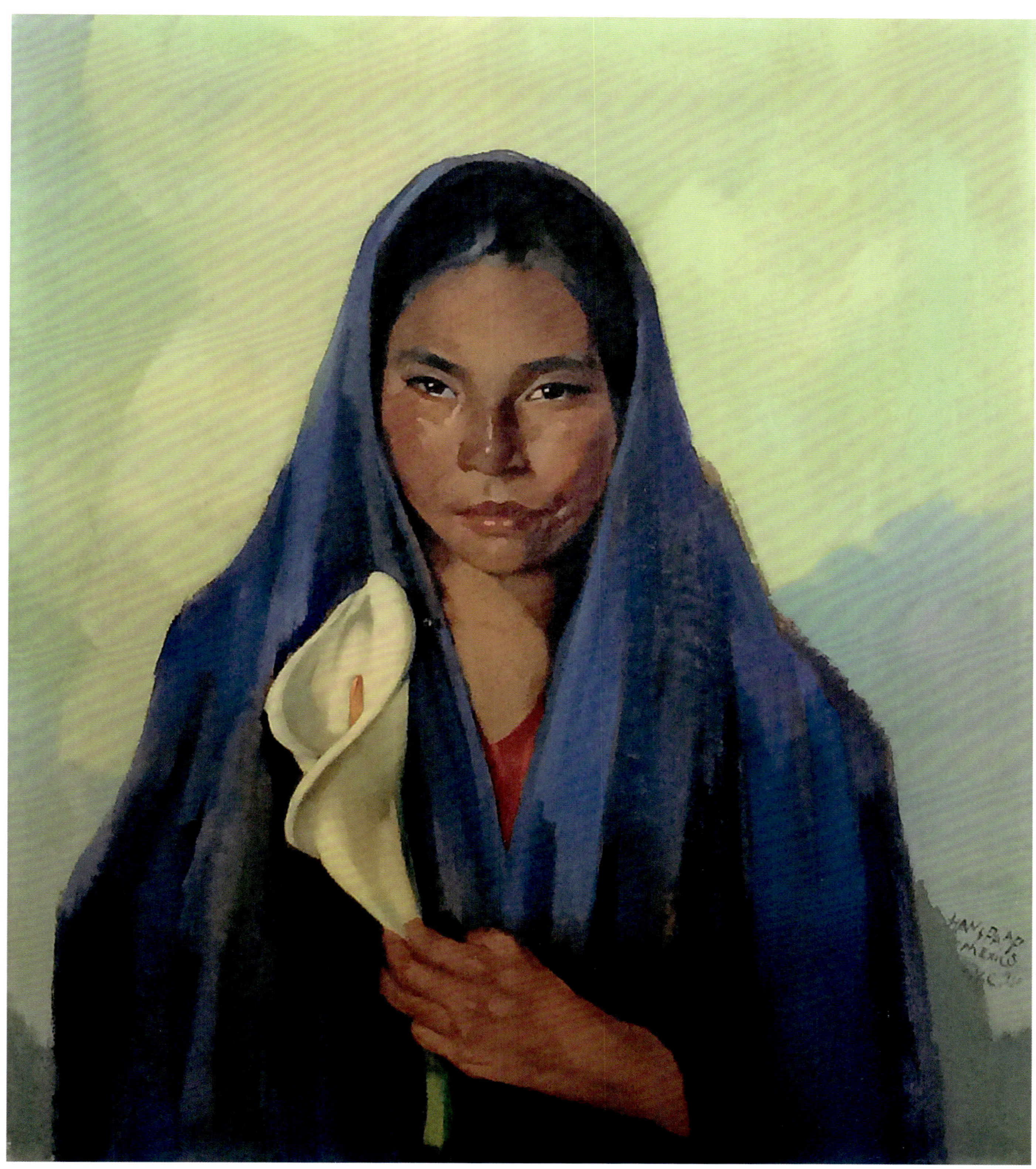

Anchorage

## California
## Hawaii
## Mexico

Kodi

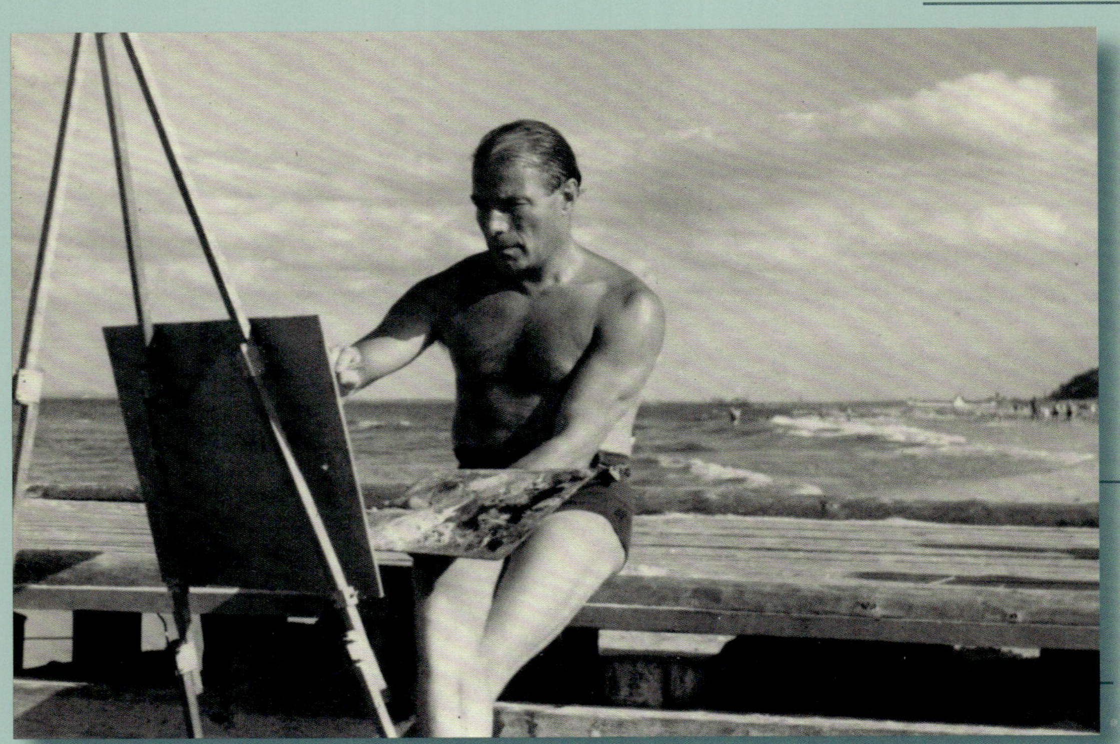

Hawaiian Islands
(U.S.A.)

PAC

**Paap painting beside the ocean**

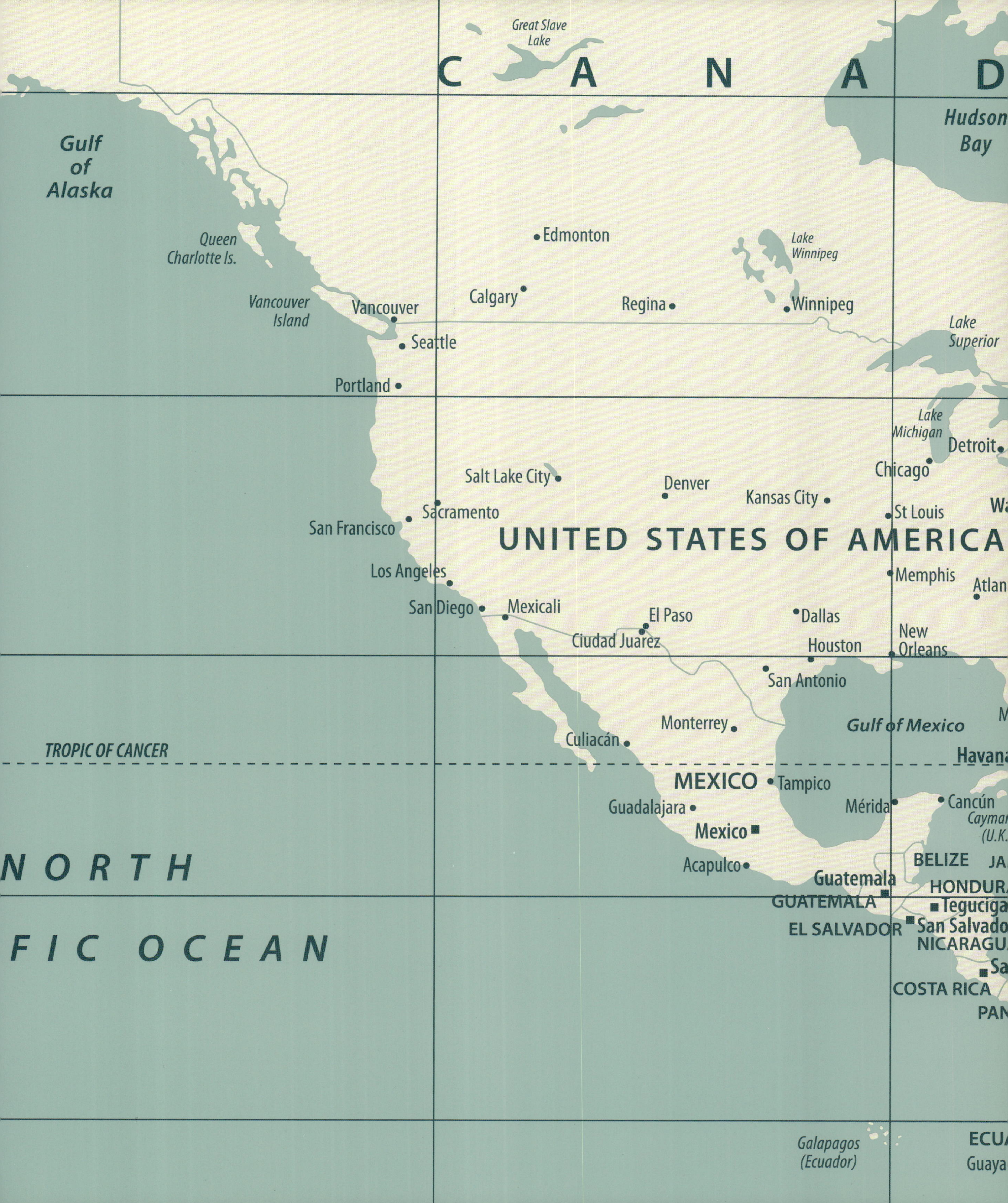
Great Slave Lake
C A N A D
Hudson Bay
Gulf of Alaska
Queen Charlotte Is.
Edmonton
Lake Winnipeg
Calgary
Regina
Winnipeg
Vancouver Island
Vancouver
Seattle
Lake Superior
Portland
Lake Michigan
Detroit
Chicago
Salt Lake City
Denver
Kansas City
Sacramento
San Francisco
St Louis
UNITED STATES OF AMERICA
Los Angeles
Memphis
Atlan
San Diego
Mexicali
El Paso
Dallas
Ciudad Juarez
Houston
New Orleans
San Antonio
Monterrey
Gulf of Mexico
Culiacán
TROPIC OF CANCER
Havana
MEXICO
Tampico
Guadalajara
Mérida
Cancún
Mexico
BELIZE
Acapulco
Guatemala
HONDUR
GUATEMALA
Tegucig
EL SALVADOR
San Salvado
NICARAGU
NORTH
FIC OCEAN
COSTA RICA
PAN
Galapagos (Ecuador)
ECU
Guaya

*Deetjen's Big Sur Inn,*
*California*
oil on canvas
20 x 16 inches
Courtesy of
Deetjen's Big Sur Inn
Big Sur, CA

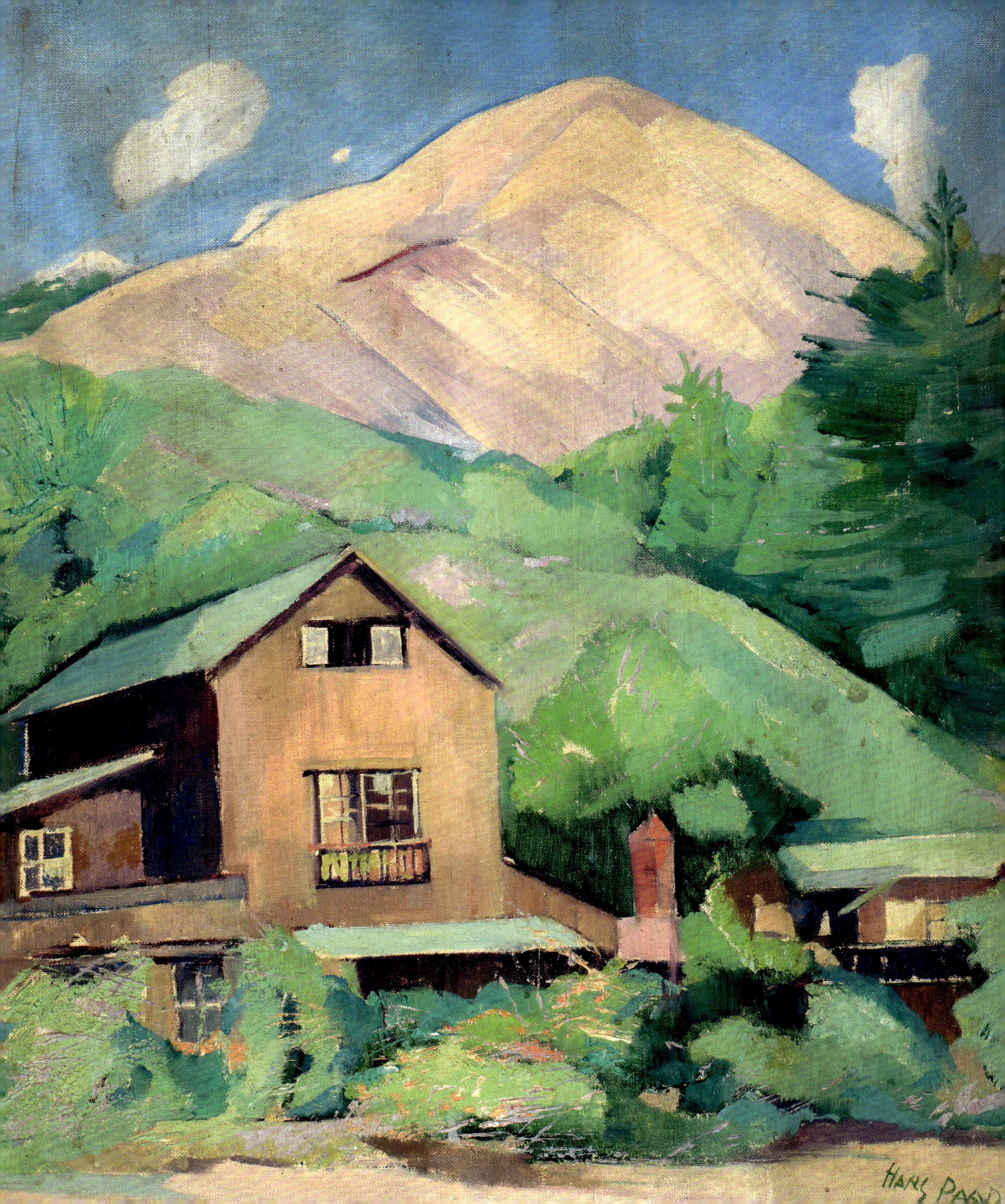
HANS

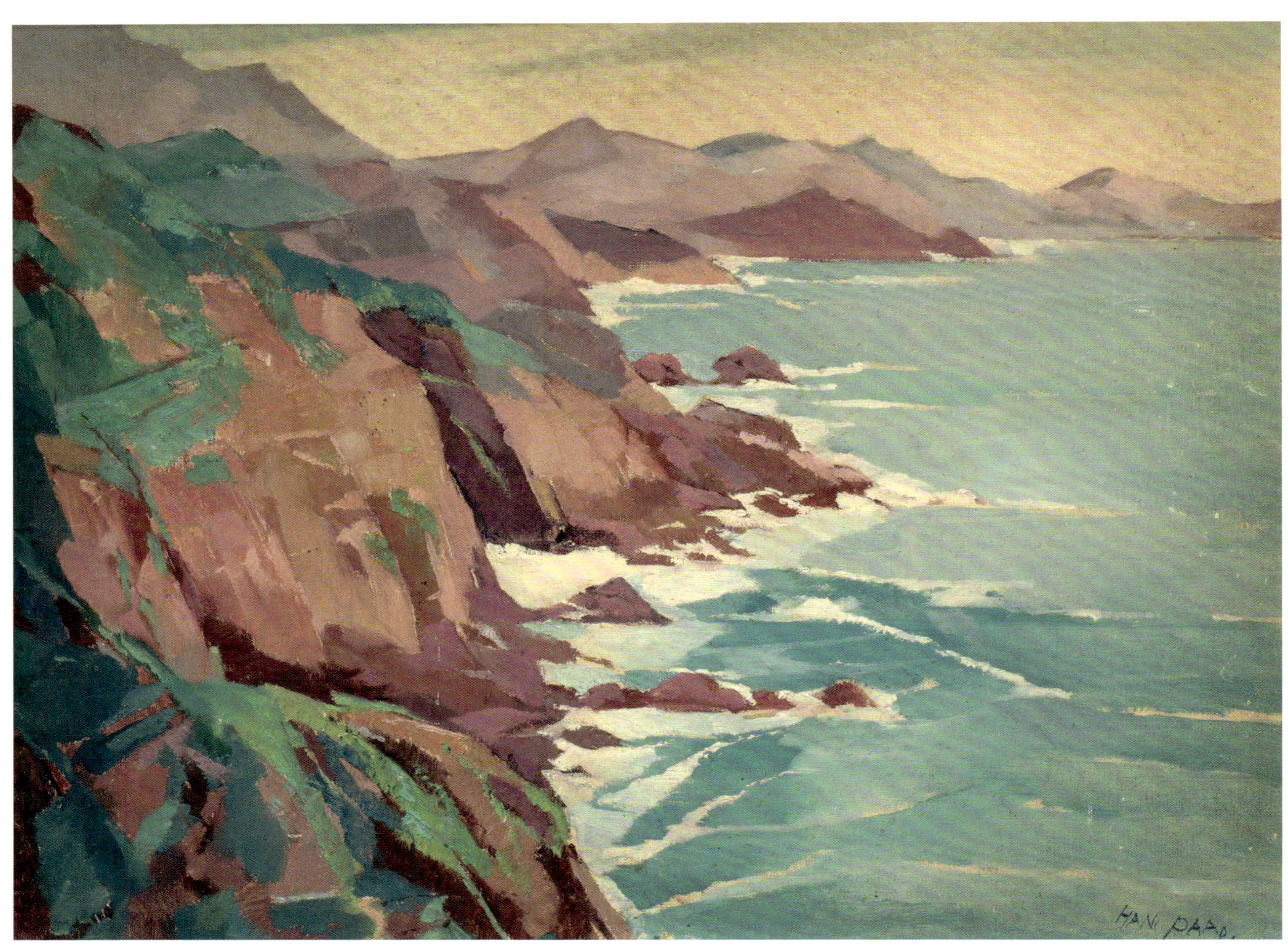

*Big Sur Coastline*
oil on canvas
16 x 20 inches
Courtesy of
Deetjen's Big Sur Inn
Big Sur, CA

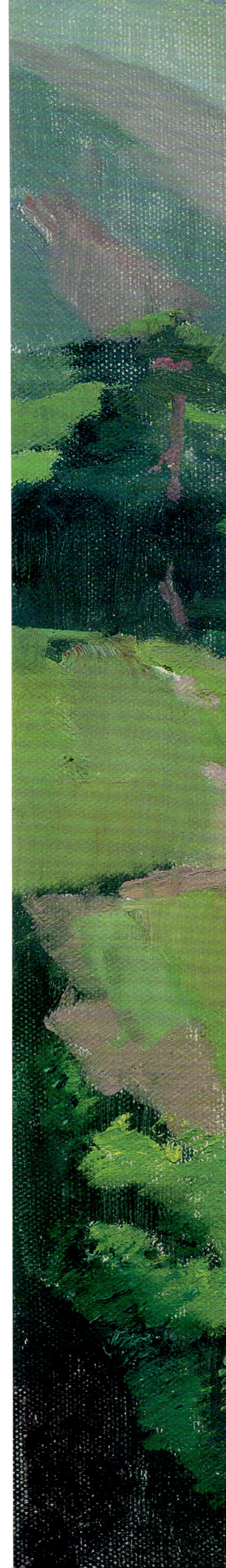

*Hawaiian Landscape*
oil on canvas
15 x 14 inches
Courtesy of Nancy Paap
Tesuque, NM

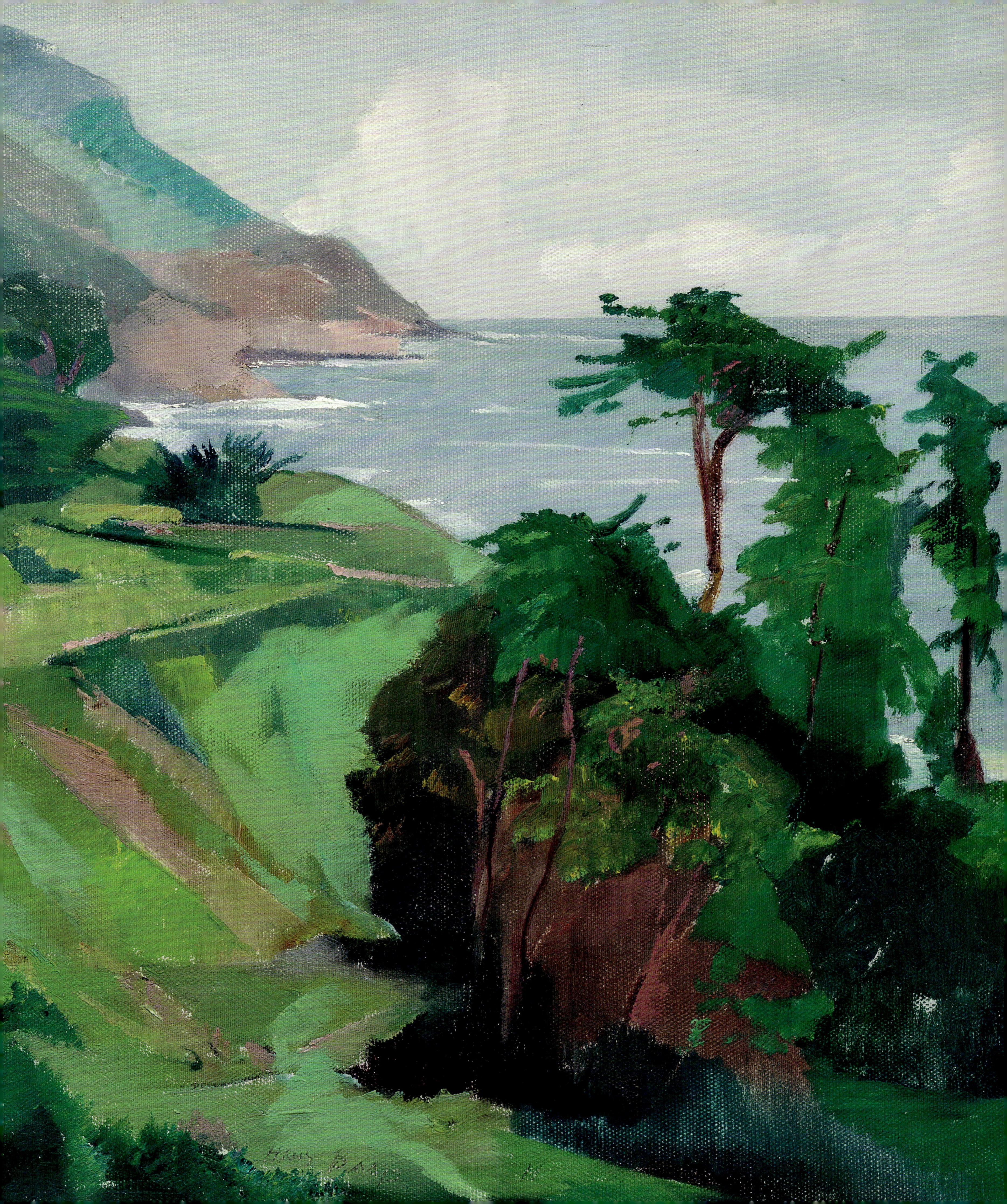

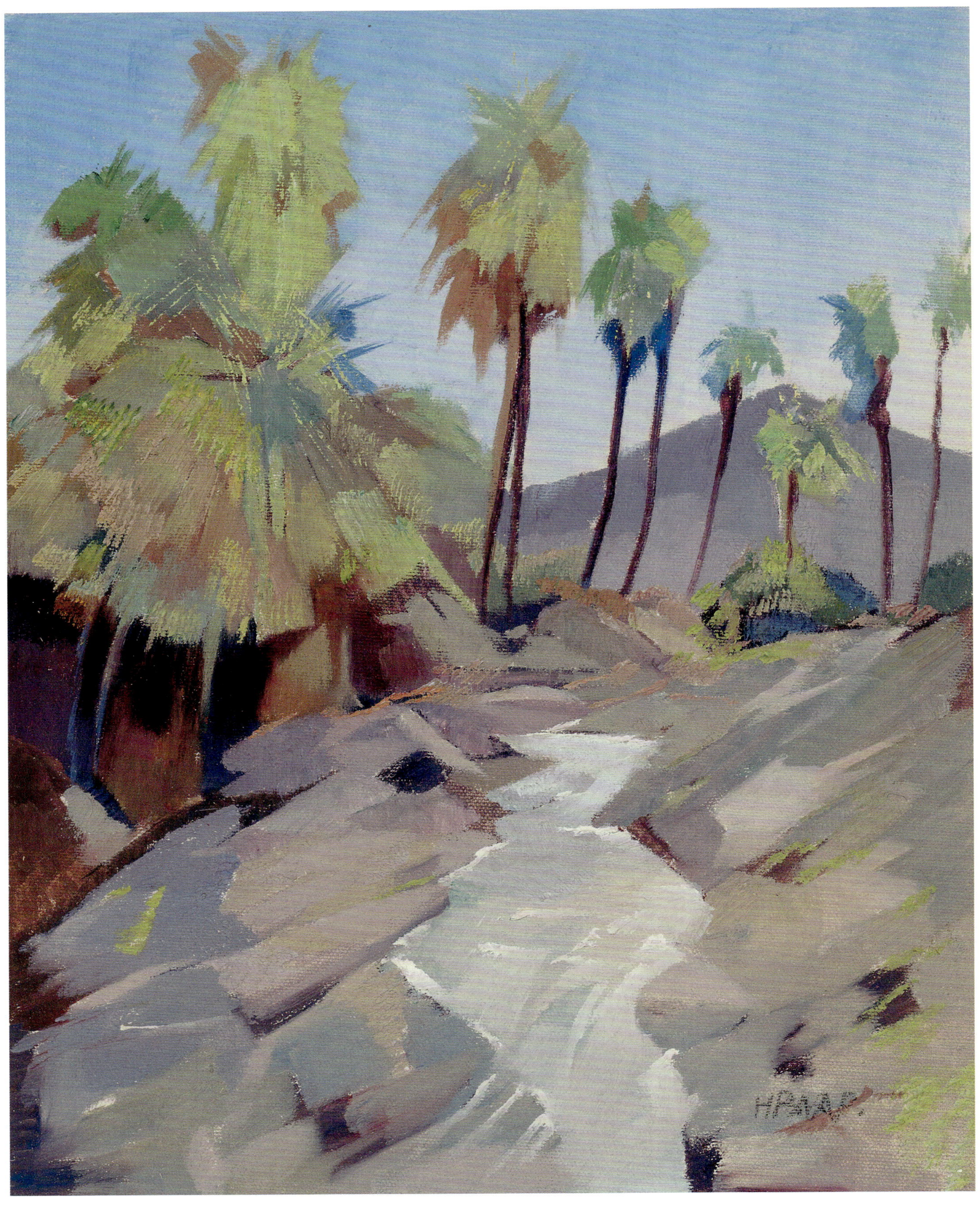

*Landscape*
*with Palm Trees*
oil on canvas
15 x 12 inches
Courtesy of Nancy Paap
Tesuque, NM

*Hawaiian Cliffs*
oil on canvas
22 x 18 inches
Courtesy of Nancy Paap
Tesuque, NM

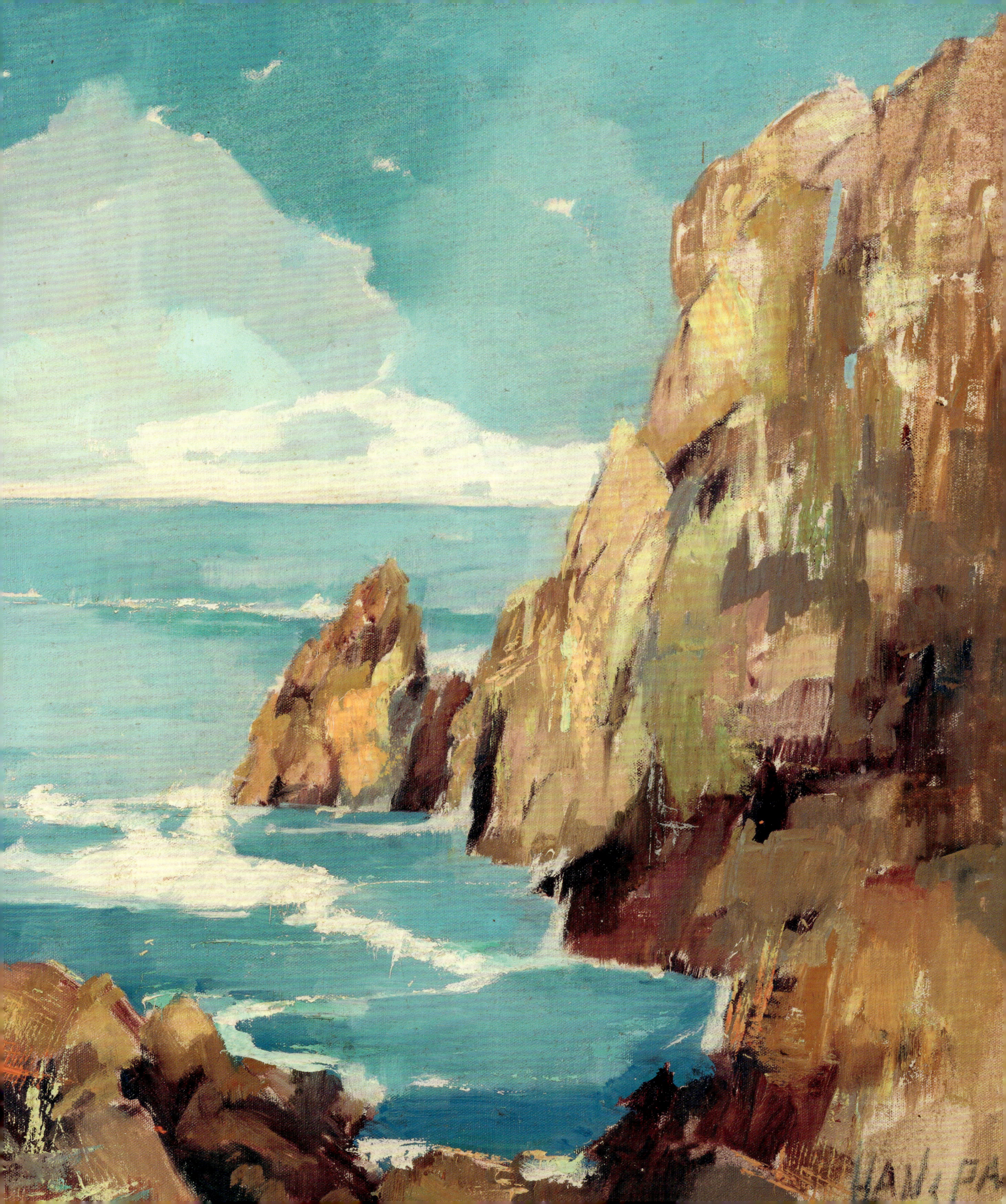

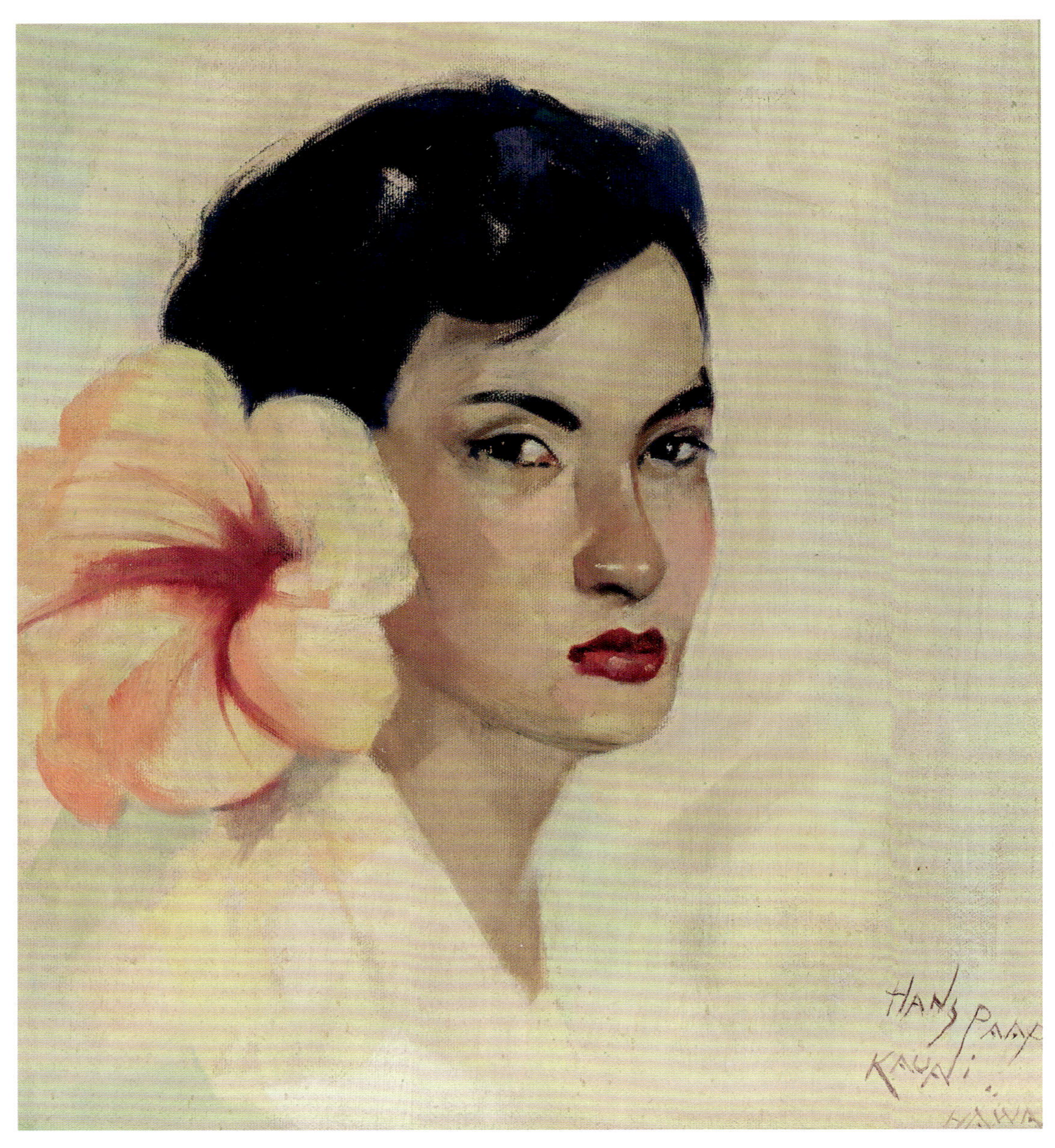


***Portrait of Hawaiian Woman with Yellow Hibiscus, Kauai, Hawaii***
**oil on canvas**
**15 x 14 inches**
**1956**
**Courtesy of Nancy Paap**
**Tesuque, NM**

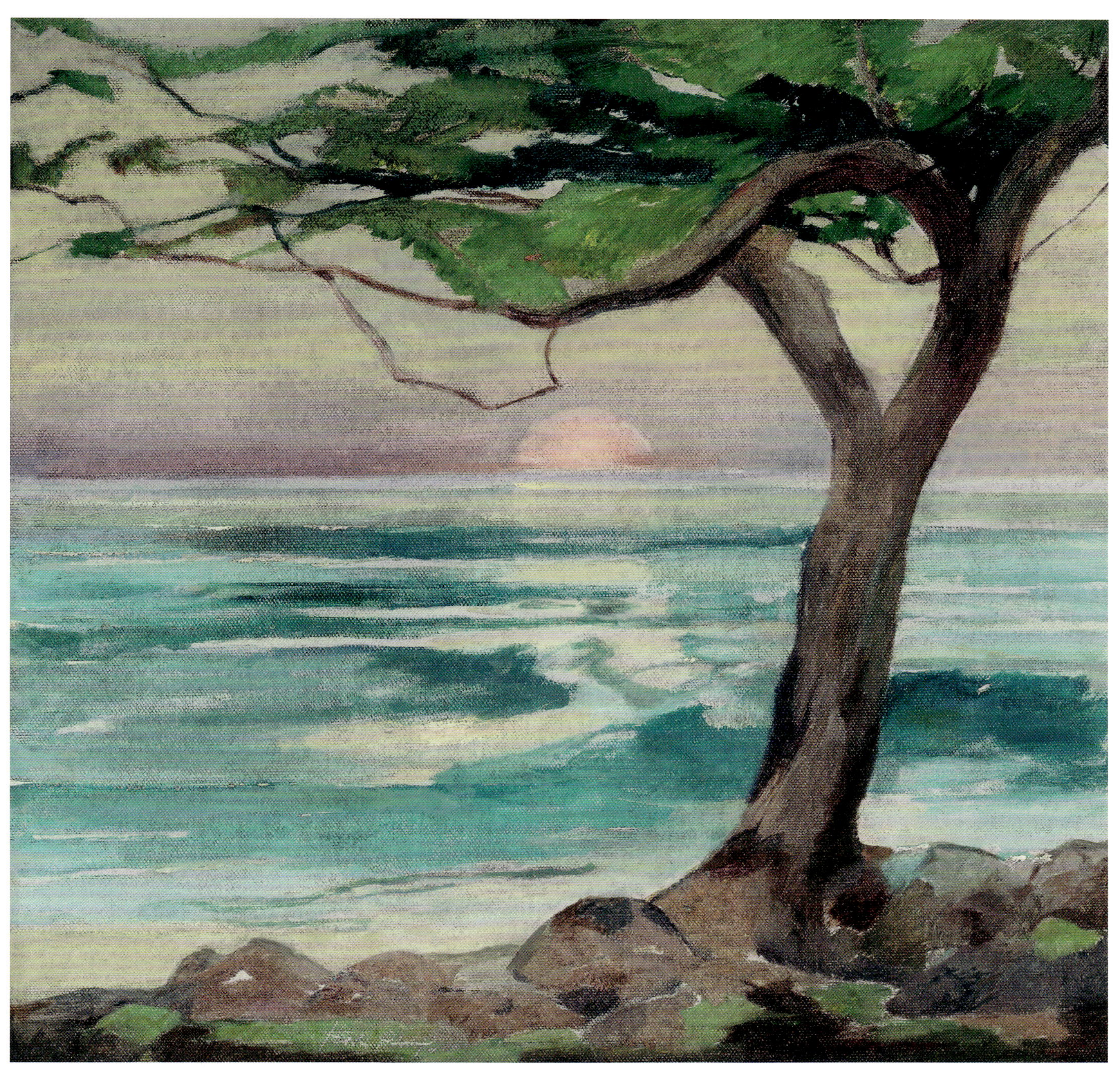

*Hawaiian Sunset*
oil on board
14 x 15 inches
Courtesy of Nancy Paap
Tesuque, NM

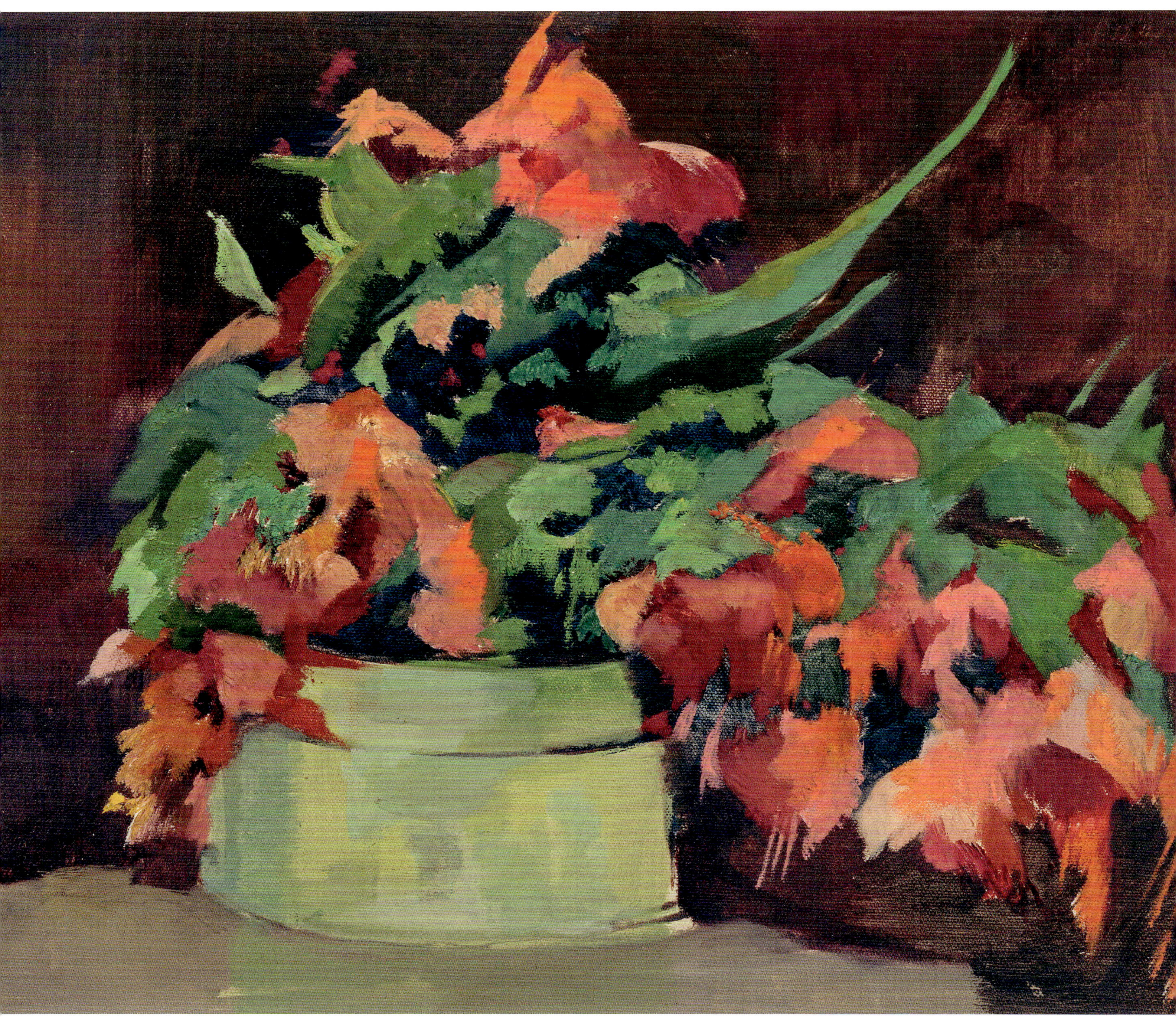

*Still Life Hibiscus*
**14 x 16 inches**
**oil on canvas**
**Courtesy of Nancy Paap**
**Tesuque, NM**

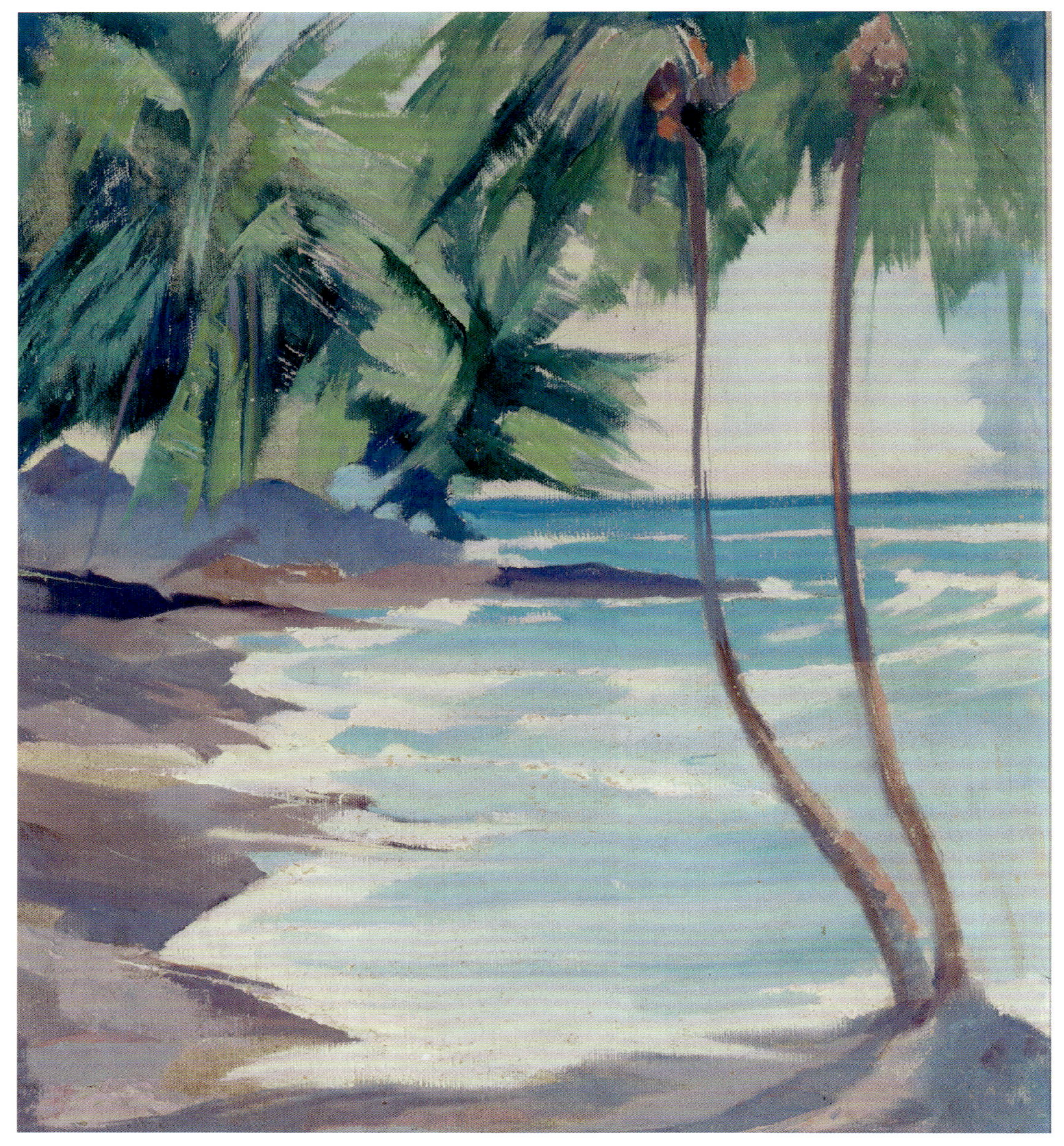

***Seascape with Foreground Palm Tree***
**oil on canvas**
**17 x 15 inches**
**Courtesy of JoAnna Paap**
**Santa Fe, NM**

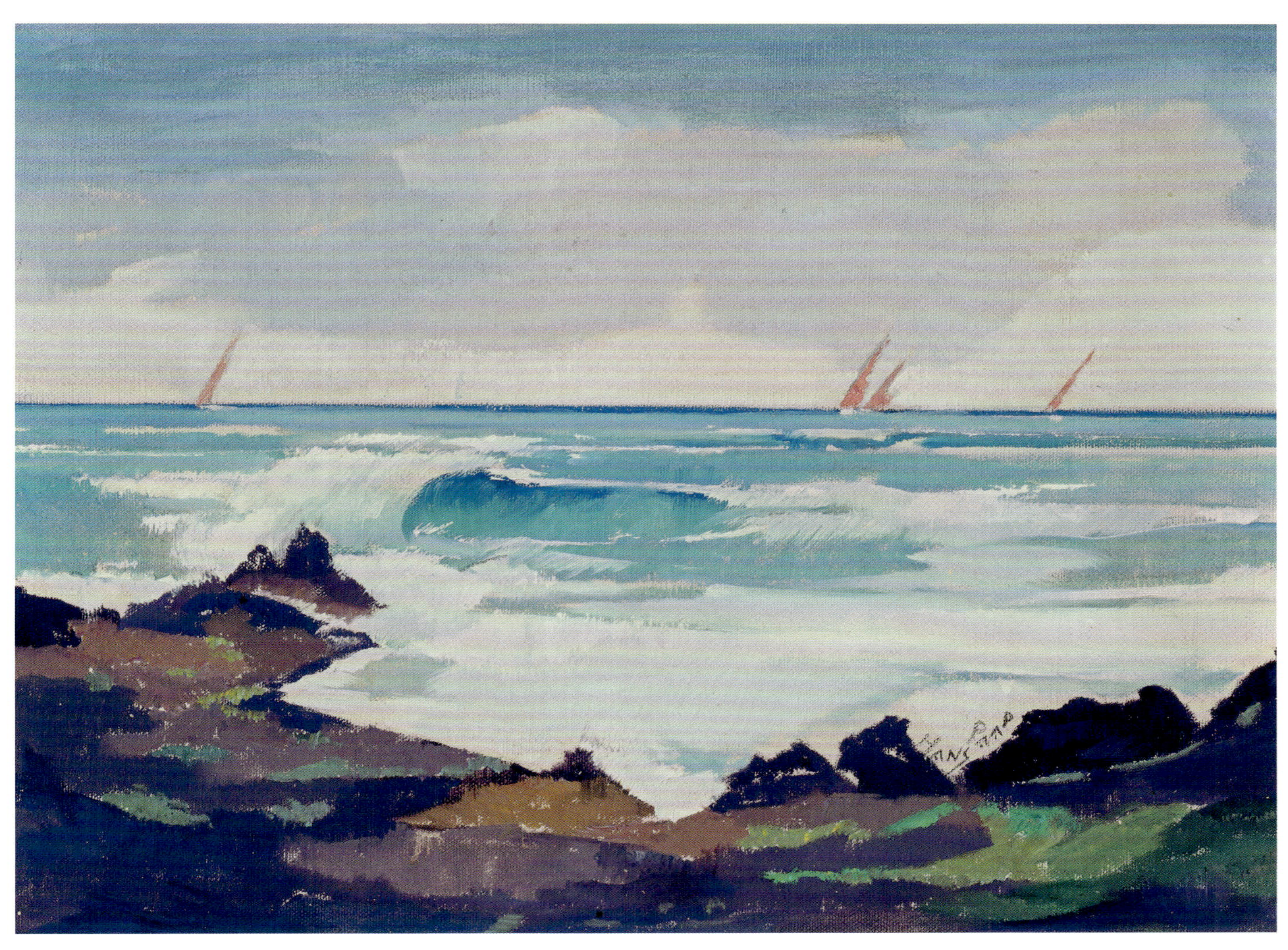

*Seascape with Four Sailboats*
oil on canvas
12 x 16 inches
Courtesy of Roy Paap
Albuquerque, NM

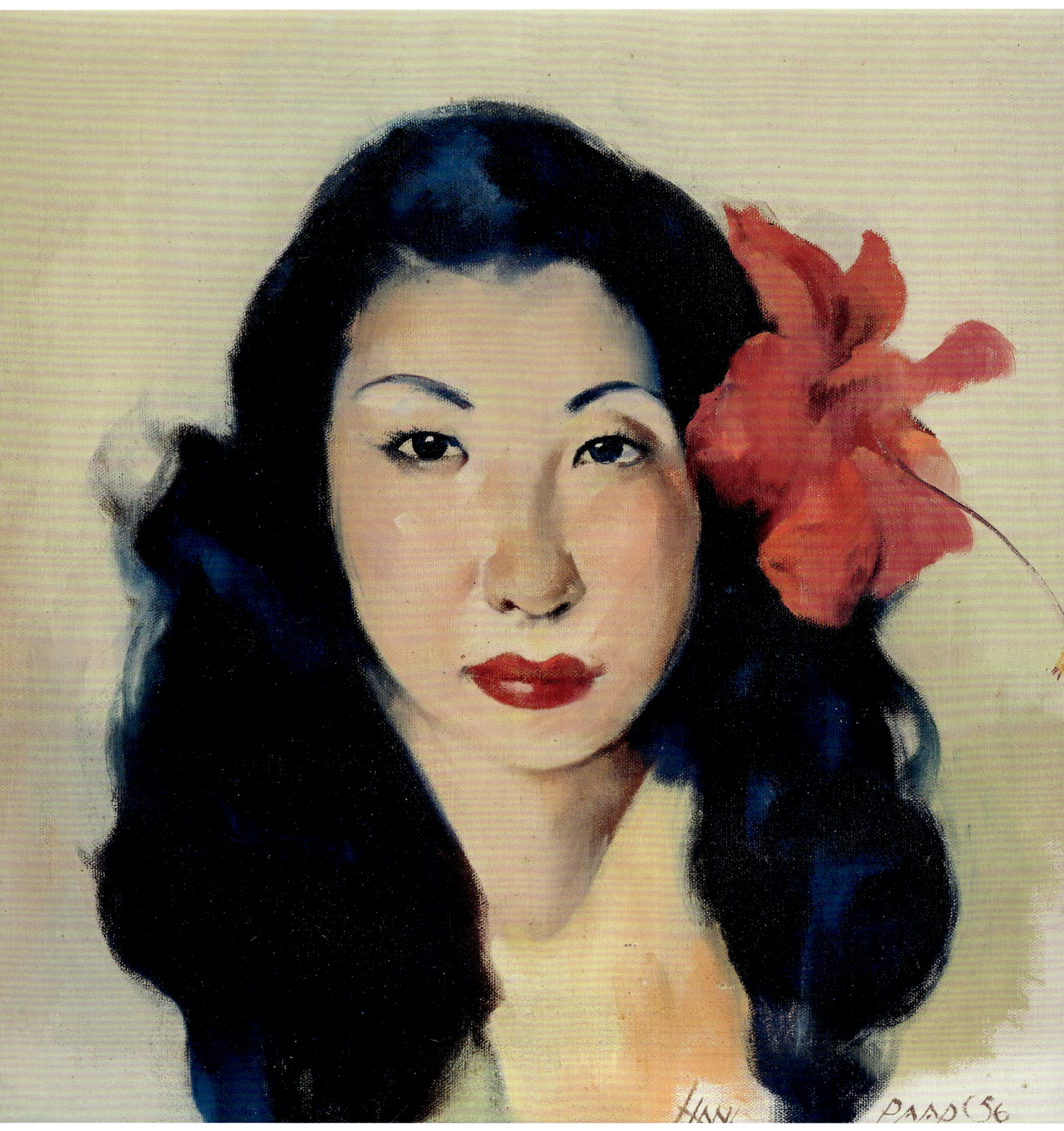

*Portrait of Hawaiian*
*Woman with Red Hibiscus*
oil on canvas
16 x 16 inches
1956
Courtesy of Nancy Paap
Tesuque, NM

*Paap lived in countless places during his life, including Europe, South America, Mexico, the United States and on various islands around the world. He returned to Hawaii several times, often going there to paint in the winter.*

***Hawaiian Seascape with Sailboat***
**oil on board**
**15 x 15 inches**
**Courtesy of Nancy Paap**
**Tesuque, NM**

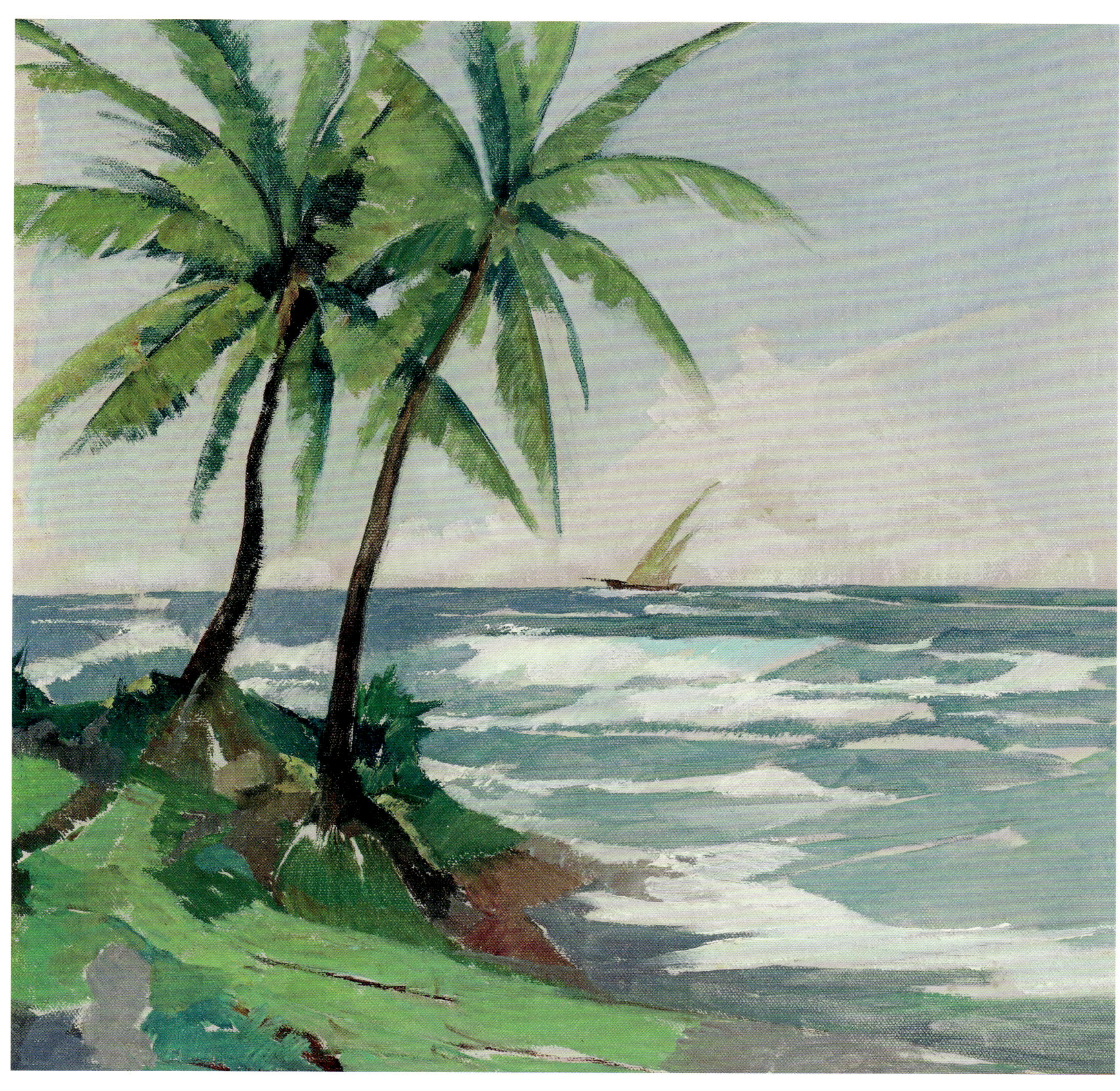

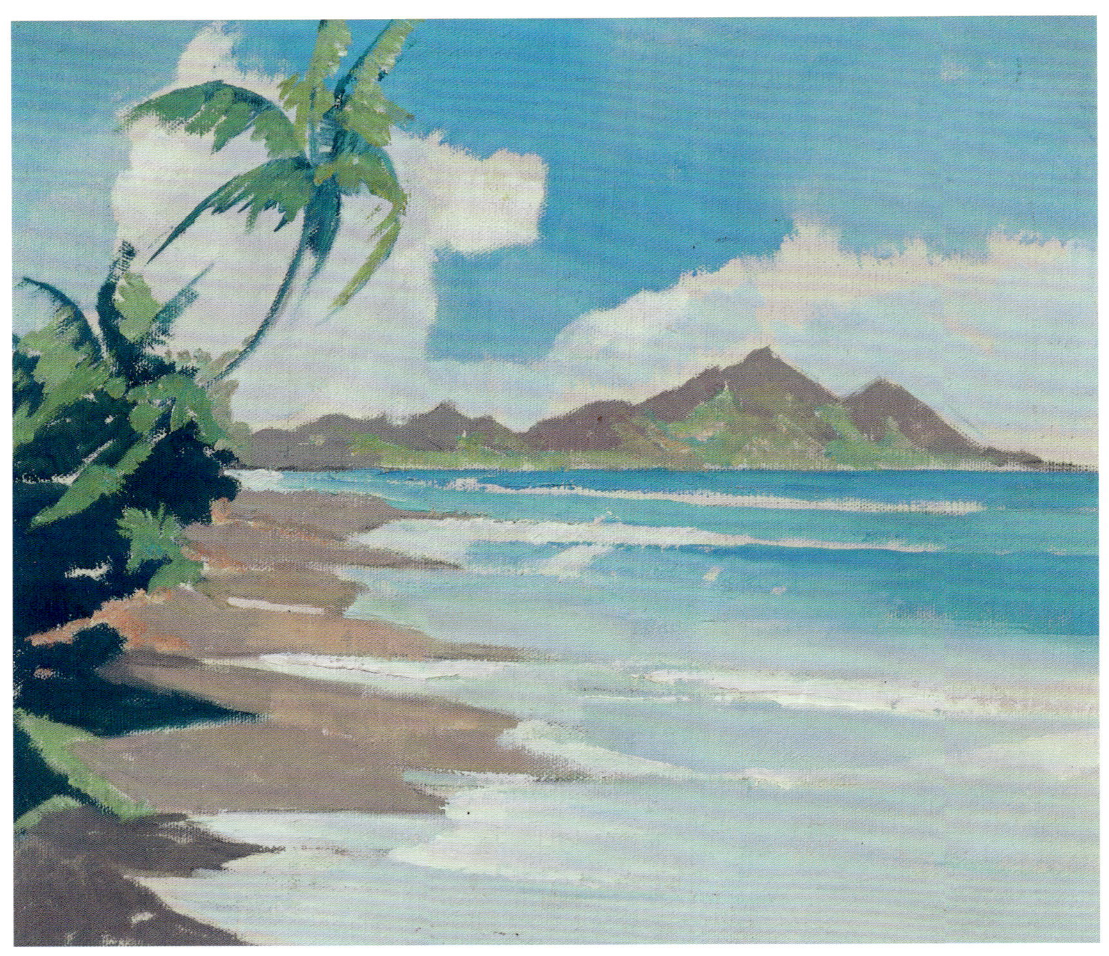

*Seascape with Mountain*
oil on canvas
11 x 13 inches
Courtesy of Roy Paap
Albuquerque, NM

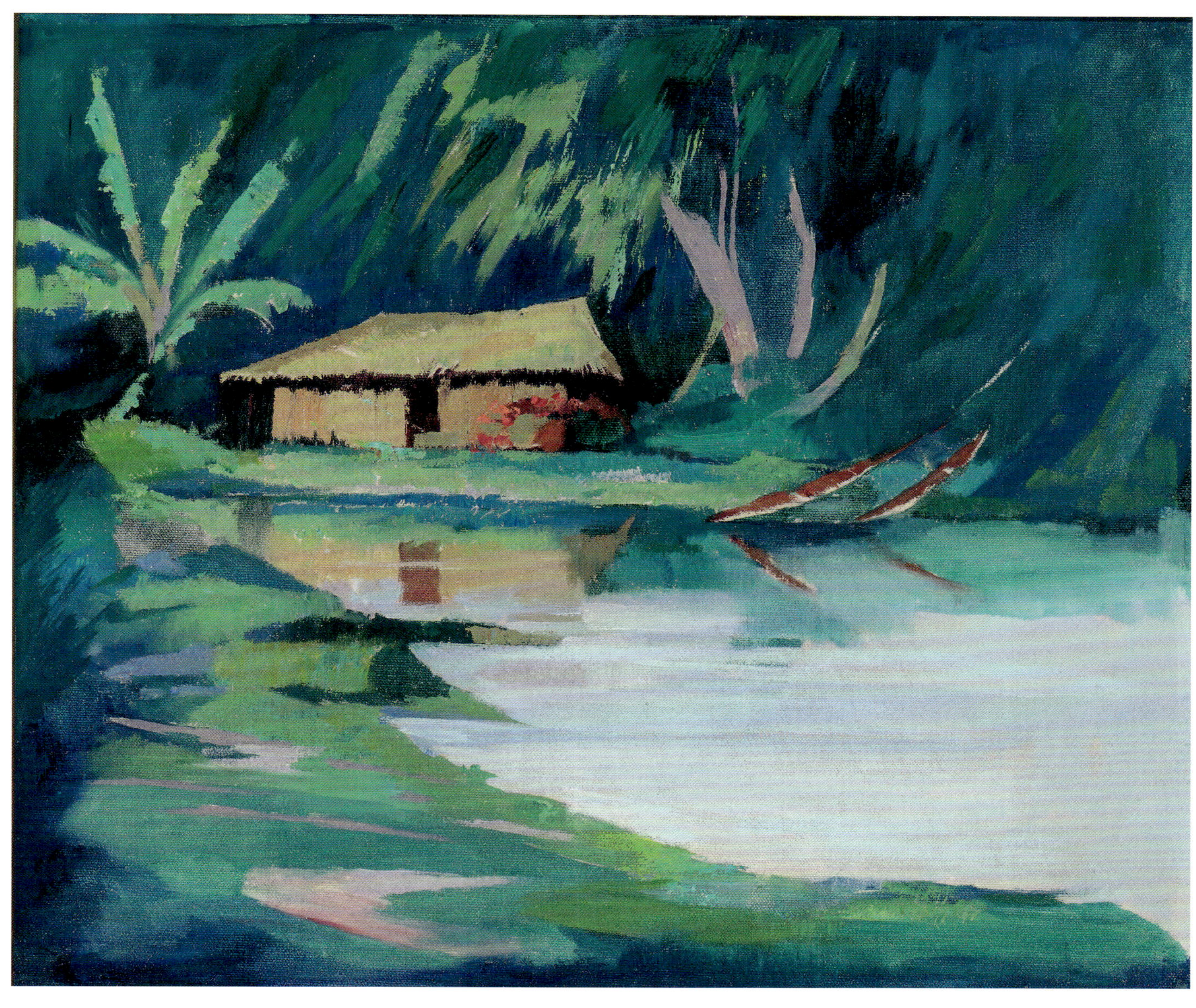

*Seascape with Hut*
oil on board
15 x 18 inches
Courtesy of Nancy Paap
Tesuque, NM

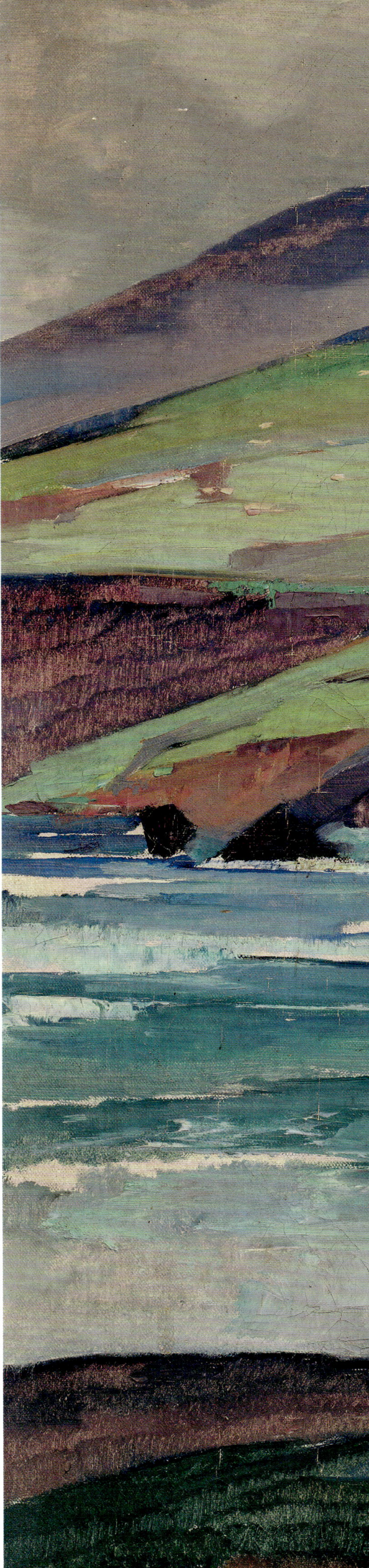

*Crashing Waves, Hawaii*
oil on canvas
28 x 31 inches
Courtesy of Nancy Paap
Tesuque, NM

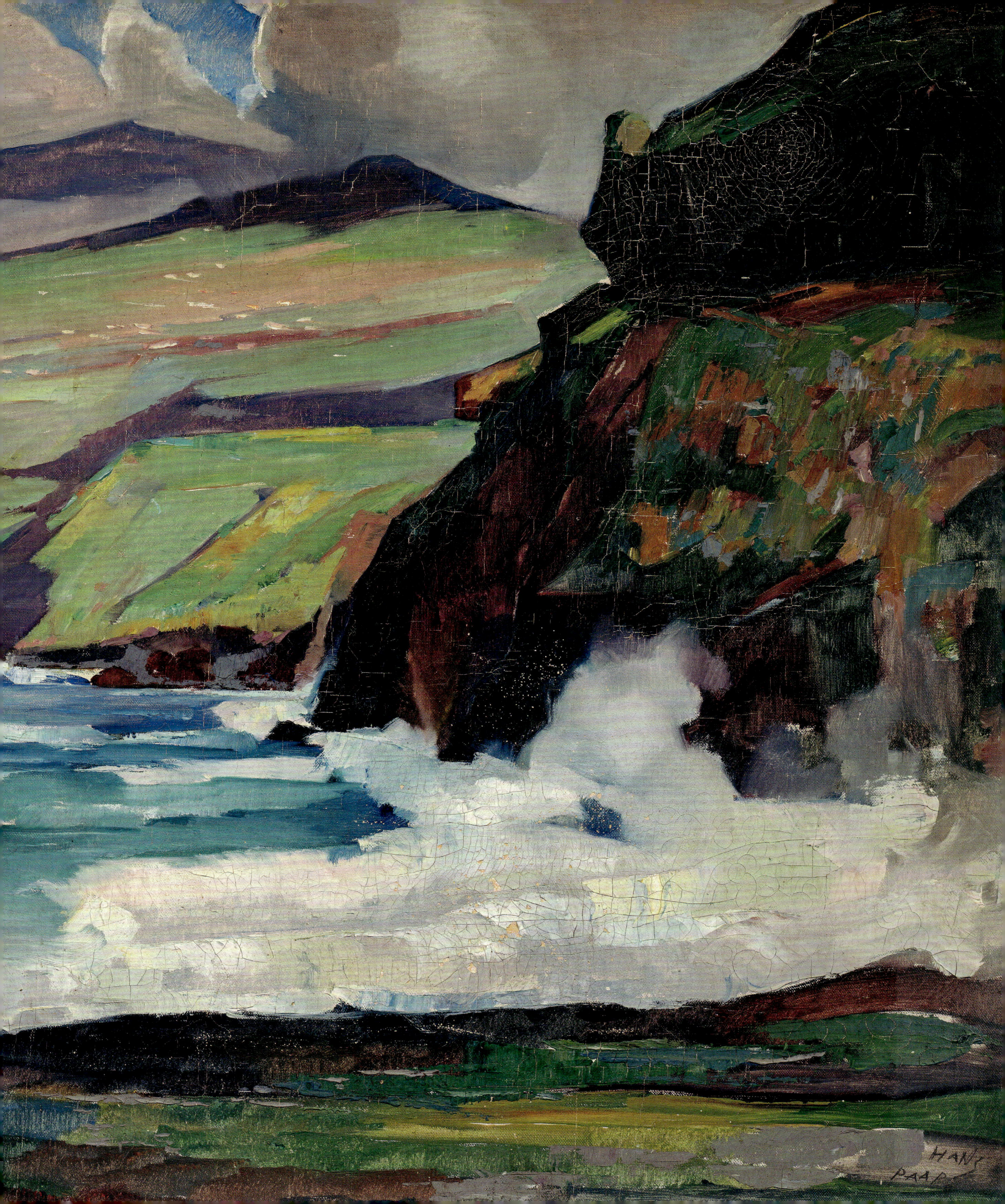
HANS
PAAP

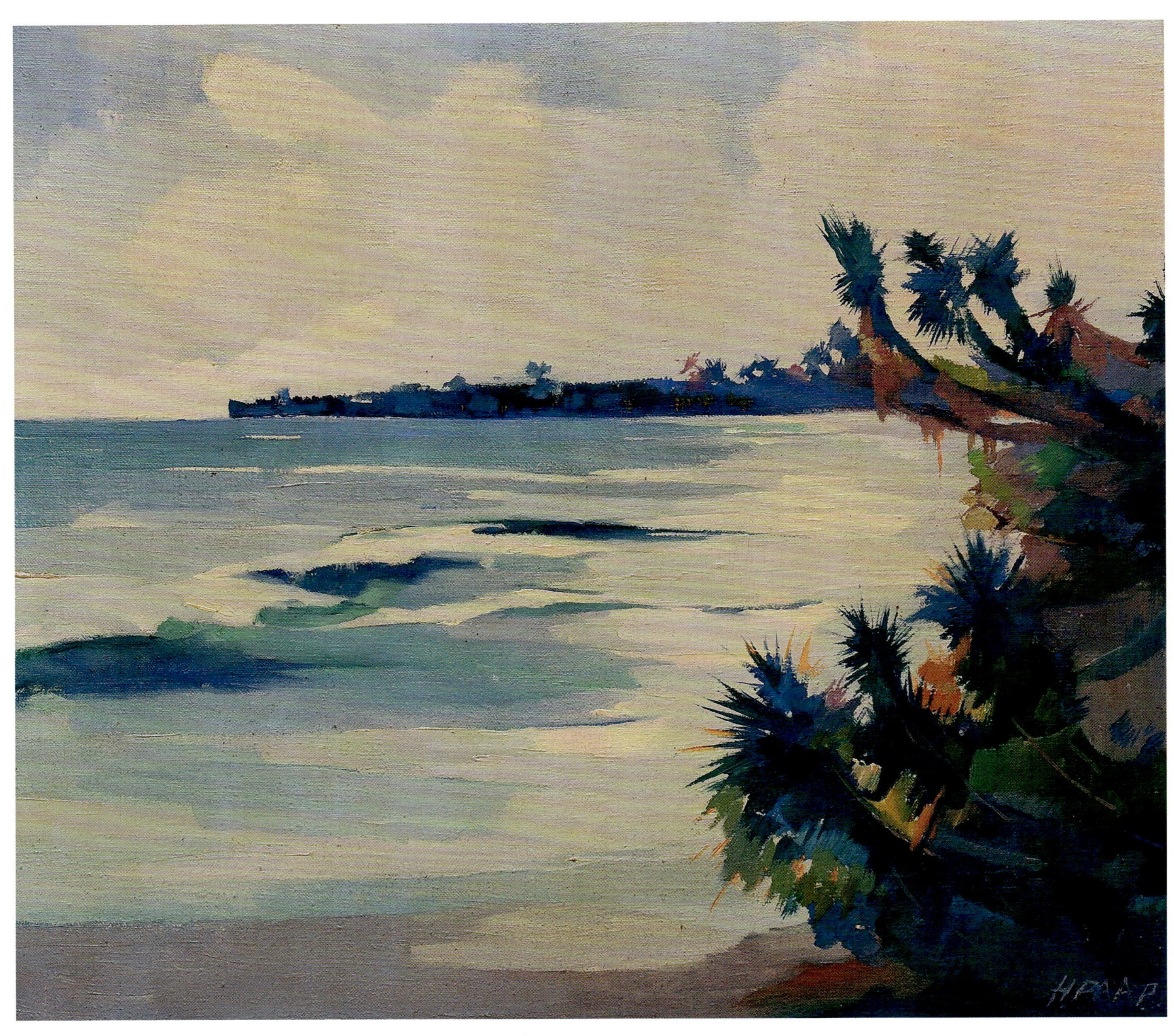

*Paisajes de Playa #1*
19 x 21¼ inches
oil on canvas
Courtesy of
Morton Subastas
San Pedro Garza García
Nuevo León, Mexico

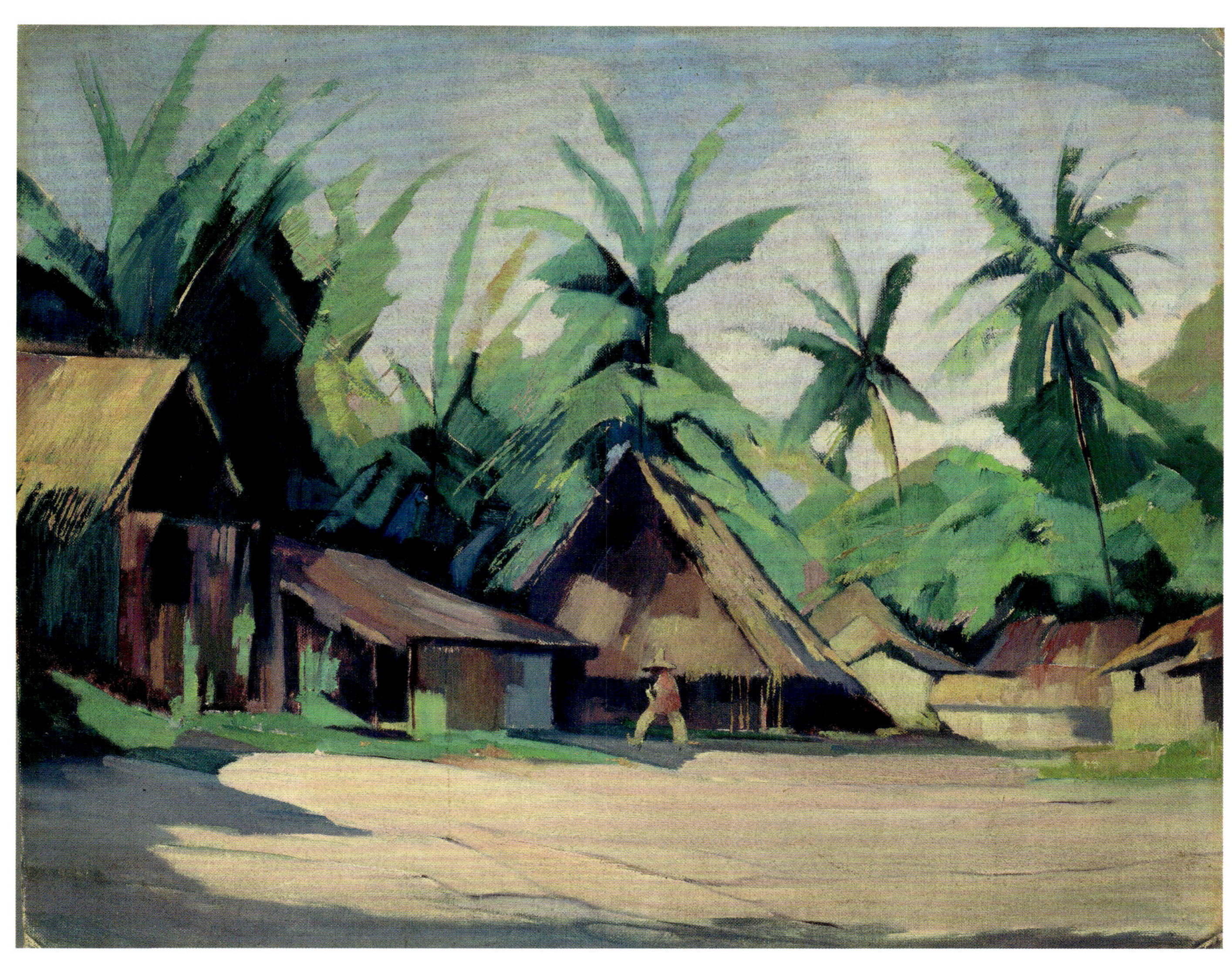

*Mexican Village*
oil on canvas
16 x 20 inches
Courtesy of
Deetjen's Big Sur Inn
Big Sur, CA

**_Paisajes de Playa #2_**
**19 x 21¼ inches**
**oil on canvas**
**Courtesy of**
**Morton Subastas**
**San Pedro Garza García**
**Nuevo León, Mexico**

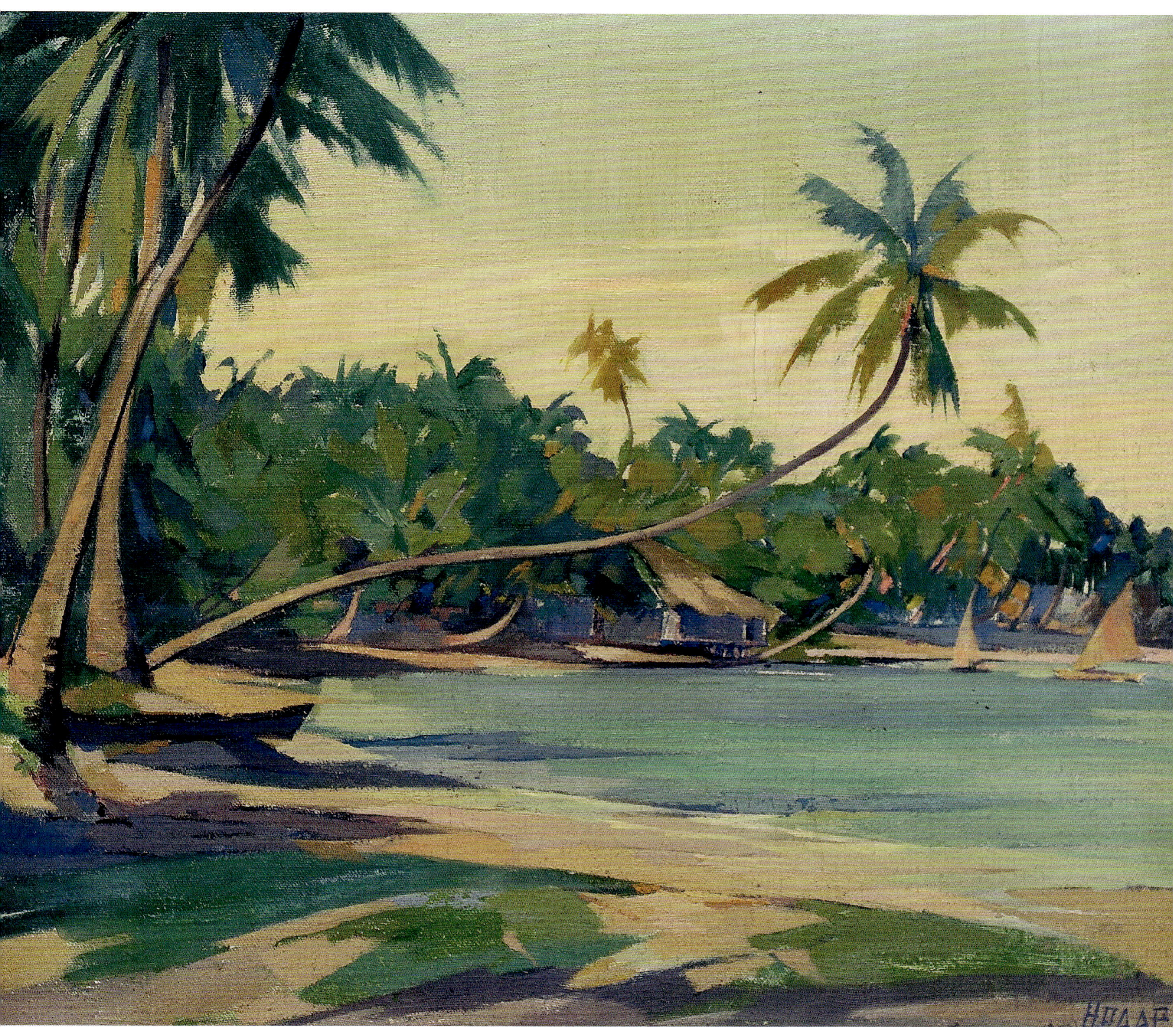

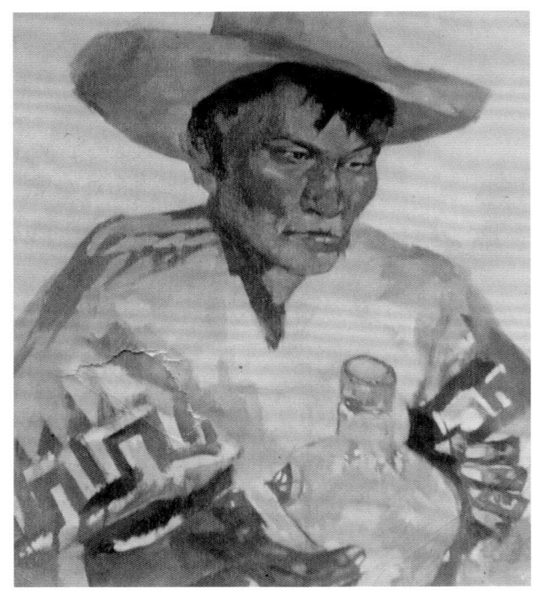

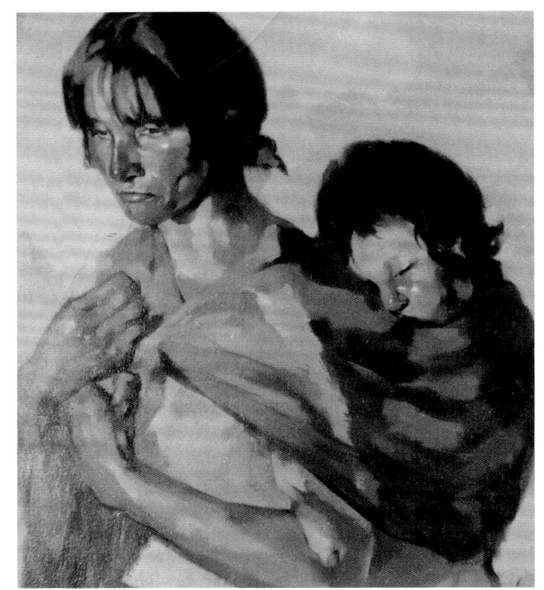

**Portraits by Hans Paap,
photographed
by Ilse Paap,
Mexico
c. 1951**

**Far Right:
*Red Roofs with Palms*
oil on board
22 x 19 inches
Collection of JoAnna Paap
Santa Fe, NM**

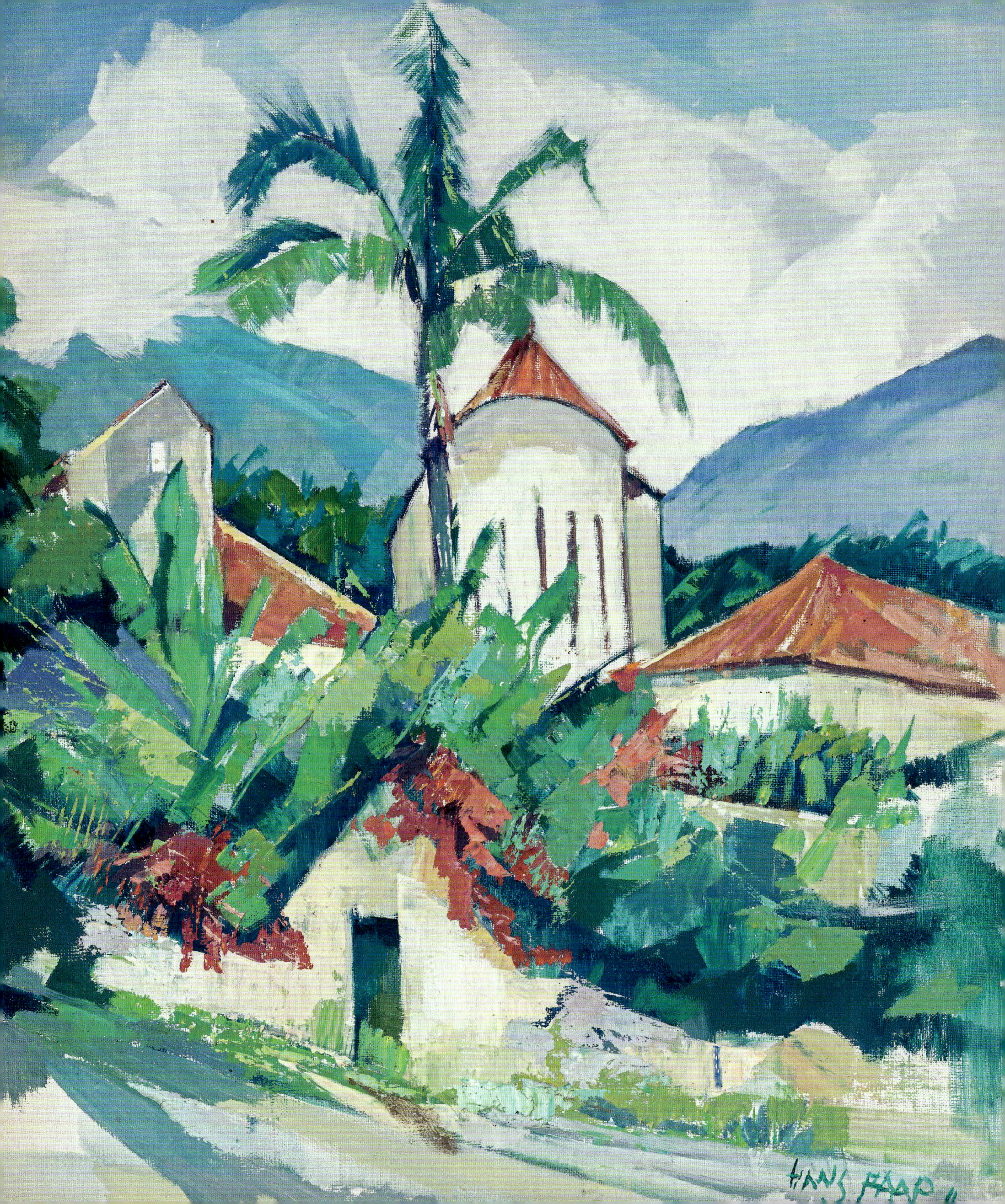
HANS RAAP

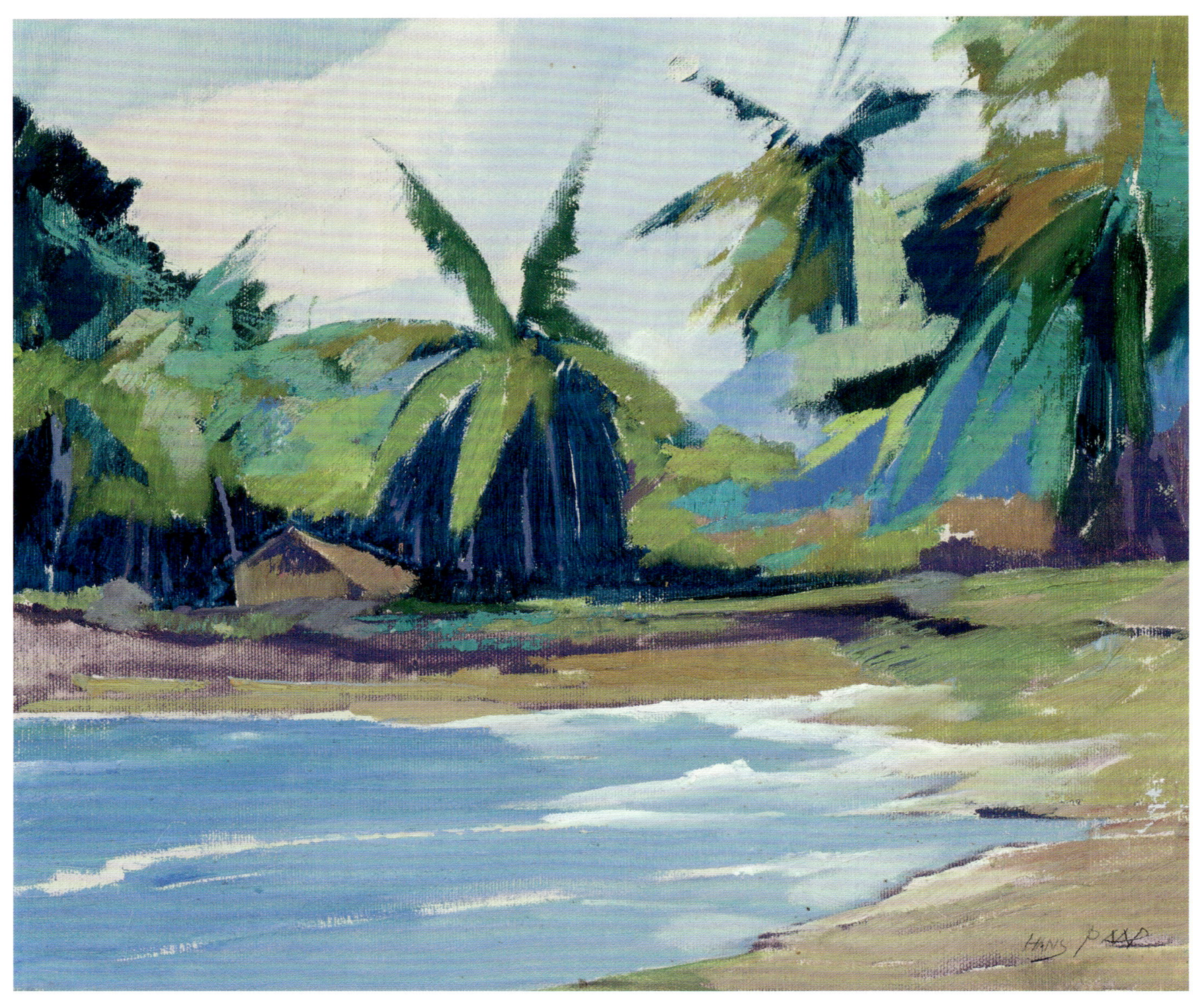

*Bay with Palm Trees*
oil on canvas
12 x 14 inches
Courtesy of Elizabeth Rice
Santa Fe, NM

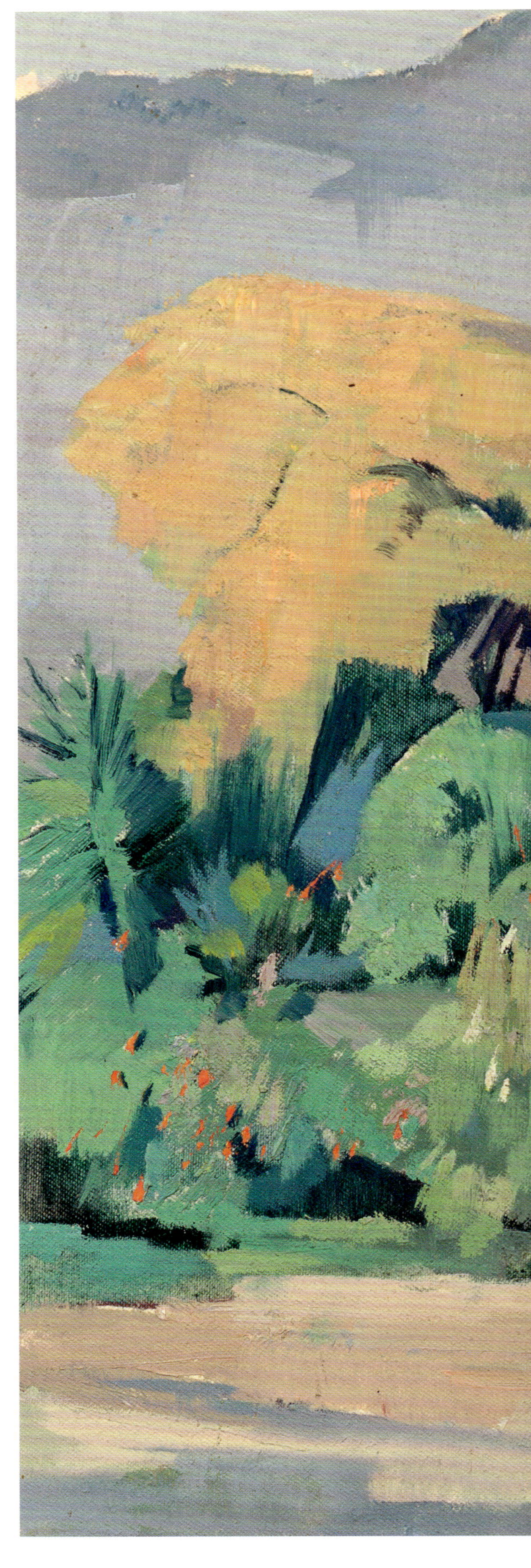

*Dos Burros, Mexico*
oil on canvas
16 x 20 inches
Courtesy of Nancy Paap
Tesuque, NM

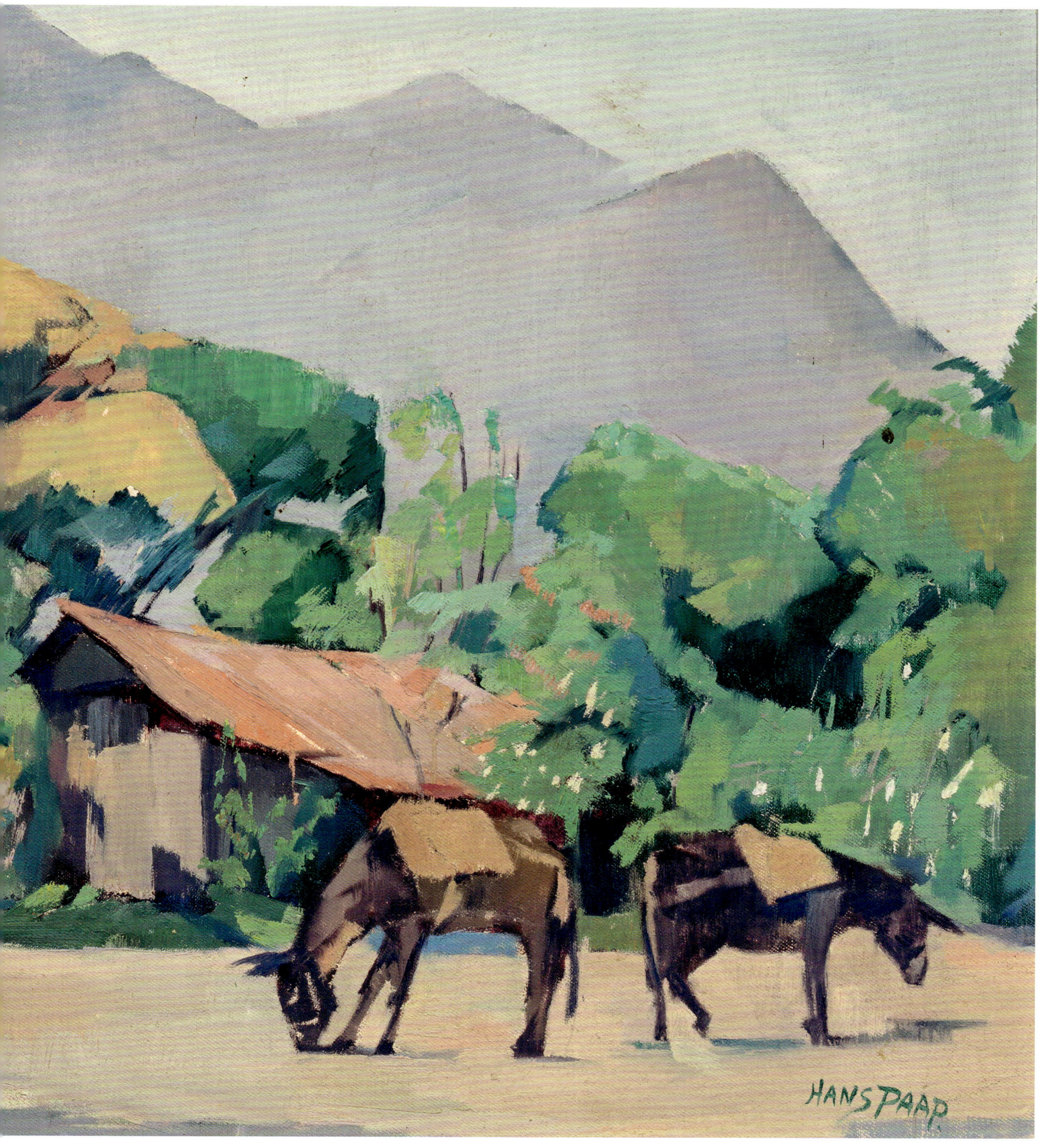
HANS PAAP.

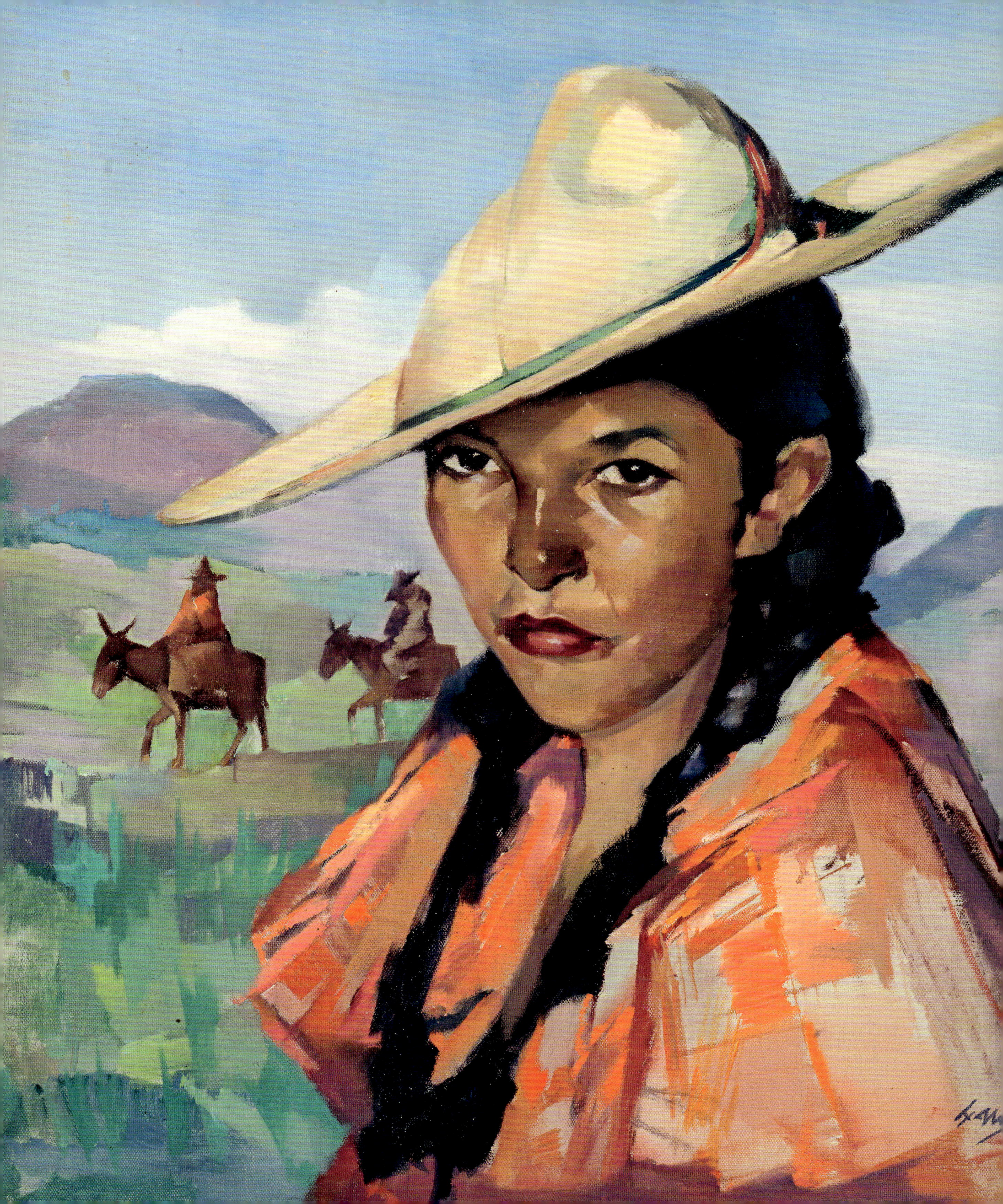

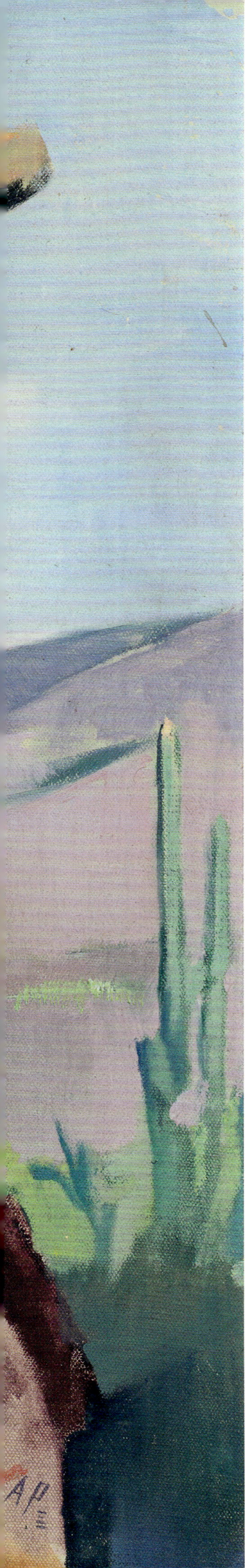

*Sí Sí, Señor*
oil on canvas
21 X 21 inches
Courtesy of Nancy Paap
Tesuque, NM

# Hans Paap & Family Timeline

| | |
|---|---|
| **1890** | • **Hans Paap born on May 5 in Hamburg, Germany** |
| **1910–1912** | • Studies at the Royal Academy of Fine Arts in Munich, Germany<br>• Studies lithography, textile printing, embroidery and leather engraving in Veracruz, Mexico |
| **1913–1917** | • Works as an art director in the nascent German film industry; Munich |
| **1918** | • Lives in Argentina and marries an Argentine woman who subsequently dies in childbirth; Paap's son is raised by her parents |
| **1920–1923** | • Professor of fine arts in Buenos Aires, Argentina |
| **1923–1927** | • Works in Rio de Janeiro, Brazil; has several exhibitions of his work, which receive awards and press coverage |
| **1928** | • Moves to Los Angeles, California; works as an illustrator for the Standard Oil Company magazine; exhibits paintings that receive press coverage |
| **1929** | • Moves to Taos, New Mexico, where he establishes himself with the Taos Art Colony; studies under Walter Ufer |
| **1930** | • Marries painter Mildred Rackley in Taos |
| **1933** | • Travels and paints throughout Europe with Mildred<br>• Has an exhibition with Mildred in Taos |
| **1934–1935** | • Lives and paints in Madeiras (islands off the northwestern coast of Africa that are an autonomous region of Portugal) and the nearby Canary Islands (an autonomous region of Spain)<br>• Has many exhibitions that are covered by the press |
| **1936** | • Exhibition at the Texas Tech Art Institute, Lubbock, Texas |
| **1937–1942** | • Returns to Hamburg to visit his mother and sister; when German borders are closed in 1939, he is unable to return to the United States |
| **1942** | • Paap's *The Westerner* added to the permanent collection of the Panhandle-Plains Historical Museum, Canyon, Texas |
| **1943** | • Marries Ilse Nitschmann in Germany, and they live in Prerow and Obergrainau |
| **1944** | • Son Pancho (later called Roy) is born |
| **1945** | • Paap, wife and son immigrate to the United States |
| **1946–1947** | • Paap and family are detained on Ellis Island for nearly two years before being permitted to immigrate to the Dominican Republic |
| **1947–1949** | • Paap family lives in the Dominican Republic, where Paap paints, exhibits and works as a Fine Art professor |
| **1948** | • Daughter Nancy is born |
| **1949** | • Paap and family immigrate to the United States, settling in Taos, New Mexico, where Paap paints and exhibits |
| **1952** | • Hans, second son and third child, is born in Taos |
| **1953** | • Ilse leaves Paap and moves to Los Angeles, taking the children with her, and divorces Paap<br>• Paap moves to Hawaii, where he exhibits and paints |
| **1955–1956** | • Ilse marries an Englishman, Ivan Waight, in 1955; the couple and her three children move to England<br>• Paap returns to Hamburg and travels between Europe, Mexico and the United States |

| | |
|---|---|
| 1963 | • Ivan, Ilse, Nancy and Hans immigrate to Cape Town, South Africa; older brother, Roy, remains in England |
| 1967 | • **Paap dies in Hamburg on July 5 at the age of 77** |
| | • Nancy lives and works in Munich from April through November, unaware her father is in Hamburg |
| 1968 | • Ivan, Ilse, Nancy and Hans immigrate to the United States, settling in Santa Fe, New Mexico |
| 1974 | • Nancy begins weaving, does Navaho rug repairs and begins collecting her father's paintings |
| 1976 | • Nancy and three friends open Santa Fe Weaving and Knitting Center on Canyon Road; Nancy continues to collect her father's paintings |
| 1979 | • Nancy and three friends open Santa Fe Weaving Gallery on Galisteo Street; she continues to collect her father's paintings |
| 1990 | • Hans Paap included in retrospective exhibition, *Inventing the Island*, in Madeira |
| 1994 | • Van Vechten-Lineberry Art Museum showcases paintings of Taos artists, including Hans Paap |
| 2003 | • Art collection of the Nicolai Fechin Home incorporates Paap painting from Van Vechten-Lineberry Art Museum |
| 2004 | • Article by Eberhard Axel Wilhelm identifies the location of numerous Paap paintings |
| 2005 | • Nancy conceives of a book about her father's life and art |
| 2010 | • Paap's *Portrait of a Cowboy* added to the permanent collection of the Colorado Springs Fine Arts Center, Colorado Springs, Colorado |
| 2016 | • Paap recognized for his contribution to Dominican Republic art and for his participation in the IV Bienal, National Gallery of Fine Arts, Santo Domingo |
| 2017 | • Nancy's mother, Ilse, dies in December at age 98 |
| 2018 | • *Hans Paap: Portraits & Landscapes* is published |

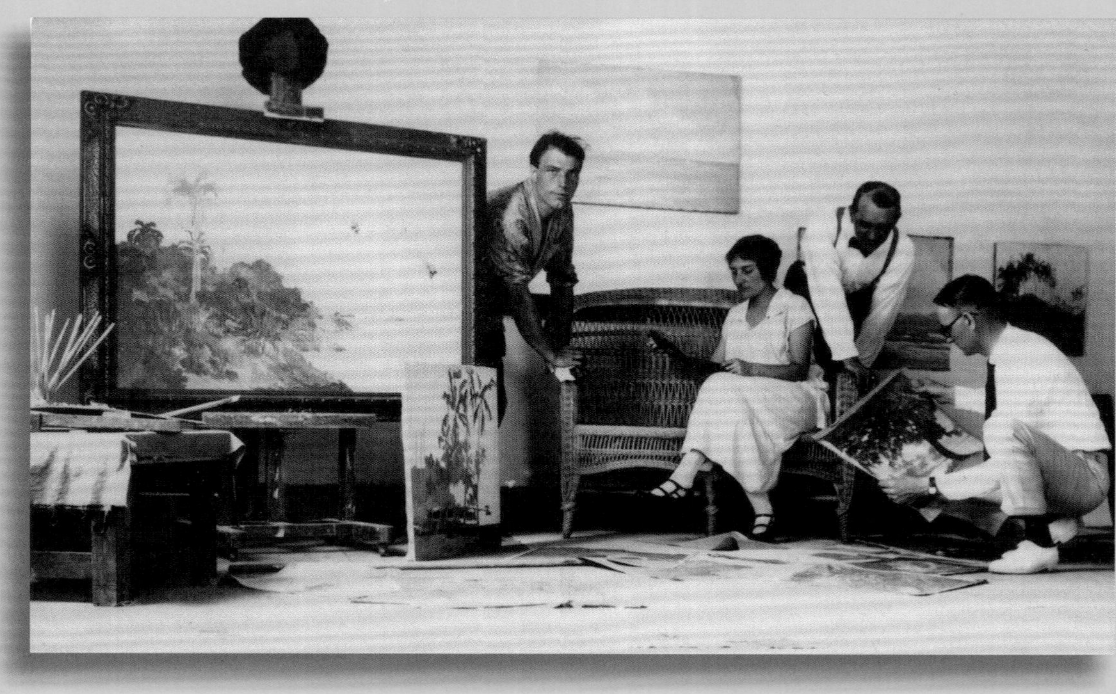

**Paap's studio in Brazil, c. 1923**

## Thank-Yous

Many people were instrumental in the creation of this book, and I am indebted to all of them.

Cyndy Tanner, the overall project manager, is the person to whom I owe the most: she was the anchor for this book. I am especially grateful for her extraordinary talent in assembling the exceptional team of Santa Fe professionals who helped create this book. She skillfully navigated the project through each phase, from research to development to execution. Without her constant vigilance, especially in the final months, the book might have floundered. I am also fortunate to have Cyndy as a neighbor, and I count her among my longtime friends.

Samantha Furgason, of ARTWORKinternational, continually amazed me with her research ability. Ever joyful and strong, she dug deep and found so much related to my father: countless photos, paintings, news articles and more. Her discoveries made us realize the magnitude of the project we were about to embark upon. Her broad and substantive findings quickly turned my simple dream of producing a book about my father into a very real possibility.

Alex Hanna, of Invisible City Designs, was everything I could have hoped for in a graphic designer. Along with his enthusiasm and talent, he brought intelligence, sensitivity and a refined sense of color, shape and placement to the undertaking. His attention to even the smallest visual detail assures that readers will enjoy every painting and photographic image in the book.

John Vokoun, of Fire Dragon Color, photographed nearly all of the paintings in this book in a way that brought them to life. Because color was so central to my father's art, it was extremely important to have a photographer who was equally accomplished in this way. In John, a master of color who specializes in art books and art reproduction, we found that person.

Bess Murphy, PhD, Assistant Curator of the Ralph T. Coe Center, wrote the overview of my father's life and art. She miraculously managed to bring together myriad scattered pieces into a coherent whole. With my father's many travels and somewhat mysterious life in far-flung places, this was no small task. In addition, her description of his paintings provides an insightful interpretation of his use of color and perspective, and through the paintings, she chronicled the evolution of his creative expression.

Janet Elder, PhD, served as our editor. I thank her for transforming my sometimes jumbled thoughts and words to express what was in my mind and heart, and for presenting them in the clearest, most informative way. Her generosity of spirit and patience never wavered as we worked to refine each piece until I felt the content and the tone were exactly right.

Kitty Leaken is the talented photographer who took the portrait of me that appears on the book jacket. What a fun experience she made it, and what a wonderful picture of me she captured.

Mary Buck Thompson, my dear friend, lent encouragement and enthusiasm from day one of this project, and I thank her. I am equally grateful to my family members, who are thrilled this book is no longer a dream, but a reality.

Although I am beholden to my entire team, I want to end where I began, with my heartfelt thanks to Cyndy Tanner. From start to finish, she cheerfully, tirelessly and steadfastly shepherded us through this fascinating, challenging and occasionally perplexing enterprise. More remarkably, perhaps, is that she did so without ever losing her sense of humor, tact and graciousness.

## Acknowledgements

I extend my deepest appreciation to those individuals who generously allowed us to include images of their Hans Paap paintings in this book. They include

- Garrett and Renee Boetsma, who were infinitely patient with me over the years as I persevered with this book. Their family, who lived in Brazil in the early 1920s, collected several of my father's earliest works.

- Susan Swift who, towards the end of this book, called me to say there was a Hans Paap painting in her partner's gallery. That magnificent painting ended up on the cover of our book!

- Curt Nonomaque, who lives in Tesuque, where I also live. He owns the wonderful portrait of Mabel Dodge Luhan.

- Margo Beutler Gins, for her generosity of spirit and delightful anecdotes about Taos and its colorful inhabitants.

- Deanna Luciani, whose beautiful portrait as a young woman came to my attention at an arts fair I attended. She saw my name and asked if I was related to a man named Hans Paap, who had painted her portrait decades ago.

- Maye Torres, who contacted me years ago about her Hans Paap painting, the portrait of a rugged Brazilian fisherman.

- Nedra Matteucci, with whom I traded my weavings for three beautiful paintings in the early 1980s.

- John Fisher, to whom I am particularly indebted. I bought many paintings from him in the 1970s and 1980s, and I remained in contact with him until his passing in 2016.

Finally, I thank the galleries here and abroad who also graciously let me include images of their Hans Paap paintings in this book.

Nancy Paap
August 2018
Santa Fe, New Mexico

## Credits – Photography

John Vokoun • Fire Dragon Color, Santa Fe, New Mexico
• Paintings belonging to Paap family members
Nancy Paap, Roy Paap, JoAnna Paap, Brendon Paap and E. Rice
• *Mabel Dodge*
• *Two Indians* (cover)
• *Still Life*
• *Church, Talpa, New Mexico*

Taylor Photography, Lawrenceville, New Jersey
• *Dusk on Brazilian Coast*
• *Tropical Fruit Still Life*
• *Dusk Seascape*

R. Boyer, Maryland
• *Paquito*
• *Ocean Cottage, Santos, Brazil*
• *Brazilian Seascape*
• *Sailing the Brazilian Coastline*

Kodiak Greenwood, Big Sur, California
• *Big Sur Coastline*
• *Deetjen's Big Sur Inn, California*
• *Baja Village*

Paul O'Conner, Taos, New Mexico
• *Brasil El Pescador Valente de Inla de Paqueta*

Betsy Wall, Salt Lake City, Utah
• *Blue Madonna*

## Credits – Production

Nancy Paap - Publisher • Tesuque, New Mexico
Cyndy Tanner • Parasol Productions - Creative Director and Project Manager
Alex Hanna • Invisible City Designs - Graphic Design and Print Production
Bess Murphy - Writer
Samantha Furgason • ARTWORKinternational - Research
Janet Elder - Editor
John Vokoun • Fire Dragon Color - Color Separations
Elcograf • Verona, Italy - Printer



First Edition • ISBN 978-0-692-16956-8 • nancypaap.com

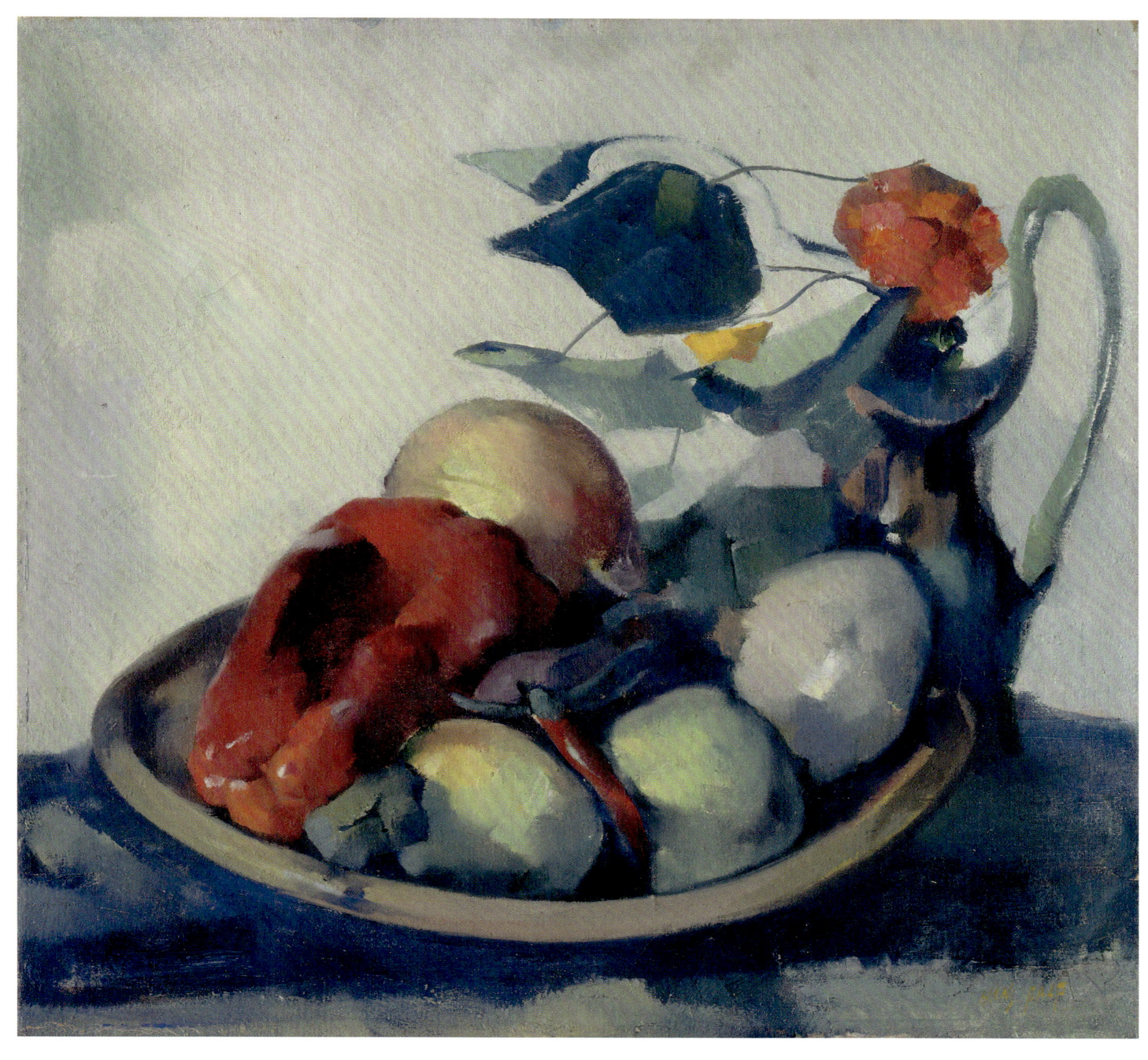

*Still Life with Fruit*
oil on canvas
16½ x 17½ inches
1932
Collection of the
Vancouver Art Gallery
British Columbia, Canada